CW00541673

CITY OF INTELLECT

During his four years as the tenth Chancellor of Berkeley (2013–17), Nicholas B. Dirks was confronted by crises arguably more challenging than those faced by any other college administrator in the contemporary period. This thoughtfully candid book, emerging from deep reflection on his turbulent time in office, offers not just a gripping insider's account of the febrile politics of his time as Berkeley's leader, but also decades of nuanced reflection on the university's true meaning (at its best, to be an aspirational "city of intellect"). Dirks wrestles with some of the most urgent questions with which educational leaders are presently having to engage: including topics such as free speech and campus safe spaces, the humanities' contested future, and the real cost and value of liberal arts learning. His visionary intervention – part autobiography, part practical manifesto – is a passionate *cri de cœur* for structural changes in higher education that are both significant and profound.

Nicholas B. Dirks served as Chancellor of the University of California, Berkeley, between 2013 and 2017. He is currently President and CEO of the historic New York Academy of Sciences, founded in 1817. Previous positions he has held include Executive VP and Dean of the Faculty of Arts and Sciences at Columbia University, where he was also the Franz Boas Professor of Anthropology and History. Professor Dirks is the author of *Autobiography of an Archive* (2015), *The Scandal of Empire* (2006), *Castes of Mind* (2001, for which he won the Lionel Trilling Award), and *The Hollow Crown* (Cambridge University Press, 1987). He is a fellow of the American Academy of Arts and Sciences, and a senior member of the Council on Foreign Relations. In addition, he has been a MacArthur fellow at the Institute for Advanced Study in Princeton and has also held a Guggenheim fellowship.

"Dirks' lavish anecdotes about evolving from starry-eyed missionary seeking a utopia of the intellect to tough-love administrator are hugely compelling, and there is no book like it. From his uncomfortable place at the top of two of America's most prestigious universities (Columbia and Berkeley), he gives us a brilliant, questing, at times very vulnerable story of the moral calling of the 'city of intellect' and its oddly conservative defense of old disciplinary pathways. His argument is troubling, invigorating, and impossible to ignore. All in all, a captivating, blow-by-blow account of the university's inner circle."

Timothy Brennan, Professor of Cultural Studies and
Comparative Literature, University of Minnesota

"*City of Intellect* is a beautifully written book that combines memoir with well-researched analysis to address the current place and crisis of the American university. Dirks tells the story of his brief and controversial chancellorship at Berkeley, while offering a full-throated defense of his actions and views that will be of deep interest to the many observers who have wondered about the details of the conflict. But the book is about much more than the highly visible and contentious battles at Berkeley. Dirks' long experience in higher education serves as the foundation for thoughtful observations about why universities are in crisis and why they seem so resistant to necessary change. He addresses, among other topics, the future of the humanities, the appropriate role of disciplines, the improvement of decision-making processes, and financial realities and possibilities. It is a call to action with a number of quite specific and useful proposals. It serves at once as a significant primary and secondary source about higher education and has important things to say."

Drew Gilpin Faust, Arthur Kingsley Porter
University Professor and President Emerita
(2007–18), Harvard University

"Professor Dirks possesses both personal and professional experiences that position him to offer a unique perspective on the broad trends shaping higher education in the United States and around the world. He uses these experiences to illustrate, analyze, and address some of the most fundamental questions facing the world's universities, both public and private. And he simultaneously contextualizes the developments he discusses within a masterfully presented history of higher education, a technique that will broaden the appeal of the volume and extend its influence. In short, this is a terrific book about which I am extremely enthusiastic."

John Sexton, Benjamin F. Butler Professor of Law Emeritus and Emeritus President (2002–15), New York University

CITY OF INTELLECT

THE USES AND ABUSES OF THE UNIVERSITY

Nicholas B. Dirks

New York Academy of Sciences

CAMBRIDGE
UNIVERSITY PRESS

CAMBRIDGE
UNIVERSITY PRESS

Shaftesbury Road, Cambridge CB2 8EA, United Kingdom

One Liberty Plaza, 20th Floor, New York, NY 10006, USA

477 Williamstown Road, Port Melbourne, VIC 3207, Australia

314–321, 3rd Floor, Plot 3, Splendor Forum, Jasola District Centre, New Delhi – 110025, India

103 Penang Road, #05–06/07, Visioncrest Commercial, Singapore 238467

Cambridge University Press is part of Cambridge University Press & Assessment, a department of the University of Cambridge.

We share the University's mission to contribute to society through the pursuit of education, learning and research at the highest international levels of excellence.

www.cambridge.org
Information on this title: www.cambridge.org/9781009394468

DOI: 10.1017/9781009394437

© Nicholas B. Dirks 2024

This publication is in copyright. Subject to statutory exception and to the provisions of relevant collective licensing agreements, no reproduction of any part may take place without the written permission of Cambridge University Press & Assessment.

First published 2024

Printed in the United Kingdom by TJ Books Limited, Padstow, Cornwall 2024

A catalogue record for this publication is available from the British Library

A Cataloging-in-Publication data record for this book is available from the Library of Congress

ISBN 978-1-009-39446-8 Hardback

Cambridge University Press & Assessment has no responsibility for the persistence or accuracy of URLs for external or third-party internet websites referred to in this publication and does not guarantee that any content on such websites is, or will remain, accurate or appropriate.

"The twentieth century was a grand century for the cities of intellect. The century, that century, is now past, never to be replicated."
Clark Kerr, *The Uses of the University*, p. 198

For Janaki

CONTENTS

PREFACE

"If we wanted **home** truths, we should have stayed at **home**."

Clifford Geertz[1]

In my first semester of college, I signed up for a freshman seminar – one in a series of team-taught courses
drawing faculty from different disciplines – called "Free
Will and Necessity." Taught by a professor of religion
and a professor of behavioral psychology, it was an
eye-opening experience. For the first time, I saw how
two intelligent and serious people could disagree about
fundamental questions, in this case concerning human
nature. Professor Crites, with a full beard, a cherubic
face – his mouth invariably clamping down on a sizzling
pipe – began by asking us to read Ernst Cassirer's *Essay on
Man*, a nearly impenetrable text that was a distillation of
Cassirer's three-volume work on the philosophy of symbolic forms. Cassirer was both an intellectual historian
and philosopher, whose focus on symbolic forms was part
of his more general effort to capture the ways in which
humans – especially in an age of advancing science – construed the world. Crites used Cassirer to introduce us to
the foundational importance of European thinkers like
Kant and Hegel and to stake the claim that human agency

---

[1] Clifford Geertz, *Available Light: Anthropological Reflections on
Philosophical Topics* (Princeton University Press, 2012), p. 65.

was primarily about the quest to find and make meaning. Professor Leaf – thin, with a wry smile and a persistent look of consternation – regaled us with stories of experiments and examples used by his teacher, B.F. Skinner, most of which were about pigeons. The upshot for him was that our behavioral patterns were conditioned by training, incentives, and discrete outcomes – nothing transcendental. Human agency, in this view, was neither free nor fixed; behavior was always circumstantial. We could be trained to do different things, rather than thinking we as humans were the product of abstract thought, ethical principles, or moral predispositions.

Even before class, I knew I was going to side with Crites. I liked the way he focused on the various components of human culture as critical factors in our humanity. I too was hailed by the importance of the creative and imaginative arts, and distrustful of what I took to be reductionist arguments that sought to explain human activity through biological or behavioral drives or imperatives. But what struck me most of all was how each of these professors made compelling cases for their view of the world. I did not know at the time how rare such amiable if impassioned debate really was, not just in the world at large but even in the university.

As the professors debated the basic premises of human nature, we not only read extensively from Skinner, we also read works written by Reinhold Niebuhr, Martin Buber, William James, Herbert Marcuse, and Jean-Paul Sartre. And as I look through my student papers, I can see now what I had actually forgotten in the years since, how during my freshman year of college I continued to use a Christian frame of reference for my budding interest in philosophy that hearkened back to my childhood religious faith. I was struck by how Niebuhr saw God's revelation in terms so different than the fundamentalist preachers I had listened to as a boy, as conveyed in large part through "the catastrophic events of history .... As the source and center of the created world against which the pride of man destroys itself."[2] For me, this was a new and compelling way to invoke the Christian message, to link revelation with the study of history and man's folly, but to do so with a sense of hope and perhaps even faith that the future would be not just a place of freedom but of progress, achievement, and social justice.

I had come a long way since the Sunday when my mother bundled me, along with my two brothers and sister, into a station wagon to attend a service in a Plymouth Brethren Assembly in Hamden, CT, near where I grew up. I must have been eight or nine at the time, and until then we had all attended a Presbyterian Church, the denomination in which my father had been ordained and in which my mother had herself been raised. My mother had grown up in Chicago, daughter of a corporate lawyer who saw church as an extension of his social aspirations, though he himself had grown up in a small Illinois town, the son of a buggy maker. When she was thirteen, she had begun attending a camp, and then a church, that was avowedly fundamentalist, and for most of her teenage years rebelled against her somewhat staid upbringing by spending as much time as possible in a community of born-again Christians. These churchgoers not only

[2] Reinhold Niebuhr, *The Nature and Destiny of Man*, vol. I, (New York: Charles Scribner's Sons, 1964), p. 141.

believed in the centrality of individual salvation, they were much more demonstrative about their faith and its life-altering significance than the Presbyterians. My mother clearly found this most compelling.

My father was born on an Iowa farm where the local German Presbyterian church was the centerpiece for the social life of the local German community, most of whom continued to speak a dialect of low German. He only left because he was born with a hole in his heart, making it impossible for him to take over the farming chores from his father. Although he wanted to go to the University of Iowa, he was only allowed to go to a local Presbyterian college when he promised his father that he would enter the ministry. He returned to his local church for his ordination but then went on to earn a PhD in philosophy at Columbia, where he studied with Niebuhr, Paul Tillich, a German philosopher and theologian who advocated for a solely symbolic – rather than literal – interpretation of the Christian message, and several of John Dewey's most illustrious students. My father later sought permission from his father to take his ministry to the university rather than be pastor of a congregation; his father assented, and he taught at the Yale Divinity School during the years I went from kindergarten up to my senior year in high school.

My mother returned to the Presbyterians when she married my father – then a guest pastor in a small Illinois church while he was studying in a divinity school in Chicago – but rebelled against the Presbyterians again ten years later when she had four young children and he was off traveling the world learning about the efforts of Christian academics in places as various as India, Japan, and Chile. While my father engaged in global dialogues about secularization and decolonization, my mother migrated back to the Plymouth Brethren and the kind of faith and community that had given her solace years before. It was because of this that I was baptized twice, first as an infant in a Presbyterian church just outside Chicago, next as a thirteen-year-old who had been persuaded to believe he needed to proclaim his faith through public immersion in the waters of the church. Although I was always troubled that I never had a clear narrative of conversion – as far as I could tell, I had always been a Christian – I was haunted by the fiery rhetoric of preachers who painted pictures of hell worthy of a twentieth-century American suburban Dante. It was only after that second baptism that I began to rebel myself, this time against the narrow-mindedness of the Plymouth Brethren, who rejected scientific understandings of evolution and seemed to distrust even the Christian credentials of my father for being too liberal. By the time I was about to go to college, I only attended church when I could accompany my father to the Yale chapel to listen to its eloquent activist chaplain, William Sloane Coffin. I had begun to resent my mother's decision to take us off to the fundamentalists, though by this time she had rejoined the Presbyterians in a progressive and politically active church in St. Louis Missouri where she had just moved. She told me later in life she found this last church the most satisfying of all she attended across her lifetime, a source of great relief to me.

At first, because of the clear continuities between my own spiritual journey and the course work I encountered, I thought perhaps that I should major in religious studies or philosophy. I also wanted to learn more about India, where I spent a magical year as a twelve-year-old. In the winter, I signed up for a course on the "Religions of India" with James Helfer, a stark but playful man with short hair and a well-trimmed mustache who was known as much for his quirkiness as for his brilliance. He dutifully taught some basic texts about ancient India and Hinduism, but made clear early on that he thought the essence of India's wisdom was to be found in Buddhism, especially in the work of the philosopher Nagarjuna, who was credited with establishing the Madhyamika school (or middle path) of Mahayana Buddhism. Helfer was taken by its emphasis on "emptiness," which he saw as the core of Buddhist thought. The Buddha had only obtained enlightenment after experiencing and then contemplating the enormous suffering in the world, which he realized was based on attachment to things that did not last: thus the emphasis on impermanence. The radical thought of Nagarjuna, Helfer argued, took up and extended the Buddha's insistence on the non-existence of self, directing us to shed the illusion that there was an enduring and ultimate principle of being in the world.

This was the spring of 1969, and there were students in the class who had come to learn about Hinduism and Buddhism as counter-cultural vehicles to fashion an alternative to the materialist preoccupations of American bourgeois life in the fifties and sixties, while imbibing the hip underpinnings of meditation and yoga. A student on the cusp of graduating sat quietly in the corner, responding to leading questions from Helfer to analogize Hindu and Buddhist thought to elements of European philosophy. He turned out to be John Perry Barlow, who at the time, despite having grown up on a ranch in Wyoming and later becoming a lyricist for the Grateful Dead and a leading theorist of the open internet, appeared more like a graduate teaching assistant than the countercultural hero he would later become. Barlow was especially interested in phenomenology, and through their exchanges I learned that Helfer himself viewed Nagarjuna through the lens of European phenomenological thinking, especially the work of Edmund Husserl and Maurice Merleau-Ponty.

Helfer was a captivating classroom professor, and he recruited some of his students to join an experimental residential hall called West College, where I lived for the next three years. Helfer was the faculty advisor, and that is where he taught a course on phenomenology the next year. He fashioned himself as a kind of hybrid guru, one part Buddhist and the other part existentialist, a stern presence with a flamboyant flair, often wearing only black, chain-smoking unfiltered Pall Mall cigarettes, and bringing two pint-sized cans of beer with him to afternoon seminars where he said that the class would go on as long as it took him to finish the beer. The more we talked, the more he would drink and the sooner it would all be over. These were different times.

We spent much of the semester reading Husserl's major work, *Ideas*, in which he elaborated the philosophical underpinnings of his project. Helfer explained that phenomenology was best captured through what Husserl meant by the concept of "eidetic reduction," an epistemological exercise – likened by Helfer to the peeling away of layer after layer of an onion – to understand nothing less than consciousness itself. The onion was the metaphor of choice because it expressed Husserl's fundamental conviction that consciousness by, or for, itself, did not exist, no more than there was a core fruit inside an onion. What Nagarjuna meant by the self, Helfer implied, was also the case for the idea of consciousness. Helfer made such an impression on me that one of the few books I took with me to India when I was doing my "study abroad" project was Merleau-Ponty's *The Phenomenology of Perception*, a hefty tome I lugged around with me for six months and read during long evenings under a mosquito net in a cheap hotel in the temple town of Madurai.

Some years before, my father had taken our family to India for a year because he had a Fulbright grant to spend the year in a small Christian college not far outside the city of Madras, where in addition to teaching he worked with the college's Principal to redesign the curriculum for a postcolonial and secular age. I was enchanted by a world far removed from the suburban comfort of Connecticut, going for the year to a local high school affiliated with the college, and roaming around the jungle terrain behind the college campus that was inhabited by leopard cats and cobras. Twice a week I left the school and traveled by bus to the back streets of Madras near the Mylapore temple, where I sat cross-legged to learn to play the mridangam, the south Indian drum, with a Tamil maestro who spoke no English and taught me Carnatic rhythms with Tamil syllables. I visited some of the great temples of south India, from Mahabalipuram to Madurai, and traveled with my parents across vast swaths of the subcontinent. It was a time when I began to ask questions about my Christian faith, in large part because I could not believe that devout Hindus – or Buddhists or Jains – should go to hell because they were brought up in different religious traditions. I became fascinated by India's culture and history and after

I returned to my school in the US I did a series of special term papers and research projects on Indian themes. This was why I had gravitated to courses in college on India, and ultimately decided to do a senior thesis on questions related to Gandhi's political entanglements with the non-Brahman movements that warred with all-India nationalism during the years leading up to independence.

In the first weeks of my time at Wesleyan I had gone to the campus church on occasional Sunday mornings. Stripped of the fervor of the Plymouth Brethren, and without a charismatic pastor like Bill Coffin whose sermons were all about civil rights and the war in Vietnam, the services seemed lifeless. Even as my studies seemed in some ways extensions of my religious quests and doubts, they also made me feel the growing irrelevance of the church. I continued to sense the force of religious faith, though it resided now in the questions and concerns that emerged out of my other intellectual pursuits and interests, not in the church. But I steadily turned away from religion, and then from religious studies, migrating instead to the study of history, politics, and economics. I decided to enter an interdisciplinary program in Asian and African Studies that would sponsor a return to India. There was a war raging in Vietnam, and because I had spent such a meaningful year of my life already in India, I decided to turn to its study in a serious way.

While my reading of philosophical texts had opened up my sense of religious possibility, I worried that this kind of phenomenological philosophizing was a dead end, providing the basis neither for faith and hope nor for political action. I hung on to the idea that there must be ultimate meaning associated with some idea of God that implied a theory of being. But life in those days necessitated taking political stands, and I felt that continuing to study philosophy and religion would be too self-indulgent. I was also struggling to understand how America had become embroiled in such an unjust neo-colonial war. While I sought to embrace an ecumenical idea of religious sensibility, I worried about the absence of a recognizable ethics in world views that I thought focused too much on renunciation or, for that matter, a rejection both of the world and of being in the world.

As much as I reacted against the fundamentalist world view, I must have been searching to find some other source of meaningfulness. My loss of faith felt at first to be the loss of a firm ground for finding meaning of any kind. Vietnam loomed large during those same years of awakening, with the recurrent nightmare of being sent to war for a crusade in Asia to fight a war that I deplored. I was convinced that American power was born both of hubris and ignorance. I wanted to counter both. As I was rethinking my relationship to God, religion, and faith, while also trying to reconcile my new preoccupation with Asian history and politics with other interests, I was also waiting to deal with a much more immediate specter. A great weight was lifted when my draft number – low enough to make me vulnerable at first – gave me a pass just the year I graduated from college. When I then went to graduate school in Chicago, I turned to the university as a place where I could not only pursue these ideas, but where I could follow a vocation, find a community, pursue a career, and live fully rather than face possible death. Chicago turned out to be the perfect university for one looking for a new secular faith. When I arrived in Hyde

Park in September of 1972, I found it to be a place where people seemed to worship ideas. I followed a path that had been well charted throughout the nineteenth and twentieth centuries by others who had sought in critical ways to make the university into their new church. Significantly for me, my father had been one of those.

I followed – without for a long time fully acknowledging it – the example of my father, who came to adopt the university as his new church, literally. I did not have to negotiate with him as he did with his father, as he approved of my growing sense that the university was an oasis that could help me reframe my childhood religious faith as the basis for a lifelong intellectual journey. This transplantation of religious faith onto the values of the liberal arts was in some ways a metonym of the larger effects of secularization on the modern university, a history that was as much a personal point of reference as it was a theme of my long university career. The university was also the place where my childhood experience of spending a critical year in India could lead to a life of reading and research about South Asia, an opportunity ironically created by the cold war and America's postwar global hegemony. But at the time I was simply grateful that I received funding to return time and time again to India to do research on the history of kingship, the development of the caste system under different political regimes, the rise of democratic political movements in the context of British imperial rule, and ultimately the overweening significance of European colonial history both for many of our traditional understandings of India and for our contingent convictions about the triumphant character of western civilization itself.

When in recent years I began thinking anew about the different trajectories that led me to and then through the university – as student, faculty, dean, and chancellor – I went back to peruse my father's papers. I realized that despite all the reasons that propelled him away from Iowa during his life, he had carried that Iowan village church with him. He had been part of a group of mostly Protestant theologians and academics who had been committed to making the university into a new kind of church, an institution devoted to education and research that could also fulfill what they saw as a uniquely Christian vocation. During the two decades after the Second World War, these religious leaders tried to counter the threat of secularization not by contesting it directly but rather by infusing university debates and institutional spaces with moral concerns and religiously based projects. They accepted and even celebrated the secularizing trends of the previous century, although they did not wish to evacuate the university of all connection with ethical preoccupations and debates over meaning. My father had worked out the rationale for why his own deep religious faith required the open inquiry of the university; and he had worked with colleagues around the world to help facilitate a global conversation about the relationship of secularization and decolonization. Once I pieced this together, my father's life seemed far less meandering than he had suggested in his short but poignant memoir that he wrote shortly before his death.

Over time I came to realize that I maintained my own relationship – however muted – with the legacy of the Protestant renaissance in which my father had played an important role. I believed that a serious moral commitment, both in teaching and in learning, was a fundamental element not just of my disciplinary commitments but of the university itself. Coming of age during protests about civil rights and the war in Vietnam, and then becoming a scholar of colonial history, my sense of "values" came to be cast in the shadow of the overhang of "power" – whether rooted in empire, politics, economic relations, cultural capital, race, ethnicity, gender, sexuality, etc. Now, however, I see a definite line from my father's emphasis on the moral dimensions of learning to my own persistent interest in understanding the larger uses of the intellectual life. Although I never thought of my own commitment to the liberal arts as in any formal way linked to religion, I confess I see the connection now, even as I would acknowledge that the secular can – even must – take up questions that do, after all, hearken back to and then in turn transform religious debates, commitments, and institutional histories into the stuff of genuine intellectual awakening. I became convinced that the encounters I had with different ways of understanding the world, and my place in it, encapsulated the significance of an education in the liberal arts.

Writing this book, I've come to accept that my meandering too was hardly accidental. My turn from the church to the university was more abrupt than it was for my father, but far less of a surprise. I had grown up in the shadow of the university, which was always there, even as it became the vehicle that allowed me to transition seamlessly away from my fundamentalist days. Once I made the move, it became a large measure of my life, though I was never content to stay in my lanes, either the ones constituted by the disciplines, or those typical for faculty who disdain the administrative life. I have always been inspired by seeing the university as a place where lives are changed, where knowledge is not only developed and transmitted, but transfused with the continuous quest to make sense of our humanity, to find meaning in life, to embrace our engagement in the world, and in doing so to decry injustice, call out the workings of power, and argue about how we might attempt to add real value to the world we share. I see this still despite all the contemporary crises around the university – and the accompanying – and very real – worry that the university is less and less the "city of intellect" Clark Kerr invoked as an ideal and saw as unable to survive the journey from the twentieth to the twenty-first century.

My invocation of the city of intellect as the title of this book may itself seem an impossible gesture of utopian folly. What I mean by this choice is to put at the forefront of my exploration of the uses and abuses of the university the intellectual values that must undergird and guide all the other things we encounter and discuss when we think about the university today. I am not joining the chorus of laments about how the university has lost its soul – whether or not they explicitly invoke the Christian origins of western universities or for that matter the place of moral education in the debates over the past, present, and future of humanistic learning. Although I tell my own personal history of losing my faith alongside the larger history of secularization, I have come to see the ever-changing intellectual dimensions and aspirations of university life not just as fundamental, but as perpetually threatened by attacks on the university from almost every side. Warranted though some of these attacks may be, it

is the image of the city of intellect that helps me identify and define the basic mission and justification of the
university.

And yet my account of the university is one in which
it never lived up to the utopian ideals I projected onto it.
How could it have? And, arguably, while I should never
have engaged in this kind of institutional transference, I
was far too critical ever to be fully satisfied, even setting
aside how much the world has changed over the last five
decades. When I was in college, I saw how impossible, and
undesirable, it was for the university to seal itself off from
a world that impinged with its full force on the intellectual capacities and ambitions of its students. The struggles over civil rights and America's war in Vietnam were
hardly epiphenomenal; they were central to everything I
did and studied during my college years. My early experience in India offered the basis for what seemed a necessary counterpoint to my American suburban upbringing,
anchoring both my intellectual curiosity about the world
outside and my growing desire to fashion a life inside the
academy. When I went to graduate school, I was able to
maintain and develop that connection, but I also encountered the fundamental limits of academic life, as the locus
of some displaced spiritual journey, as tied to institutions
that professed values and yet maintained old and sometimes rigid hierarchies, privileges, and exclusions, and
as an expression of the peculiar need to assert a kind of
professional authority over a place and set of issues that
always and inevitably outpaced whatever I – or any of us –
could learn in our education and research. The university
could no more seal itself off from the world than master
it through knowledge. And the preoccupation with the

professionalized trappings of disciplinary knowledge only made the university less intellectually adventurous than it should, and could, have been.

Getting a job out of graduate school, at Caltech no less, was the realization of a dream, but during those same years I saw many talented colleagues lose out and leave the field. I also watched the egregious behavior of some senior mentors who wielded enormous influence over my future, a reminder of the indignities of academic hierarchy and a distillation of the vagaries of the many academic judgments on which any academic's future in the university invariably depends. Once I had tenure, I felt as if I had been set free. My time at Michigan thereafter was the most satisfying stretch of my intellectual life as a newly licensed academic. Even as I later felt I needed to move on from Michigan, away from a failed marriage and to a major city, I took to administrative work primarily to expand both my institutional and intellectual life. One thing led to another, though never in an uncomplicated way. I saw how intellectual commitment and camaraderie were by no means sufficient to overcome the slights and anxieties of university life; and later how a move into senior administration further expanded but then complicated my fundamental relationship to the university and the communities I had built there.

As I came to see the university in a more synoptic way, with the incredibly good fortune to work in leadership roles with colleagues in a succession of preeminent universities across an expansive array of disciplines and perspectives, I also came to see the limits, the constraints that institutional constituents and commitments as well as ideological passions and principles imposed on efforts to sustain the city of intellect. That collision took place in a far more intense way as chancellor of a great, if imperiled, public university. I came to realize the need for an increasingly expanding sense of the public good. I also ran up against the limits of state funding, the recalcitrance of public university governance, the self-enclosed worlds of faculty colleagues, and the skepticism of the public itself, among much else. I confronted the limits of institutional work, the ineluctable disappointments of projecting too many of my own ideals and ambitions onto the political realities of the contemporary university.

While tempted at times to plot this story of the university as one of decline and fall, that would be to forget the early origins of my own relationship with the university. What began for me in the fall of 1968 with confusion, skepticism, and critique continues to unsettle me, and that is as it should be. Besides, as I make clear in this book, I continue to believe in the need for change, even when it might war with the personal nostalgia that inevitably flowers over the years. At the same time, I'm no fan of the easy talk of disruption, the certainty among so many that the university has outlived its uses in our new world. While I've become critical of some parts of the history of an institution to which I've dedicated most of my life, I've also realized that the very survival of what is most important about the university will certainly require serious self-critique, and along with it the capacity to let go of the past, while rethinking and reimagining altogether new futures. But I would be the last to advocate abandonment. The university still stands for that capacity to believe in the liberatory potential of new knowledge: new to students who learn, and new to scholars and researchers who engage in the quest to tackle new problems, understand new ideas, ask new questions, and disagree about them all. As we detach our sense of the future uses of the university from the history of the actual university, I have no doubt that the past will live on, in good ways as well as bad.

I am far from alone in thinking of the university as a sometime utopia, or at least as a place that still affords the hope one can work towards utopian goals, however contradictory, evanescent, and disappointing that may be. I tell many stories here, and most of them draw their sustenance from this idea, nurtured by a rich and varied history, that even though the university will always fall short, it will continue to be a vital and lasting institution in our future world. But I revert now to my scholarly position as critic and observer, returning from the fray to my academic vocation to share my reflections about both the world and my experiences in it. The archive I use in this book – like that of my earlier books as well – is anthropological and historical, a proliferation of narratives, texts and documents that are as much about the experiences I've had across the different roles I have held in universities as any historical and analytic accounts I've consulted. Although the book that results reads in places like memoir, the intention is to use personal struggles to animate my description and evaluation of the present crisis of the university and to connect my reflections and commentary to the different ways I've lived in the university over many years. If my narrative sounds at times defensive, I mean it less about myself than about the institution that enabled both my education and my intellectual life. Throughout this book I talk about the need for change, and in the final chapter I make specific recommendations for what in some cases are major changes. I confess that some of these changes would not be entirely comfortable for me, even as I've come to acknowledge the necessity to think differently about the future than we think about the past. And yet, I necessarily leave it to others to decide whether the proposals I make here are remotely adequate for the future survival of the university, leave alone to ensure the flourishing of the city of intellect it represents.

Introduction

∽

"The American University generally ... [is] ... for its academic staff
and many of its students the last remaining utopia."[1]

Edward Said

The walk to my office in California Hall from University
House – the house on the Berkeley campus where I lived
when I was chancellor – was idyllic. After walking down
the formal front steps of the Italianate mansion, past the
two sleeping stone lions that graced the front porch, the
path cut off to the left where smaller steps led down to a
wooden bridge across Strawberry Creek. A steady stream
of water flowed most of the time, except in the late summer months of a drought year. The sound of the water
was soothing even when I clutched at my phone to catch
the clips of the morning university news reports that usually hit my email a few minutes before eight just as I was
on the walk. The bridge was shaded and pleasant even
on the hottest days, and I often recall stopping there not
just to stare at the phone but to glance up at the towering
sequoias that rose from the back garden of the house and
spread their pine wings across the tangled banks of the
creek.

It only took ten minutes to go from door to door, but
until the last few steps I arranged my route to be mostly

---

[1] Edward Said, *Reflections on Exile and Other Essays* (Cambridge, MA:
Harvard University Press, 2000), p. xi.

I

undisturbed. I needed that quiet since the days were anything but – and as I look back there always seemed to be one crisis or another brewing. Issues only came to my notice when they were difficult – otherwise they were taken care of without the need for my attention – but there seemed to be a growing succession of those issues. On days when I had a few minutes to linger before the meetings and calls began, I would stop by the Free Speech Movement café to pick up a cup of coffee, taking my first sips while reading the headlines from the front pages of newspapers around the world that were displayed in glass cases just outside the café. It was good to be reminded of the more global crises that were always there to distract me from the local ones, though they faded from mind and view as I walked into the administration building and said good morning to the police officer who was invariably sitting at the front desk, next to signs announcing that protest was one of the core values of the Berkeley campus. If there was to be a major protest, the officer gave me updates, sometimes telling me that my building would be on lockdown or inquiring about my movements later on in the day.

When I walked around campus I frequently was asked by students to take a selfie with them, and was routinely greeted by salutations of "Hey Chancellor Dirks." After a few newspaper stories announcing my arrival, I became a public persona, identified by my distinctive round glasses and the shock of now fully grey hair that became a meme before I knew what the word meant. I didn't mind being so recognizable, but it made me cherish the quiet of the wooden bridge, not to mention the few evenings in the house when there weren't public events either there or somewhere else at the end of the day's invariably packed schedule. I especially enjoyed those few evenings when I could walk home and sit with my wife, Janaki, and our two Labrador retrievers on the back porch. It was soothing to look out on the vast expanse of green lawn where on many days we would have tables set for receptions or events, flanked by the row of sequoias and live oaks that bordered the creek just outside the compound's fence. I never sat for long, however, without taking phone calls or responding to the emails that kept filling my inbox.

The house was hardly a real retreat, situated as it was on the heart of the campus, and designed as it was for a regular succession of events, from lunches with the faculty senate, fireside chats with groups of students, evening receptions, and dinners with faculty, alumni, and donors – in addition to the regular visits of protestors, sometimes with the intent of breaking into the house or calling me out for rebuke. I soon came to realize it was an extension of the public role I had taken on and became a steadily more cloying embodiment of it. At Columbia, where I had spent the previous sixteen years of my academic career, the walk from apartment to office door was also a quick ten minutes, but until I took on the role of chancellor I experienced a far clearer separation between public and private roles. My time at Berkeley seemed to bring to a head both the aspirations and the contradictions of university life as I experienced them across a lifetime in different roles.

For many years I had no interest in doing anything administrative. I immersed myself in teaching, organizing workshops and conferences with colleagues, and writing articles as well as books. My research work was all-consuming. I moved several times, but wherever I was, the university at which I worked felt like home. At Caltech, I taught courses in Asian civilization to students of science and engineering. When I moved on to Michigan, I was preoccupied with the two departments in which I had appointments, and soon was working to create an interdepartmental PhD program in anthropology and history. Although I worked with the administration to do this, I'm sure I carried with me all the righteousness of a young academic assuming that I was invariably on the side of justice and truth, knowing better than any administrator what the university needed. Because of the success of the new program, nine years after moving to Michigan I was asked to chair the anthropology department at Columbia – the site of the first department in America in the discipline – and offered the chance to rebuild the department.

Janaki and I moved to New York and took up residence in Edward Said's old railway apartment on Riverside Drive with a commanding view of the Hudson sweeping from the Hull Oil Tanks straight across the river in New Jersey up to the George Washington Bridge to the north. We had been married just the year before, at which point Janaki left a position as an editor for an academic press and decided to return to graduate school, first at Penn and then at Columbia. As we began to live in the same place, I began to build a new department, recruiting faculty from around the world – Calcutta, Capetown, Kingston, among many other ports of call – and from different disciplinary backgrounds, as I tried to create the first genuinely postcolonial anthropology department in the US. I did so in the face of resistance from some

4

otherwise progressive faculty, however, realizing for the first time how difficult it is to try to change departmental culture. My primary focus in those days continued to be my scholarship. I was finishing a book on caste I had worked on for years, and then wrote a book I called *The Scandal of Empire*, focusing on the impeachment trial of Warren Hastings, the British colonial Governor-General of India who was later impeached by Edmund Burke, in the late eighteenth century.

In the spring of 2004, Columbia's new president, Lee Bollinger, asked me to take on the role of the Vice President and Dean of the Faculty of the Arts and Sciences. It was not an easy job. My predecessor, David Cohen – who had been provost at Northwestern before taking on this role – told me that administration at Columbia was a full body contact sport. Faculty, he told me, resorted to "principle" when all else failed; I told him I already knew that; I had done it myself. I was hit almost as soon as I started by the impingement of the politics of the Middle East on campus life. But I had the opportunity to build a range of departments across the arts and sciences. These were years when Columbia returned to the glory days it had occupied as one of a handful of preeminent universities in the world before the troubles of 1968, when it had been a center of intellectual vitality and ferment, and a powerhouse of research and discovery. Within a few years, I began to be asked if I was interested in becoming a provost or a president at another college or university. I was flattered but felt a great deal of ambivalence about making that kind of move. In 2012, however, eight years after I started as dean, I accepted an offer from Berkeley to be the tenth chancellor of the university.

I knew that Berkeley had been in significant distress as a result of state defunding during the great recession; the *New York Times* had carried stories about the furloughing of faculty and the removal of phone lines from offices. By the time I was interviewed for the position I also had heard that the fortunes of California's economy were back on the upswing, and I was assured that Berkeley was back in business. Meanwhile Janaki, who had been awarded a tenured position at Columbia a few years earlier, was recruited to the history department – a big deal since the department had earlier declined to offer an appointment to a chancellor who was a historian – and we decided to make the move.

My time as chancellor was intense. The times turned out to be even more turbulent than the years before, with a steady crescendo of crises that were far more vexing than anything I had encountered at Columbia. Berkeley was the scene of steady and escalating protests, some ending in violence. There was turmoil, agitation, and protest around football and intercollegiate athletics, sexual assault and harassment on campus, tuition increases and student debt, and the manifest tensions between the university's commitment to free speech and the widely felt need to combat hate speech. And all this took place with the backdrop of escalating, and at times staggering, budget shortfalls and challenges.

Students complained about high costs, growing precarity, and insufficient resources. Faculty complained about administrative overreach – the imposition of reforms in the name of efficiency that made life ever more bureaucratic and difficult – as well as about what they saw as administrative "bloat." Deans suspected that when I proposed a new system for organizing fundraising I was preempting their local authority. The two chairs of the Berkeley Faculty Association publicly declared I was a "spiralist," a professional administrator who went from job to job with the sole intent of depriving faculty of their right to govern themselves. The faculty, discouraged by years of budget cuts, began to demand more resources to support new centers, additional faculty, and a return to Berkeley's storied past. And then I became caught in a political showdown between long-time California governor Jerry Brown, a Berkeley alum who was committed to cost cutting and austerity measures, and Janet Napolitano – former Governor of Arizona and Secretary of Homeland Security – who came in as President of the system with the mandate that she do a better job of dealing with state politics than academic leaders had been able to do, despite our worry that she was using the job as a platform for her next political role.

In this strange and sometimes alienating landscape, I began to re-evaluate everything I had thought about the university. When I first moved to Berkeley I channeled Clark Kerr, who after having worked to solidify his famous "Master Plan" of 1960, began to think in his own way about the need to stay ahead, or at least with, the times, and to change Berkeley in the process. Because the levels of funding were so high, Berkeley prospered, even during the turbulent political decade of the sixties. Brought down in 1967 by the newly elected Governor Ronald Reagan for his (initially grudging) approval of the Free Speech Movement, Kerr continued to write for years about the changing currents and needs of higher education. I too ran aground against the headwinds that have made the utopian desire to preserve the lofty aspirations of great universities in a public system of higher education such a deeply contradictory and often impossible task.

I have seen all but the wealthiest colleges and universities begin to fray under the weight of constant budget cuts, political scrutiny, public disaffection, student protest, faculty unrest, and growing disillusionment with everything from the cost and utility of higher education to the very idea of "elite" research universities – regardless of how public and open they are. I have seen the culture wars shift from the debates over canons and academic fashions to a fundamental interrogation of the liberal assumptions that have governed university life since World War II. Whereas students fought for freedom to exercise the First Amendment on campus in the early sixties, they now often hold the belief that free speech can only really be exercised by those with power, that the old conceits of academic freedom and open inquiry mask the structural inequities that make the university a fundamentally unsafe space for the marginalized. The terms of many academic debates have been turned upside down, with many conservatives and liberals alike bemoaning what they see as a fundamentally inhospitable campus culture, a place where students are coddled and safe spaces are created and cordoned off from the world. In these views, the university has been taken over by new generations of self-proclaimed "victims" who have sought to convert their oppression into forms of power that reject and intimidate those who hold onto the older values of university life.

Meanwhile, I have watched campus life become the mainstay of conservative media outrage while faculty

8

and administrators both have been viciously attacked on social media and Fox News. What once might have been arcane stories about professors teaching Marxism, or feminism, are now the mainstays of cable television diatribes, amplified and disseminated by social media, the outrages yielding quickly to even more outrageous ones. In recent years, long overdue interventions in our political and legal theories that finally acknowledged the outsized role race has played in US history are being caricatured and outlawed in political attacks against "critical race theory" – and sometimes any mention of race at all. At the same time, there is a small but vocal group – some of them at the most elite universities – who bemoan the fact that diversity doesn't mean an equal number of right-wing professors as those on the left – assuming bizarrely that the mainstream political spectrum in the US should be the measure of the university's intellectual diversity.

And yet universities have also come under attack from many on the left, for being profit-maximizing neoliberal institutions run for the benefit of administrators and trustees rather than either faculty or students. The university, in this view, has been corporatized and runs on the cynical combination of student debt and labor exploitation. Meanwhile, faculty increasingly express concern that they cannot speak freely either in class or outside for fear they will be cancelled, by the "left" as well as the "right" (however misleading these political labels have become). But the crises don't map neatly onto a standard political map of blue and red. While Stephen Salaita was prevented from taking a position as a professor of ethnic studies at the University of Illinois because of tweets on the subject of Israel, Laura Kipnis, a progressive feminist professor at Northwestern, discovered that even questioning the administrative protocols of important offices like Title IX in articles or books can lead to a mysterious investigation into the traumas induced by critical intellectual interrogation by a member of the faculty of the workings of that office.[2]

Like many other university presidents, I struggled to negotiate the cacophony of political laments about campus politics. I've listened to the growing disaffection with the liberal arts and in particular the humanities on the grounds that they are either irrelevant or at best a costly luxury suited only for the elite. I've also seen the education gap between those with and without college degrees not only widen but map onto the growing polarization of our politics, our discrepant views about science, and our growing levels of socio-economic inequality. But it would be a mistake to assume that universities are exempt from any blame for compromising their own professed values, whether about how meritocracy works or about how fairness is implemented on campus. The recent "varsity blues" scandals associated with college admissions have shone an awkward light on the ideas of meritocracy that seem to be repeatedly betrayed by universities even as they seek greater economic, racial, and ethnic diversity among their students.[3]

---

[2] Laura Kipnis, *Unwanted Advances: Sexual Paranoia Comes to Campus* (New York: Harper, 2017).

[3] For an excellent recent study of college admissions, see Jeffrey Selingo, *Who Gets In and Why: A Year Inside College Admissions* (New York: Scribner, 2020). For important studies on the history of college admissions, see Nicholas Lemann, *The Big Test: The Secret History of the American Meritocracy* (New York: Farrar, Straus and Giroux,

And yet these same scandals make clear that alongside the growing public disaffection, there is an even greater desire on the part of many members of the public to secure admission to the top universities given their singular role in producing elite status and financial opportunity. Even as all but a few of the wealthier public universities reveal the extent to which the future of public higher education hangs in the balance, so also does the idea that the intellectual life should not be restricted to the universities that have the largest endowments, or to individuals who don't have to worry about their careers or finances. Many other public and private universities alike have begun to retrench under financial pressures and the increasingly competitive landscape in which securing "paying enrollments" has become increasingly challenging. This is an age of mergers, acquisitions, and peril for experimental but excellent liberal arts colleges as various as Marlboro, Hampshire, and Mills. It is also a time when the humanities are in decline, and when opportunities for employment as tenure track professors across many fields have become more and more remote, while universities rely on a growing cadre of adjunct instructors who have understandably become increasingly disaffected.

I have written this book in part because I have lived through, as they say, "interesting times." The second decade of the twenty-first century – the very years I was chancellor at Berkeley – was a time when the campus culture

1999); Jerome Karabel, *The Chosen: The Hidden History of Admission and Exclusion at Harvard, Yale, and Princeton* (New York: Houghton Mifflin, 2005); and Daniel Goldin, *The Price of Admission: How America's Ruling Class Buys Its Way into Elite Colleges – and Who Gets Left Outside the Gate* (New York: Three Rivers Press, 2006).

wars became far more intense than they had been before. Structural changes in the economy and in American politics led to cultural conflict on a scale not seen since the Civil War. The great financial crisis of 2008 and the resulting cuts in state funding necessitated major tuition increases, almost doubling tuition in the UC system from around $6,500 a year to around $12,000 three years later. Although this was still far less than Columbia's tuition (then) of $50,000, it has led to persistent unhappiness and major protests on campuses against the university system. Before long, the still smoldering resentment against the university merged with the national Occupy movement, leading to another round of protests and confrontations at UC Berkeley, UC Davis, and elsewhere. Meanwhile, the Tea Party movement arose in response to both the immediate aftermath of the recession and the resentment against "big government," coastal elites, Obamacare, and Obama himself.

Although the Occupy movement soon fizzled out because of a lack of clear aims and various breakups within the coalitions that had been forged in its early days, it – and the continuing effects of the financial crisis that had led to it – left a significant residue of ill feeling about elite institutions of all kinds, including universities. Universities came to be seen simultaneously as exclusionary places that reproduced elite privilege and as engines of financial greed that held back a generation of students who were consigned to a life of hardship, uncertainty, and massive debt. In 2011, the level of federal student debt climbed up above $1 trillion (in 2022 it is close to $1.6 trillion), during the same years that educational degrees seemed less and less useful for those seeking jobs and careers that would allow the pursuit of middle-class life-styles with manageable mortgages and a sense of economic progress. In the short term, the recovery in California's economy and the booming tech industry made it seem as if the recession was in the rear-view mirror by 2012. In the longer term, however, it became clear not just that inequality was on the rise but that even California's economic prosperity was won at the expense of the growing percentage of the population left out, including many students for whom housing became more expensive, food security more challenging, and hope for the future steadily more tinged with fear and anxiety.

It was no accident that this was also the decade of Black Lives Matter and Me Too. It was the time when the acquittal of George Zimmerman in the shooting of Trayvon Martin in 2012, and the shooting of Michael Brown in Fergusson, Missouri by the police, led to major and sustained protests, further provoked by the ubiquity of video footage displaying repeated instances of police violence against African Americans. It was also the decade when there was increased focus on sexual harassment and violence, among students as well as faculty on college campuses, in the entertainment industry, in politics, and in business. Me Too, a slogan that had been coined in 2006, took off after multiple accusations against Harvey Weinstein in 2017, but well before that there was a growing insistence on changing the rules – on college campuses as well as elsewhere – for mitigating the scourge of sexual abuse. While protests over Black Lives Matter took place on urban streets, Me Too unfolded in social media. Increasingly, social media was used to call out and disseminate bad behavior of many kinds across just about every walk of life, along with a growing level of vitriol that amplified and ventilated political and cultural differences. The election of Donald Trump in 2016, after his verbal abuse of Latinos and the disabled – among many others – and then the Access Hollywood tape in which he boasted of his own sexual assaults, escalated the rhetorical war around virtually every issue in American life, from "political correctness" to xenophobia, from issues around race, ethnicity, gender, and sexuality, to just about everything else. Everyday life was weaponized, and politics became polarized in ways that elicited fears that the country was headed for a civil war.

If all this made for "interesting times" in general, the times themselves seemed amplified at a university that was always a primal scene of political contestation. When I was Chancellor of UC Berkeley, I believed – perhaps naïvely – that it would be possible to chart a path in which I could work to advance the distinction and excellence of a great university in the midst of political turmoil of a kind that had undone many a previous leader, from Daniel Coit Gilman (the first President of the University of California) to Clark Kerr (the first Chancellor of Berkeley), while still fulfilling the public goals that had been fundamental to Berkeley's history. I had fallen into institutional work because I sensed the opportunity to combine the intellectual and the institutional, to put ideas to work – to make things happen, as Auden famously quipped poetry did not. And when I realized that the best public university in America was in dire budgetary circumstances and needed to be reimagined, I not only recited the words of Gilman and Kerr, I took them seriously.

In my inaugural speech at Berkeley, I spoke about the power of the utopian ideal, how in imagining a new future

for a great public university we were "all utopians now."
In hindsight, I see that it may be time to put the idea of
utopia aside. Even as I experienced how universities resist
change with all the tenacity they can muster, I also came to
see how the crises and contradictions of the university are
still critical components of what is most important about
them. If, indeed, the university continues to be a site for
the advancement and dissemination of knowledge as well
as for the age-old struggle with meaning, the "good life,"
and the "public good" – about knowledge as well as about
what knowledge is for – it will not be able to avoid serious
disagreements about fundamental questions.

The reports from the frontlines of university life I provide here are intended to be as much about the future
as they are about the past. The narratives I tell lead to a
series of reflections about how universities have changed
over time, and to my suggestions about why universities
need to change at an even faster rate today and in the
future to remain vital. But I need to go back to how I
got involved with university life in the first place. Before
saying more about Berkeley, I will provide some sketches
of my life as a professor and then as a dean. These were
the experiences that shaped both my time as chancellor
and the perspectives on the university that predicate my
analysis of its past as well as my hopes for its future.

PART I
A PERSONAL HISTORY

≈

I

The Professor

~

Culture is an instrument wielded by professors to manufacture professors, who when their turn comes will manufacture professors.[1]

Simone Weil

There is a kind of "guild mentality" in the academic profession, as in many others. The guild was isolationist toward society, devoted to producer as against consumer sovereignty, and committed more to guild rules than to quick adaptation to popular demand. The guild was egalitarian, full of senatorial courtesy, selective of its own members. It was also a 'sort of club...'"[2]

Clark Kerr

When I was young, I thought I would be a farmer when I grew up. I admired my father's relatives, who lived a life in harmony with nature (so I thought at the time) in central Iowa. When I was a teenager, I abandoned that idea, but – again betraying my father's influence – thought I might become a minister, though one who could combine my budding interests in philosophy and theology with the social activism that seemed required in an age of civil rights and the Vietnam war. When I later went to college and shifted from course work in intellectual history and religion to a program in the history and politics

[1] Simone Weil, *The Need for Roots: Prelude to a Declaration of Duties towards Mankind* (New York: Putnam's, 1952).
[2] Clark Kerr, *The Uses of the University*, 5th edn (Cambridge, MA): Harvard University Press, 2001), p. 73.

of Asia, it seemed only natural that I would mirror my father again – this time to become a professor, though not one of religious studies. From the time I made that decision, all I really wanted in life was to secure a regular faculty position in a college or university. I could think of no better future than one in which I could teach, read, and write for a living.

India was also an important part of this, and key by now to my academic interests. After spending six months in southern India doing research for my senior thesis in college, I knew I wanted to keep going back to spend time there and try to understand it better. I decided to pursue a PhD in the history of India at the University of Chicago, where I did most of my course work in the South Asian area studies program, made up of disciplines across the humanities and social sciences. Area studies had emerged as an important component of university education and research after World War II, when the US realized its universities had little systematic knowledge about the world outside Europe and North America. During the war, FDR commissioned William C. Donovan to create an intelligence gathering and analysis body, which he created as the Office of Strategic Services. That office hired academics as various as W. Norman Brown, a Sanskritist from the University of Pennsylvania, and John K. Fairbank, a historian of China at Harvard, but for the most part found a paucity of academic resources for understanding the world at large. Many of the academics who worked for the OSS (as well as some other fledgling intelligence agencies) went on to become the founding figures behind the growth of area studies in the postwar university. The effort to understand Asia, the

Middle East, Africa, Russia, and Latin America received major funding from foundations such as Carnegie, Ford, and Rockefeller, while generating significant support from the Defense Department and then from the State Department.[3] Dominated by the social sciences, it also entailed important investments in language, literature, and cultural study. Despite the extent to which its support during the postwar decades was motivated by the exigencies of the cold war, area studies introduced serious interdisciplinary study to US universities, and ultimately spawned important opposition to US foreign policy when the US shifted from focusing on the Soviet Union to fighting a war in Southeast Asia. I credit my education in area studies with my continued commitment to interdisciplinary perspectives both in college and in graduate school – a disposition I've carried throughout my academic career.

My advisor, Bernard Cohn, an anthropologist by training, completed his PhD in the early 1950s after a stint in the army that took him to India and sparked a lifelong interest in the subcontinent. With his muttonchop whiskers and a perpetually wry sense of humor, he was a young chair of the storied Rochester anthropology department before being recruited to teach history at Chicago in 1963 (where he also held a professorship in the department of anthropology), a reflection both of Cohn's cross-disciplinary work and of the paucity of trained South Asian historians in the US at the time. In the late 1950s he began writing

---

[3] For more, both on the role of the OSS, and on support for area studies after the war, see Nicholas B. Dirks, *Autobiography of an Archive: A Scholar's Passage to India* (New York: Columbia University Press, 2015), pp. 265–90, 303–20.

a series of papers on questions that concerned key anthropological questions but were framed historically, with a special focus on the eighteenth and nineteenth centuries. Over time, he argued that the British developed a "colonial sociology" of knowledge that served imperial interests, representing Indian categories and values in distinctly empire-serving ways. He saw anthropological categories as shaped largely by historical forces, and specifically by colonialism, strongly influencing my work, while allowing me to develop my interest not just in both disciplines but in larger questions about the interplay of categories of knowledge and the forces of history.[4]

I followed Cohn's example by choosing a dissertation topic that required both archival research and anthropological fieldwork. I spent two years away from Chicago, mostly in Madras but also in villages and towns in the southern part of Tamil Nadu that were situated in earlier kingdoms. I lived for two months in the guesthouse of a run-down palace, formerly a British colonial residency, where I observed the continuing forms of deference and power that circulated around the royal family. I rode a motorcycle to villages across what had been a "princely state" and began to see places and traces of references I read about in the local archives. I studied the relationships between royal families and their forms of rule and the development of caste structures. I came to see that caste was shaped as much by the exercise of political power as it was by any set of scriptural ideas about ritual

---

[4] See Bernard S. Cohn, *An Anthropologist among the Historians and Other Essays* (Delhi: Oxford University Press, 1987); Cohn, *Colonialism and Its Forms of Knowledge: The British in India*, intro. Nicholas B. Dirks (Princeton University Press, 1996).

purity and pollution. I also came to see the extraordinary impact of British colonial rule in India, not just in macro political and economic terms, but in its effects on the very organization of social relations through colonial policies around land tenure, legal systems, and indirect rule. I wrote a massive dissertation that, after several revisions and finally wearing down one member of my committee who had decided not to pass the thesis at first because I disagreed with him, made me realize I had to return to the princely state for additional fieldwork.

There were no jobs in South Asian history when I started looking for one in 1978, my graduate funding about to expire and a baby on the way. The academic job market had contracted markedly in the late 1970s and I was not at all sure I would be able to pursue an academic career. I began looking at applications for law school while wondering if I should take the foreign service exam. Just when I thought nothing would happen, I was offered a one-year position at Caltech to teach science and engineering students an introductory course on Asian civilization. One year led to two, and then, after a contentious search, a tenure track position. Five years later I was awarded tenure, just as I completed my book and appeared to have persuaded both historians and anthropologists that I had made a significant scholarly contribution. I could not believe my good luck. My students sometimes fell asleep in class – although they unfailingly apologized by saying that they had stayed up all night doing their physics homework – and I could not teach advanced courses for majors or graduate students in my field. But Caltech was a fabulous place to be, especially as a junior professor. The teaching load was reasonable and I had plenty of time to learn what my colleagues in fields from comparative literature to political science were working on, to participate in local reading groups, travel to conferences, and to do my own work. Although I missed the intensity of Chicago, I soon began to understand the seductive pleasures of life in southern California.

I also began to meet colleagues in the sciences, taking advantage of the round table tradition in the Atheneum. This was a glorious Spanish-style mansion that had been built as a faculty club not just for Caltech but for the Huntington Library and the Hale Observatory. Two round tables were never to be reserved, and the custom was to take a seat next to whoever else was there. I found myself sitting with some scientific luminaries, Richard Feynman, Murray Gell-Mann, and Max Delbruck among them. Feynman, the most popular physics lecturer at Caltech, was a notorious raconteur, an amateur thespian, and a voracious lover of life. Gell-Mann, who had discovered the quark (he had QUARK engraved on his California license plate), was interested in early Indian philosophy, and asked me to chat with him about the differences between monism and dualism in Indian thought. Delbruck, who was trained as a physicist, went on to win the Nobel Prize in Medicine. They were all curious about India and were pleased to know that I was acquainting their students with the thought of figures as various as Gandhi and Mao Tse Tung.

Although I felt the absence of undergraduate majors and graduate students in my field, I was able to focus on my own research. I was given leave to spend another full year in India to do fieldwork that supplemented my dissertation work. I was also able just a few years later to go off for a full year to England to begin a new research project on the colonial sociology of knowledge – research that ultimately led to my second book on the history of the caste system in India. I was pulled into some local academic politics, not least because one of the senior historians – a medievalist who believed in the bicameral nature of the brain (which in his view explained medieval mysticism) and attempted to prove his scientific chops by using advanced imaging techniques to determine whether Heloise and Abelard were really two people or just one – had disapproved of using a line in the department for a historian of India. He seemed to have taken a deep dislike to the kind of critical theory and cultural history I did. Modeling himself – so it seemed – on Kingsley Amis' creation of the senior historian as cruel curmudgeon in his novel *Lucky Jim*, he frequently invited me to lunch only to berate me in front of other colleagues for my clear historical apostasy. Happily, there were other supportive colleagues.

Robert Rosenstone, a historian of radical movements in the US, had recently spent a year teaching in Japan. He became an early supporter of expanding Caltech's offerings in fields related to Asian studies. He also was an academic who loved LA. Among other things, this meant that he lived outside Pasadena – a departure from the Caltech norm. He had served as the historical consultant for a film based on his book about John Reed directed by Warren Beatty.[5] Robert would regale us with stories about Beatty as well as about the ways Hollywood worked, including noting the blatant disregard for history

5 Robert Rosenstone, *Romantic Revolutionary: A Biography of John Reed* (New York: Knopf, 1975).

on the part of filmmakers who were more driven by spectacle and filmic narrative than factual accuracy. Driving his Alfa Romeo, he wore designer jeans and sported a stylish mustache; he was astounded that I might feel any nostalgia for Chicago. He had a house in Laurel Canyon that he had rented to Nick Nolte while in Japan (Nolte had not been a good tenant), with a hot tub in the back in which we were invited to strip down and have a good soak during an evening party (we did not). He was curious about new theoretical trends in historiography, and began writing probing articles about film and history that raised fundamental questions about historical representation. We became friends, and I began recommending that he read the work of theorists such as Hayden White and Michel Foucault. He encouraged me to start inviting speakers to Caltech to talk about these issues, set up a small reading group, and soon began to work on extending my appointment for another year.

He was helped by Peter Fay, whose India sabbatical had led to my first one-year teaching gig, and who was very much in favor of hiring someone on a regular appointment who could teach Asian history. Peter, whose sharp New England accent suggested a patrician past, himself had been trained as a British historian but he had been hired in earlier days by Caltech not for his scholarship so much as his impassioned teaching. He had written a gripping historical narrative about the Opium War and was now at work on a history of the Indian National Army.[6] Peter had spent a year in India in the late sixties,

[6] Peter W. Fay, *The Opium War, 1840–1842* (Chapel Hill: University of North Carolina Press, 1975).

teaching at the new Indian Institute of Technology (IIT) at Kanpur. While there he befriended a couple, Prem and Lakshmi, who had both been prominent followers of Subhas Chandra Bose, the founder of the Indian National Army during World War II. Bose, a nationalist leader from Bengal who was more militant than Gandhi and Nehru, had decided to collaborate with the Japanese during the war, forming a nationalist army with Indian prisoners of war from Singapore and elsewhere to attempt an assault on British India across the Burmese border in the waning months of the war.

Peter received a grant to return to Kanpur for a year, and he was now determined to use the personal stories he had heard from his friends to anchor his larger history of this "forgotten army."[7] This was the year I was hired to teach his courses, and the basis for my fledgling relationship with Caltech. Peter was doubtless anxious to have an Indian historian around when working on this project after his return, but he also believed strongly that Caltech students needed to learn about the world beyond the US and Europe and to do so from someone who had been trained in the languages, history, and culture of Asia. Robert and Peter (from afar) together managed not only to persuade Caltech to extend my contract, but, after Peter returned, to consider mounting a search for a historian of Asia during the next year. They succeeded not just in authorizing the search, but ultimately in hiring both me and a historian of China. I became aware of how

---

[7] Later published as *The Forgotten Army: India's Armed Struggle for Independence against the British in World War II* (Ann Arbor: University of Michigan Press, 1994).

important it was to have senior mentors and advocates in the world of the academy.

After another year teaching, now finally on a tenure track, I returned to India for an additional year of ethnographic work. I could have used the time simply to revise the dissertation – I had plenty of material for a book that had covered most of the available archival material for a history of a south Indian kingdom – but when doing my dissertation research I had sensed that if I could do more extensive fieldwork in the kingdom I would come much closer to an anthropological as well as historical understanding of the basic dynamics of kingship and caste. I wanted my book to fully capture the ways in which political structures of power had influenced the development and articulation of caste relations in the region, as well as the cultural forces that were fundamental to the ways in which power itself was exercised by the royal caste (an important key, I thought, to figuring out how the caste system really worked). This caste, one that in other parts of southern India had been denominated by the British as a "criminal tribe," had established itself as a dominant social group through a long history of using its military prowess to secure ritual privileges and entitlements associated with legitimate forms of Hindu kingship and sovereignty. I thought that if I could embed myself in the kingdom, I could unlock a much more complete understanding of the relationships of culture and power that had been so mischaracterized by British colonial accounts and subsequent anthropological and sociological analyses of Indian social structures.

To do this work required spending a full year in a small town in a remote part of southern India, a place where there was little for my then wife and three-year-old daughter to do aside from spending long evenings back at the palace with the royal family, where we played volleyball, watched cockfights, ate sumptuous dinners of spicy food that often featured snipe, pheasant, and wild boar, and, on rare occasions, secured strong enough signals from a distant Sri Lankan television station to allow my daughter to watch Sesame Street and Miss Piggy on the only black and white television set in the old kingdom. It was not an easy year, made even more difficult by an outbreak of viral encephalitis in the region that targeted children and was spread by pigs and birds, plentiful species in the environs in which we lived. We rented a large empty house from the former king of another little kingdom to the south, but struggled to find sufficient water for basic purposes and spent most of our time trying to entertain our daughter and find a cook who could use the single kerosene burner we had to provide meals not just for my family but for the entourage we assembled. This included research assistants, an old retired civil servant who introduced me to the local histories of the kingdom, and the steady stream of visitors who, having met me in one village or another, came to tell me about their side of a quarrel in a story that they assumed I would be able to set right when I published my book. I returned to Pasadena after the year with boxes of extraordinary field notes and an exhausted family. We were all relieved to be back in California. Anthropology – at least this kind of anthropology – was not always a comfortable affair.

It all seemed worthwhile when I finally finished my book, to which I gave the Shakespearean title, *The Hollow*

Crown.[8] But anthropological immersion as an outsider in a local society can be disconcerting, and, as I've learned throughout my career, it is not only hard for families but for coming to terms with one's own identity as a responsible scholar. There is a kind of strategic dissembling that goes with the role, an inevitable instrumentalization of social relationships predicated on multiple forms of privilege. On the one hand, that year earned for me the right to call myself a proper anthropologist, and I had direct experiences of rural life in southern India that were invaluable for my understanding of the social life of the subcontinent. On the other hand, however, the year exemplified how strange and unnatural the experience of fieldwork can be, replete with the peculiar contradictions (or should I say conceits) of participant observation. Perhaps I should have learned then to foreswear the ethnographic life. But I am getting ahead of myself.

Although I had been hired by Caltech to teach courses in history, I was again in an interdisciplinary unit, able to interact daily not just with other historians but with literary critics, an art historian, an anthropologist, and colleagues in political science and economics. I was especially pleased when the literature group recruited some exceptional faculty, most crucially Jerry McGann, a romanticist whose work ranged from Byron's poetry to an early interest in using digital techniques for textual editing. McGann, who had a Byronic flair himself, used Caltech to host lectures and workshops and recruit new faculty in literary history, becoming a valued interlocutor as we read new theoretical

[8] Nicholas B. Dirks, *The Hollow Crown: Ethnohistory of an Indian Kingdom* (Cambridge University Press, 1987).

works – Baudrillard and Barthes, Derrida and Foucault – and tried to create a new kind of research cluster for the motley group of humanists. It was fun while it lasted, but McGann ultimately decided he needed the support of a research university with strengths in the humanities and soon began to make plans to leave for the University of Virginia.

Once I was awarded tenure I too decided that for professional reasons I should, if possible, move on to a university where I could teach graduate students and be in a setting where both history and anthropology were important fields for research and advanced training. I was fortunate to be recruited to the University of Michigan, where I not only was given a joint appointment in the two departments but encouraged to create a new interdepartmental PhD program with my Michigan colleagues. This was the first program of its kind in the US and allowed us to train students in both anthropology and history with a lively sense of the importance of interdisciplinary research from the start. I had creative and committed colleagues in both departments and the sense that I was at the cutting edge of new comparative, interdisciplinary, and theoretical currents in several fields. Life as a faculty member in one of our excellent research universities is an extraordinary privilege. Now, for the first time, I began to spend more of my time on institutional work, creating the new PhD program, then directing the area studies center in South and Southeast Asian Studies. I began to learn about administration for the first time, though I thought of it solely as adjunct to my intellectual and professional interests.

Although the formal work load was always modest – we only taught two courses a semester and could for the most part avoid significant administrative assignments if we wished – there was always a sense of pressure: to write more, teach new courses, secure invitations to lecture at other universities and give papers on panels at conferences, find resources to use for inviting colleagues from elsewhere to do the same, attract more graduate students to work with us and crowd more undergraduates into our lecture halls to make the case for our need to have more graduate students, and demonstrate not just how "cutting edge" we were but how signally important our particular perspectives on the disciplinary issues of the day really were. We felt we were at the center of the university, and – like my colleagues even today – that we deserved recognition and support from the administration because of the sheer intellectual importance of our work. Each year felt busier than the year before, and I remember that even as I was tempted to join departmental or university committees, I was worried that any investment in institutional "service" might detract from the time and energy I needed to finish my next article or book. The work of research and scholarship – for that matter of teaching – was never done, as we seemed to create a world in which the satisfactions of a tenured position – being paid to study the things that had preoccupied us since college and graduate school – had to be balanced by a kind of persistent anxiety that we weren't doing enough to justify our good fortune. And yet we enjoyed a world of intense academic exchange that gave us a constant sense of the importance of our intellectual work and our scholarly accomplishment.

There were occasions when this kind of academic exchange became too intense, causing rifts among faculty who otherwise agreed about most important matters. And there were other times when academic quarrels leaked out of the academic bubble to collide with a more chaotic – and skeptical – world outside. As part of an interdisciplinary program that was organized around the themes of "culture, power, and history," I was charged with organizing a conference on culture. As I sought to expand the remit of the conference beyond the "cultural" turn in history, I invited top scholars in fields associated with the new "cultural studies," not just in anthropology and history but in literary studies and critical theory. It was going to be one of the major Michigan events of the fall, and we decided to follow a convention of cultural studies – taking popular culture as the subject of academic analysis – by designing a poster based on a contemporary Benetton advertisement. The image was intended to highlight some of the major themes around race, gender, sexuality, identity, commodification, and representation that would be discussed in the conference papers.[9] To my great chagrin, and I confess as a sign of my own insularity and insensitivity, I was so focused on the themes the poster represented that I did not anticipate that the image – featuring a black woman breastfeeding a white baby – would have been seen as offensive by those outside the critical theory circle. We learned in no uncertain terms that irony and critical distance depended on the same rarified academic culture that we thought we were critiquing. It was a wakeup call, leading me not just to apologize but to accept that I had to work much harder to understand the limits as well as the obligations imposed by my identity and subject position. I began to think differently about the ethical dimensions of both my own scholarship and my academic vocation more generally.

[9] The papers were eventually published in Nicholas B. Dirks (ed.), *In Near Ruins: Cultural Theory at the End of the Century* (Minneapolis: University of Minnesota Press, 1998).

It was hard after that not to recognize the enormous chasm between academic and non-academic worlds, not to mention the growing ruptures in the academic world itself. Cultural studies purported to take the stuff of everyday life as the proper subject of academic scrutiny, and yet frequently began by ignoring the inevitable mismatch between academic modes of knowledge and the outside world.[10] The conference showcased an extraordinary showdown between two anthropologists – Mick Taussig and Fernando Coronil – who both insisted on radically different accounts of the same ritual event in Venezuela, an argument that displayed a growing critique of the way anthropologists from the west asserted privilege over indigenous accounts using theory as a hegemonic academic weapon.[11] Authenticity and issues of identity as well as representation were at the root of the quarrel, and were fast becoming grist for other major debates in anthropology. When I edited the collection of papers for publication, I invoked Michael Ondaatji's elegiac novel, *The English Patient*, that set out a stark picture of the ruins of western civilization after World War II, ruins that contrasted sharply with the promise of the world after decolonization, first in South and Southeast Asia, then in Africa. I was referring to the world of cultural value after

[10] I am referring here to certain tendencies in cultural studies that came more from literary theory than from social or historical analysis. For a moving memoir about one of the most important founders and practitioners of cultural studies in the UK, see Stuart Hall (with Bill Schwarz), *Familiar Strange: A Life Between Two Islands* (Durham, NC: Duke University Press, 2017).

[11] Subsequently published as Fernando Coronil, *The Magical State: Nature, Money, and Modernity in Venezuela* (University of Chicago Press, 1997); Michael Taussig, *The Magic of the State* (New York: Routledge, 1997).

two European wars and the massive upheavals that came as imperial Europe confronted nationalist resistance and insurgency across the world. By the time of the conference, the image of ruins could have applied just as easily to the field of cultural studies itself, since, in its attempt to encompass the contemporary world as its subject, it had increasingly mistaken abstruse theoretical gestures for concrete political action. Little did I know at the time that the campus culture wars had just begun.

I should not have been surprised when the conference was featured in an academic satire, published a few years later by a young novelist who had been there in the audience. The novel, titled *Publish and Perish*,[12] set one of its three narratives at the scene of a conference that began with a controversy over a poster, though the novel itself was about a different academic controversy having to do with Captain Cook. This was a reference to the epic arguments between the anthropologists Gananath Obeyesekere of Princeton and Marshall Sahlins of Chicago that had erupted into print at about the same time. That dispute – it took the form of dueling books – was not unlike the one that took place at the culture conference, where questions of cultural authenticity and identity and anthropological interpretation – and theory – were sharply contrasted and debated.[13] I was flabbergasted when the novel came out because at first

---

[12] James Hynes, *Publish and Perish: Three Tales of Tenure and Terror* (New York: Picador, 1997).
[13] See Gananath Obeyesekere, *The Apotheosis of Captain Cook: European Mythmaking in the Pacific* (Princeton University Press, 1992); Marshall Sahlins, *How Natives Think: About Captain Cook, for Example* (University of Chicago Press, 1995).

I worried that the lead figure, an academic by the name of Gregory Eyck, was modeled on me, though the satire was a grab bag of caricature and parody that made little specific reference to me aside from the poster and my role in convening the conference. That was a good thing, since Gregory – an academic star whose private life was at sharp odds with his public renown – ended up perishing in a macabre end that gave the title to the novel itself. While the novel took cheap shots at academic life, it had a point. The more the academy took on the world in initiatives like cultural studies, the more it seemed to become self-parody. Older preoccupations in cultural theory, in which fields such as anthropology worked hard to understand cultural particularity and difference, were increasingly being jettisoned by a new, exhilarating but ultimately self-referential theoretical virtuosity. These same issues would come back to haunt me once I moved to Columbia and tried to rebuild the department of anthropology some years later. By then I was no longer nearly as compelled by the pleasures of cultural studies, instead far more interested in what it meant to decolonize anthropology, trying to teach students to do solid historical and ethnographic research with deep contextual sensitivity, respect, and attention to local knowledge.

Over the next few years, I spent more time trying to consolidate support for the interdepartmental PhD program and worked with colleagues to set up an ambitious new project to create an International Institute at Michigan. The recognition that this kind of interdisciplinary scholarship was reframing many central debates both in the discipline of anthropology and in the fields of area studies led to a compelling offer to move to

Columbia to chair their flailing anthropology department. Franz Boas established the first department of anthropology in a US university at Columbia in 1896, and for years it was the most important department in the country. Boas, who had been trained in Germany as a geophysicist, worked at the American Museum of Natural History and Clark University before he began to teach at Columbia, where he created and then chaired the department for forty years.[14] Training some of America's most influential anthropologists, he indirectly spawned other anthropology departments through his students as well, for example at Northwestern with Melville Herskovitz, and at Berkeley because of A.L. Kroeber. Boas famously mentored Ruth Benedict and Margaret Mead, as well as Zora Neale Hurston, and he collaborated with W.E.B. DuBois in the establishment of the NAACP. He did rich empirical ethnographic fieldwork, while developing a theory of culture that he used to refute the role of biological features in creating social differences. He worked to unite the humanistic and social sciences with the natural sciences and used anthropology to debunk claims about racial inferiority. His was quite the legacy for anthropology, and it was an honor for me to take on his mantle, especially given the fact that I had received my PhD in history rather than anthropology.

[14] See the wonderful new two-volume biography by Rosemary Levy Zumwalt, *Franz Boas*, vol. I: *The Emergence of the Anthropologist* and vol. II: *Shaping Anthropology and Fostering Social Justice* (Lincoln: University of Nebraska Press, 2019–22). Also see Charles King, *Gods of the Upper Air: How a Circle of Renegade Anthropologists Reinvented Race, Sex, and Gender in the Twentieth Century* (New York: Doubleday, 2019); and Lee D. Baker, *From Savage to Negro: Anthropology and the Construction of Race 1896–1954* (Berkeley: University of California Press, 1998).

The Columbia department had continued for some decades after Boas' death to be one of the most highly ranked departments in the US, but for years it followed Boas in far too literal a fashion, remaining committed to a holistic "four-field" approach long after it began to cause ruptures in the discipline at large. It continued to have outsized personalities, including Marvin Harris, Elliot Skinner, and Robert Murphy (Margaret Mead had an office and an affiliation, but never a tenured appointment), though by the late 1980s and early 1990s it had descended into rancorous quarrels over the direction of the field. When David Cohen was recruited to Columbia in the mid-1990s as the VP of Arts and Sciences to rebuild many of Columbia's most foundationally important departments, he began with the project of remaking anthropology. Taking the department under "receivership" (meaning that the dean assumed full control over departmental affairs), he sought to recruit notable anthropologists from departments first in Chicago and then in Michigan. At some point he landed on my name, and asked me to be chair, and to assume the Franz Boas professorship.

I was able to use the department to recruit an array of postcolonial scholars – from Africa, Asia, and the Caribbean at first – who began to turn the tables on older anthropological modes of understanding the world, even as we recruited faculty in global feminism and African American studies. It was a heady experience to build a different kind of department, but it also led to conflicts, including with some of my colleagues who had initially talked me into coming to Columbia. Even academics who professed a strong commitment to postcolonial perspectives resisted recruiting postcolonial scholars if they came from outside their own networks of training and interaction within the anthropological world of US academia. As I developed an appetite for institutional work – trying all the while to build my intellectual commitments and values into actual academic structures – I realized how institutions – and faculty – were fundamentally resistant to major organizational changes, and that existing structures of academic governance militated against change as well. I also realized that despite all the talk about interdisciplinarity, my own views about the limits of disciplinary categories and protocols were not always widely shared.

The role of chair is strange. For years, I had tried to avoid the position, fearing that it involved a numbing amount of bureaucratic paperwork, a significant distraction from research and writing, and little actual discretion over decisions aside from selecting committee members and every now and then putting a very light thumb on the scale of a contested departmental decision. I only found the job appealing when I was given extraordinary latitude at Columbia as chair of a department that had been taken under "receivership." As I soon realized, however, it was not an easy job under any conditions; one had to put one foot in the administration while keeping the other one firmly in the faculty, trying to keep one's balance astride the fault lines of university governance. Chairs had to represent themselves to their own departments as battling solely for the departmental good, while finding ways to negotiate with administrators who had to frame their own decisions in relation to university-wide goals. When the relationship was good, it tended to pull the chair further into an administrative mindset, but when it became antagonistic, as was too often the case, it encapsulated the worst of university modes of governance, in which chairs and deans blamed the administration and set departments against the university at large.

I soon began to wonder whether a department was the best way to organize academic life, leave alone provide the basis for real intellectual community. I missed the hybrid chemistry of the Anthro-History program at Michigan. Faculty too often thought of themselves as citizens of single departments rather than of universities, projecting onto the screen of departmental life a set of hopes, desires, expectations, and convictions that seemed more than a single administrative unit could or should bear. The department would often see itself in a fundamentally oppositional relationship to the rest of the university – fighting over scarce resources in a putatively zero-sum environment. Faculty with joint appointments were seen as less valuable to each department because of their multiple loyalties and because their academic duties were divided between departments. The department was the principal community for faculty, their fundamental identity and point of reference. And yet that same community was governed by rigid hierarchies and protocols and plagued by long-standing quarrels and resentments, none of them conducive to actual intellectual community. Senior faculty judged junior faculty; they were asked to vote on whether junior faculty members should receive tenure – lifelong membership in the community – after these faculty were already long-standing members of the community, sometimes for as long as seven years – a longer span of time than it took many of them to get their PhDs. Votes on appointments or tenure decisions were often taken personally rather than as inevitable intellectual judgments and disagreements, and routinely fractured social relationships and friendships.[15]

I read with interest a report written by the historical sociologist Immanuel Wallerstein (among others)[16] in which he recommended that all faculty have at least two departmental appointments. The idea was that this would change the dynamic of departmental governance and enable faculty institutionally as well as intellectually to engage with broader currents across the university world. Awkward though the Anthro-History program at Michigan had in some ways been, it was based on the establishment of multiple affiliations for students as well as faculty. I had always found my own cross-disciplinary appointments to broaden institutional relationships across a larger world within the university, and I wished more of my colleagues had that same experience. But perhaps I was swimming against too strong a tide. Faculty, especially at top research universities, often speak about the "department" as their real academic home, far more so than the university itself. And they live their professional lives with a single-minded focus on the discipline, gratifying when they feel things move in their direction, alienating when things don't go their way. Within any one university, the

---

[15] Louis Menand has written that, "It is easy to see how the modern academic discipline reproduces all of the salient features of the professionalized occupation. It is a self-governing and largely closed community of practitioners who have an almost absolute power to determine the standards for entry, promotion, and dismissal in their fields." See Menand, *The Marketplace of Ideas: Reform and Resistance in the American University* (New York: W.W. Norton, 2010), pp. 104–05.

[16] Immanuel Wallerstein *et al.*, *Open the Social Sciences: Report of the Gulbenkian Commission on Restructuring the Social Sciences* (Stanford University Press, 1996).

department was both the chimeric signifier of "community" and the primary locus for discontent.

After four years of chairing, I took a sabbatical to spend a year away from New York. We had a one-year-old son, and Janaki needed time and quiet to write her dissertation. I was completing my book on caste and beginning a new project on the eighteenth-century impeachment trial of Warren Hastings, prosecuted by Edmund Burke. It was wonderful to spend a full year in the quiet of the Berkshire hills, reading and writing, walking through all four seasons in the New England woods, some distance away from departmental life. We came back to New York, feeling refreshed by the year away, a week before September 11th, the day that my caste book was slated to be published.[17] It – and much else – was eclipsed that day by the attacks on the World Trade Center, and we began to adjust to a city and a world that seemed forever changed. Meanwhile, a few weeks later, Columbia appointed a new president, Lee Bollinger, who had been president at Michigan and whom I met once when I gave a lecture on caste at Michigan before leaving for New York.

I continued to work on my book on Burke and Hastings, thinking that this project – combining as it did imperial history and political theory – might begin to allow a slightly broader role for myself in New York's intellectual life. In the department, earlier struggles over the appointments of faculty I had nominated gave way to a more normal ebb and flow, and I began to think about passing over the administrative baton to one of my colleagues and spending more time on my writing and teaching. I had terrific graduate students working on anthropological

---

[17] Nicholas B. Dirks, *Castes of Mind: British Colonialism and the Making of Modern India* (Princeton University Press, 2001).

and historical issues and found my seminars more stim-
ulating than ever, especially the one I began to teach on
a regular basis with Partha Chatterjee, a brilliant scholar
of anti-colonial nationalism and colonial modernity in
India. We complemented each other in our intellectual
styles and backgrounds, while joining forces in training
a new generation of students studying South Asia. I also
found intellectual satisfaction from doing more comparative work in British imperial history with colleagues in
the history department.

The biggest crisis I had to deal with in the department after returning from leave revolved around a young
anthropology faculty member, who in a faculty event
organized to protest the American invasion of Iraq in
the spring of 2003 declared that there should be "a million Mogadishus now." He meant by this to call for the
ambush of American troops as a deterrent to the war,
horrifying many of his fellow faculty who worried that he
had hijacked their anti-war event by celebrating violence
against the US. He certainly captured the attention of
Fox News and other right-wing media and began to get
death threats that seemed genuinely credible. As chair of
the department, I was one of several administrators who
were instructed by politicians and media commentators
to fire him immediately. I also began to get threatening
messages on my phone (this was well before Twitter); I
started watching my back as I walked between the office
and our apartment. One caller left a message on my office
phone every two days, in a kind of countdown suggesting
that he would come after me if I did nothing before his
deadline. I worked with the president's office to move the
junior faculty member into a new apartment in a building

with a twenty-four-hour doorman where we could post university police protection.

This was my first personal taste of real political controversy outside the university. I defended free speech and academic freedom but experienced for the first time how those who found these terms to be mere alibis for irresponsibility could put menacing pressure on the administration. It was disturbing to be targeted with death threats, even as I saw echoes of earlier controversies. Franz Boas had been targeted by President Nicholas Murray Butler during the First World War when he spoke out against the war. And in the midst of the hearings of HUAC under the zealous anti-communist crusade of Joseph McCarthy in the early 1950s, President Greyson Kirk found a way to fire Gene Weltfish, a lecturer in anthropology who had been called to testify in Washington for alleged communist sympathies.[18] It was not the first time the anthropology department had been caught up in the political struggles of the time.

As I stepped down from my second term as chair, I was relieved to leave these struggles behind. Meanwhile, I went out for dinner with Lee Bollinger and was impressed by his intellectual seriousness as well as his grand plans for Columbia. I began to think how interesting it would be to work with him on ideas we discussed over dinner, creating new interdisciplinary and global projects, expanding Columbia's engagement with New York and the world, bringing the arts into a prominent position in the university. I worked with him as he brought the Royal Shakespeare Company to Columbia to

[18] David Price, *Threatening Anthropology: McCarthyism and the FBI's Surveillance of Activist Anthropologists* (Durham, NC: Duke University Press, 2004).

44

stage a production of Salman Rushdie's acclaimed novel, *Midnight's Children* – a book I knew well and admired greatly – and gave a series of public lectures about India's modern history. I didn't know at the time where all this would lead. But I was intrigued as I gossiped with colleagues about how Bollinger might form his own administrative leadership group.

Even as I thought for the first time about what it might be like to be a dean or a provost, I was fully embedded in faculty life. I never thought that an administrative position would compromise my fundamental academic identity. Although I hadn't been able to understand my father's move from a university to a foundation back when I was in college, I had been more than happy when my father returned to the university, this time to the new campus of the University of California in Santa Cruz, as a dean. That is when I realized that deans – my father was the dean of humanities there – could do intellectually engaging work, in his case recruiting the historical philosopher Hayden White to the History of Consciousness Program. He worked with another important thinker whose work had been inspirational for me, Norman O. Brown, while helping this unconventional interdisciplinary program rebuild in the changing intellectual environment of the 1970s. Having been a chair who was able to hire some extraordinarily interesting intellectuals to Columbia, I began to think that I might end up following in my father's footsteps once again.

I have met college and university presidents who decided early on in life that such a role was what they aspired to have. I was not one of them. For years I only became involved in institutional work when it was directly related to my own academic interests. It was only after my experience of chairing the department at Columbia that I began to think more broadly about the university, and how interesting it might be to become more involved outside my own departments. I did carry with me some strong ideas about how universities needed to change. But I was also interested in taking a broader view because my own intellectual interests had never been fully congruent with single disciplines, and because they kept shifting. I had always been interested in how knowledge was produced and organized around disciplines; now I was interested in exploring not just my own disciplines but the intellectual protocols of academic knowledge more generally. Besides, I had recently been denied permission to continue to do primary research work in India because I had been seen as asking a few too many questions about the then Chief Minister of Tamil Nadu, where I was doing my ethnographic research. I was restless and ready to take on new intellectual projects and try on some new roles in the university. Given my interest in the sociology of knowledge, it seemed to be a natural extension of everything I had done so far. A different kind of fieldwork, perhaps, but not a different intellectual calling.

2

The Dean

∾

"Wasn't a college dean a kind of executive?"[1]

Saul Bellow

"Governance is a form of class treason, a leap from "we" to "they,"
and a betrayal of our primary mission – teaching and research.
For this reason also, it is crucial – once a decanal or similar post is
attained – to give evidence of continual suffering."[2]

Henry Rosovsky

So You Want to Be a Dean?

From the point of view of university faculty, deans are
a looming presence, far more critical for their everyday
lives than presidents and provosts. Most faculty want to
befriend them, while always distrusting them; after all,
they make arbitrary decisions, dispensing favors and
judgments, exercising their power with an infinite pot
of money at their disposal that they invariably deny by
talking about the need for budgetary stringency. When
I was a faculty member at the University of Michigan,
I soon came to learn that the Dean of Letters, Sciences,
and the Arts played a critical role for everything from
our salaries to any hope we might have to influence hiring, program development, and departmental prospects.

[1] Saul Bellow, *The Dean's December* (New York: Harper & Row, 1982).
[2] Henry Rosovsky, *The University: An Owner's Manual* (New York:
W.W. Norton, 1990), p. 243.

When I was recruited to Columbia by David Cohen – he was both Dean of the Faculty and in charge of six schools, from the College and the Graduate School to the School of the Arts – I saw that deans can have enormous influence over the fortunes of departments, especially when they became so dysfunctional that they were taken under "receivership," as was the case with anthropology. Columbia's Dean of Arts and Sciences – who was also a Vice President – seemed especially powerful. When I went to Columbia the yearly budget of the Arts and Sciences was close to half a billion dollars.

It was only much later that it occurred to me I might one day move into David's office as his successor. When the phone rang late one evening in the spring of 2004, seven years after I had moved to Columbia as a chair, I knew it was the new provost, my colleague from the history department, Alan Brinkley, on the line. Alan, a highly esteemed historian of twentieth-century American politics and son of the legendary TV newscaster for NBC, David Brinkley, had taken on his new role just the year before. He had told me that Lee Bollinger was thinking of asking me to become the next Vice President and Dean of the Faculty of the Arts and Sciences. He was calling now to make sure I was still interested in the position. I told him I was in. I had spent the year away from being chair and was not missing it. I had become intrigued, however, both by Bollinger's ideas, and by the work David Cohen had been doing, not just what he did in anthropology but across a range of departments. Cohen had created the Academic Review Committee, on which I had served, that oversaw the periodic reviews of departments and major centers or programs. He had invited eminent scientists to evaluate the basic science departments, with the request that they prepare a white paper proposing what it might take to return Columbia to national prominence across the sciences. Reading that report I learned about other sides of the campus I knew little about.

As chair I had begun to have a slightly broader view of the university, but I was excited by the prospect of learning more about areas of university life far removed from my own. I also had begun to develop a more synoptic sense of what I thought Columbia could achieve, and I was intrigued with the idea of working with Bollinger, a gifted scholar and intellectual as well as an administrator. I realized, however, that the principal job of a dean is to raise the rankings of each department – increase the quality of faculty and in turn of graduate students, competing with other universities for the best of both. That gave only limited leeway for more idiosyncratic pursuits. I had been lucky with the anthropology department to have been able to indulge my own interests while still raising the profile of the department.

When I started the VP job in late August of 2004, I moved into a corner office suite in Low Library, the neo-classical domed building at the center of the Columbia campus that had been modeled by architect Charles McKim on the Pantheon in Rome. My office was just down the hall from the offices of the provost and the president, and I enjoyed walking up the steps and into this splendid building each morning just after eight, on my walk back from dropping my son at the Columbia School at the corner of 110th and Broadway. Taking up residence in Low, however, meant a major life change. I no longer had control over my time; my calendar was now a public document stretching out weeks, and even months, in advance. Used to the flexible rhythms of academia, I found myself living what seemed a corporate life, usually wearing a jacket and tie to look the part. Even more jarring, Roxie Smith, my new chief of staff, told me that I should learn to accept that I no longer had friends at Columbia. She looked at me with great seriousness, trying to persuade me that while I doubtless thought that I could keep all my collegial relationships fully intact, something fundamental had changed. Everyone at Columbia would begin to think of me instrumentally, not as their old colleague and friend, but as someone who could dispense resources, influence, and information. I remember looking at her in mock horror, thinking that she was not just exaggerating, but failing to understand that the whole reason I had taken the job was to continue exactly the kind of work I had already done as a faculty member and chair. Of course I would keep my friends, and develop new friendships along the way.

There were the usual jokes about crossing over to the dark side – *pace* Henry Rosovksy's quote at the top of this chapter (he had been the Dean of the Faculty of Arts and Sciences at Harvard) – but administration for me seemed to be defined in large part by the people who did these jobs. George Rupp, who was president when I first came to Columbia, was a scholar of Sri Lankan Buddhism. Jonathan Cole, the provost, was a sociologist of science who had played a key role in developing the use of citation indices to measure scholarly impact. And now, Lee Bollinger was a distinguished constitutional scholar who had led the University of Michigan in its legal efforts to maintain affirmative action; and Alan Brinkley was a leading American historian with award-winning books on Huey Long and American liberalism, and a half-completed manuscript on Henry Luce. Most of the deans before David had rotated back into their positions on the faculty; I assumed that Roxie was really reflecting on her own experience working with him. When I raised the question with him, he laughed it off, and said that he was friends with the faculty he wanted to be friends with, though he didn't name any names. Even though I didn't believe Roxie at the time, her comment stayed with me, and I came, in time, to acknowledge the tensions that can develop between administrators and faculty colleagues.

The first thing I had to do as dean was come to terms with the fact that I was responsible for a total budget of what in 2004 was close to $650 million. In the anthropology department I had managed a small budget, which, aside from salary lines for the four full-time office staff and office expenses, consisted mainly of a $30,000 block grant for departmental activities. At this point I assumed responsibility for a budget that was, so the saying in academic administration had it, a tub "on its own bottom." That is, I had to balance the expenses of faculty salaries, financial aid for undergraduates and graduate students, taxes to the central administration for our share of "central services" and other costs related to facilities and debt service, with the revenue that came in from tuition, endowment payouts, contracts and grants, and other miscellaneous sources of income. Day after day I studied spreadsheets and budget memos; in the evenings I would sometimes stop by David Cohen's apartment for advice and, at the beginning, simple reassurance. I learned that the budget had been balanced with "aggressive" (that meant, I learned, unrealistic) assumptions about the projected profits of the new School for Continuing Education. I began a long period of creative financing that mostly meant seeking additional funding from the central administration for initiatives of which they might approve and perhaps even bankroll.

Soon after the beginning of the fall term, I began to hear about the David Project. It started as rumor, in the first instance about a video that had been circulating called "Columbia Unbecoming." For some time, I didn't actually see it, but I heard that it made a series of charges against a small group of faculty in the Department of Middle Eastern Languages and Cultures (MEALAC). The David Project was a somewhat indistinct group, loosely linked to "Campus Watch," an organization set up by Martin Kramer and Daniel Pipes to call out anti-Israel sentiment on American college campuses. Finally, I saw the video, and it was an astonishing piece of propaganda. Faces that were blurred spoke about the terrible climate of anti-Semitism in MEALAC, identities obscured because, so the charge went, those who spoke out were in danger of being punished for their views. The video was constantly edited and changed, partly for new audiences, and partly as new charges against Columbia were unleashed. We began to hear from trustees, and soon from journalists, asking what we were doing in response to these allegations. Anthony Weiner, then a Congressman who was launching a run for Mayor of New York, called on us to fire the offending faculty – especially an untenured professor by the name of Joseph Massad – immediately. In late November, *The New York Post* ran an article about the climate of hate at Columbia. Columbia trustees began to ask the president and the senior administration what we were going to do to respond to the charges, some of which involved classroom situations, in which the traditional protections of academic freedom also included various guarantees about welcoming different points of view.

I was new to the job but aware how this kind of crisis could escalate, and what the stakes would be for me now that I was the relevant dean. I was already deeply concerned about the role of Campus Watch and other organizations in creating a growing climate of intolerance and surveillance, having watched the attacks on Edward Said over his criticisms of Israel (which he never engaged in, by the way, in classroom situations, while exercising his First Amendment and academic freedom rights outside as all faculty were ostensibly allowed to do). Given my own background, academic freedom was extremely important and a critical condition for making the university the kind of intellectual space I wanted to work in.

I began reading about the history of academic freedom and how it was connected to the turbulent history of American universities. In the nineteenth century and for the first two decades of the twentieth, university administrators and trustees had the ultimate authority about issues ranging from faculty hiring and firing to curriculum. When Mrs. Leland Stanford (then chair of the board of trustees at Stanford) fired the faculty member Edward Ross from his professorship in 1901, there was a major uproar. Seven other faculty quit in protest, including Arthur Lovejoy, who went on, with some key faculty from Columbia, to establish the American Association of University Professors (AAUP) in 1915. That organization worked both to secure certain general protections for faculty, including specifying the meaning of tenure, and to articulate the principles of academic freedom. These principles, widely ratified across the larger ecosystem of higher education, stipulated that faculty should be seen as free citizens in a democracy and should not be evaluated or penalized on the basis of political opinions they held and expressed outside of the classroom. They also, however, "should be careful not to introduce into their teaching controversial matter which has no relation to their subject."[3] This statement – later amended in 1970 to clarify that it was not ruling against controversy but rather against material not related to the subject matter of the course – was clear in conferring curricular authority on faculty, seeking as it did to protect them from political influence either from the administration or outside forces including trustees. At the same time, it emphasized that professional rather than political criteria should guide what was taught, meaning that faculty would be the ones to judge the appropriateness of classroom content, though within the confines of their professional associations and authority, not as an expression of their political views.

While most of the charges in the David Project's film had to do with general statements of the kind that were clearly governed by the protections of free speech and academic freedom, some went after what were alleged to be unprofessional comments in the classroom itself. This was a deliberate acknowledgement, as the then director of the Columbia/Barnard chapter of Hillel had said, after collecting 33,000 signatures for a campaign against the

---

[3] American Association of University Professors, "Statement of Principles on Academic Freedom and Tenure" (1940).

divestment proposal, that the "battleground regarding the Middle East at Columbia University has shifted to the classroom."[4]

After much internal discussion, we accepted that we had to investigate the charges, but that we would do so by constituting a committee of fellow faculty, following the protocols of faculty governance. Floyd Abrams, a distinguished constitutional lawyer who specialized in First Amendment rights, was brought in, at first to serve on the committee, but soon afterwards, to my relief (it could have been seen as a violation of faculty governance to have someone not on the faculty be part of this committee), to be an advisor rather than a member. The committee consisted of highly regarded faculty; it was chaired by Ira Katznelson, a professor of political science who had been interim VP, and four others, including two who had signed the divestment petition. The committee met for months and took the testimony of sixty-two students, professors, and administrators (reading written submissions from sixty others), ultimately finding no evidence of any statements made that could reasonably be "construed as anti-Semitic" and in particular "no basis for believing that Professor Massad systematically suppressed dissenting views in his classroom." Although in looking at three alleged instances of intimidation it found that two were "credible," it found no violation of any policy or of guidelines about classroom instruction. While Massad and some other members of the department were critical not just of the committee and its investigation but also of

---

[4] Quoted in Scott Sherman, "The Mideast Comes to Columbia," *The Nation*, March 16, 2005.

its findings (demanding a much more robust defense), a number of students who had called for the investigation were even more dismissive, though for different reasons. This included Bari Weiss, an undergraduate who wrote that these "students were intimidated because of their ideological positions, a fact that was willfully neglected in the report."[5] The fact remained that the students, like Weiss, who complained most about intimidation were among the group of students most effective in using outside groups to put political pressure on faculty, and on the administration.

The report was nevertheless critical of the lack of clear and robust grievance procedures, either in the Arts and Sciences or for that matter across the university. Although many faculty well beyond the Middle East department had been upset that we had responded to the allegations at all, I learned that the university had been ill equipped to deal with issues of this kind, especially when a grievance had been filed by Columbia students. We would have fared much better had we not had to invent the procedures for the committee from scratch. To faculty critics I argued that the new robust grievance procedures would in fact work to protect academic freedom in the future. Even though I agreed with them that the David Project itself, along with Campus Watch, was an insidious effort to infiltrate the university and stifle political criticism of Israel, I held that the university had to be responsive to concerns on the part of students, whether or not they used outside groups to prosecute their case. In my view,

---

[5] Quoted in Gabriella Doob, "Columbia Report Addresses Anti-Semitism Charges," *Brown Daily Herald*, April 6, 2005.

the university was on stronger ground once it conducted its own investigation, on the basis of which it could evaluate and confirm or dismiss the allegations. From that time on, however, I began to see evidence that some of my friends on campus seemed less – yes Roxie – friendly.

The crisis had other immediate effects as well, however, especially on the internal functioning of the Department of Middle Eastern Languages and Cultures. After a deeply fractious meeting of the department in which I was present, I decided that I needed to take the department under receivership. Senior members of the faculty were not wrong to feel they were under attack, but they were in sharp disagreement with each other about most everything else, to the point that routine departmental governance was in abeyance. Given the number of other departments that had recently been under receivership at Columbia, this did not seem to me at first a radical move, though it was in fact hugely controversial. The leadership of the department began immediately suggesting that I was playing the role of Lord Balfour, who had declared that Palestine was a Jewish homeland in 1917. Their reaction conveyed a general distrust of the Columbia administration, while also charging that my interest in expanding MEALAC to include South Asian and African studies was intended to muzzle – or at the very least overwhelm – advocacy for Palestinian causes in the department.

Leaving aside questions about the claim that the department should have an explicitly political agenda, it had long been the case that the department had little serious interest in expanding its ranks to cover South Asia beyond the two faculty positions – one in Sanskrit and one in Hindi-Urdu – that traditionally resided there. Most in the department were also, at least initially, opposed to including African studies because, they complained, it would take away from their focus on the Middle East. Given my interest in expanding the global reach of the Arts and Sciences, MEALAC was in fact the only real departmental space that could house South Asian and African studies, and there was little appetite for creating a new department in the Arts and Sciences. I made clear, however, that no expansion would be undertaken without a further expansion as well in our commitment to the study of Middle Eastern subjects.

In subsequent years, the long, drawn-out, and highly politicized tenure case of Joseph Massad drew widespread attention both from those who were still expressing concern about Massad's public political profile and from many scholars across the academy who were convinced that Columbia could not conduct a neutral evaluation of his candidacy. Massad was finally recommended for tenure by Alan Brinkley: one of the last acts of his time as provost. The process had been excruciating, and although it was in the end a clear sign of Columbia's commitment to academic freedom, it also left many people from different political positions disgruntled and critical of the university and the administration.

Like many others who went off to college in the late 1960s, I had believed that the university was an inherently political institution, and that it needed to distance itself from the military-industrial complex and make courageous stands on issues ranging from the unjust war in Vietnam to civil rights. As I went through the stages as a student and then a professor, I continued to believe that on issues of the day, whether an unjust war in the 1960s and 1970s, or apartheid in South Africa in the 1980s, or the need for affirmative action when it came under political attack in the 1990s, universities could no more adopt positions of neutrality than knowledge itself could be completely objective and apolitical. This was not a casual view on my part. In my scholarly work, I wrote extensively about the politics of knowledge, and had been consistently concerned with the distortions of colonial forms of knowledge on western academic understandings of India, and for that matter on many anthropological representations of the world.[6]

And yet, first as chair and then as VP and dean, I came to recognize that while the university was inevitably thrust into political disputes – ranging from affirmative action to the Middle East – the protection of academic freedom also required a professional commitment on the part of the administration to fairness, open-mindedness, and good faith efforts to operate with as much neutrality of judgment as possible. This was necessary in the first instance around differing disciplinary standards concerning academic knowledge, that required opinionated – and, yes, polemical – academics like me to adopt far more capacious frames for academic judgment given the wide provenance of the Arts and Sciences. It was also necessary, however, around a conception of politics itself, whether viewed in academic terms concerning questions having to do with scholarship or pedagogy, or more broadly in the external political contests, whether over domestic political issues or, say, around the question of Palestine. I did not

---

[6] See my introduction to Cohn, *Colonialism and Its Forms of Knowledge*; also see my *Castes of Mind*.

like the way the David Project had fashioned its attack on Columbia, but I had to learn how to take a broader view, grappling with the implications for the university at large rather than the political demands of a single department or group of faculty colleagues. In the process, I not only struggled to make clear distinctions between political and intellectual judgments, I also thought more broadly about the historical significance of academic freedom as it had developed in the American context. This entailed considerable deference to professional communities of judgment, much as had been insisted upon by Arthur Lovejoy and John Dewey as they first formulated the principles of academic freedom. But it also entailed going back to the writings of Max Weber, who argued in his "vocation lectures" against the university as a place for tendentious opinionating and sermonizing, while recognizing and embracing the inevitable and necessary place of moral and political values in all serious intellectual work.[7]

During my entire first year as VP and dean, I was not sure how long I would last in the role. The political pressures were difficult to negotiate. I knew that if I was asked to take certain stands by the trustees I would have little choice but to step down. As we drove back and forth from the city to our home in the Berkshires, on occasional weekends and

---

[7] Max Weber, *Charisma and Disenchantment: The Vocation Lectures*, ed. Paul Reitter and Chad Wellmon, trans. Damion Searls (New York: Penguin Random House, 2020). I had never accepted Weber's view that the separation of fact and value should be a founding principle of social science – indeed, many of the most problematic efforts to make social science "scientistic" in the postwar American context cited Weber as the authority – but I was also appreciative that Weber had taken great pains to stress the need to study and evaluate values while maintaining as much distance as possible from any given value position (pp. 34–41).

for the thanksgiving holiday, I talked with Janaki about how disappointing it would be if the administrative experiment couldn't continue, since I was engaged by other parts of the role. Even as I believed I was pushing back against political pressures, I worried about where to draw the line between what I should do and what I might be asked or pressured to do. I also began to develop a more nuanced sense of how universities approach political controversies, while I worked to fashion my own approach, albeit one that was not always approved of by all of my faculty colleagues.

That is not to say that there weren't times then – and since – that I haven't felt conflicted in these kinds of situations, or when I had conversations with some donors, alumni, and political figures in which I had to work hard to suppress my own personal views. Fortunately, I had already had some relevant experience from my days of doing fieldwork, when I had no choice but to listen to a village elder speak about caste as a natural system of inequality without reacting or arguing back. Now I could be more responsive, however, and I came to see that controversies on campus could on occasion provide openings to defend a broad idea of the university, an idea that stressed disagreement and debate. Indeed, there were times I could listen to concerns from those who were seriously troubled by the views or statements of some faculty (or students) and then push back not on their own views so much as on how they thought we should respond to their views. I explained why it was that wildly discrepant ideas had to be protected. General support for the commitment to free speech enshrined in the First Amendment of the US constitution made this easier, as I could make the case that the principle of free speech was only really tested when one confronted speech acts one found abhorrent. At the same time, I realized that it was sometimes even more difficult to argue with friends from my more immediate academic world, who could not accept the ways in which I tried to enact a kind of administrative neutrality. Friends who had celebrated when I became dean became less friendly when they realized I wasn't always going to support their agenda. Faculty culture made it easy to see the administration as a malign force, even (perhaps especially) when individuals approved of and benefitted from the general initiatives that I or others had advanced.

By the time my new book on the British empire came out in 2006, however, I had settled into the role.[8] The book itself was deeply critical of the foundational myths of empire, connecting my analysis of British empire to the assertions of some – both in the Bush administration and outside – that the empire might serve as a useful model for US foreign policy.[9] The book generated a lively debate, finding most of its critics in Britain where I found myself criticized mainly for having trespassed into the field of British history (and for taking too negative a view about empire). I should perhaps have spent more time following up in the ensuing debates, which themselves had only grown more urgent both with the war in Iraq and with global crises around immigration, nationalism, and post-imperial political and economic regimes, but I also had to keep up with the grueling pace of my day job – the sheer number of hours that were booked for meetings and formal events

[8] Nicholas B. Dirks, *The Scandal of Empire: India and the Creation of Imperial Britain* (Cambridge, MA: Harvard University Press, 2006).

[9] For an academic account that took this line, see Niall Ferguson, *Empire: How Britain Made the Modern World* (New York: Penguin, 2003).

each day never failed to take my breath away. I relished the opportunity to do extensive hiring across multiple departments and schools at Columbia – through the new diversity funding as well as other initiatives to rebuild key departments and use New York's newfound allure to make some critical senior appointments. It was a heady time to be a dean at Columbia, as I worked with departmental chairs to identify "targets of opportunity" to help rebuild their departments, and with Jean Howard, a feminist scholar of literature who led the diversity initiative, to diversify them. I learned a lot about the individuals we recruited – or tried to recruit – often discovering more about their personal circumstances than I might have wished. And truth be told, it was often these logistical issues that made a recruitment possible. Since I also played a role in assigning apartments to faculty, I learned about pregnancies, marriages, divorces, and, well, a lot of other things too.

I also inherited an initiative from my predecessors to rebuild the economics department, with a major financial commitment from the president's office. When I started, the initiative had yielded one new hire, but had then stalled. The problem with hiring top economists in a department that at the time was ranked around fourteenth nationally was that they were typically not inclined to leave top five (or for that matter top ten) departments even for an Ivy League job in New York City where they could live in a spacious Columbia apartment with a river view. They had their own term for this – risk aversion – as well as a much more clearly ranked list of the best economists than existed for other disciplines, not unlike the NBA draft. During my first year, we decided to try a technique we called "cluster hiring," authorizing a large number of offers with the hope that faculty would accept if they also believed they were coming with a cohort of other top economists, which would translate into higher rankings for the department. I decided we needed to be bold to have any chance at success and authorized ten offers with the belief that we would probably at best manage to recruit three, which is what we thought we could afford. The indefatigable chair, Don Davis, kept coming back to the office with new names and possible hires that he implored me to pursue. Given the lack of success in earlier years, we kept giving him the green light, and by the end of the recruiting season I had agreed to make eighteen offers. Had we had that many acceptances, our budget would have been in freefall, but while we avoided that outcome, we brought in a talented group that began the serious work of building momentum. By the time we were done, we had moved the department into the top ten.

Although recruiting great faculty in any field was always rewarding, by far the most gratifying part of the job was when I was able to recruit leading intellectuals and writers whose work I had read and admired. Orhan Pamuk – after he had taken up residence in New York when some comments he made about the Armenian genocide to a German publication in the winter of 2005 met with sharp reactions in Turkey, including book burnings and criminal indictments – readily accepted a regular appointment at Columbia. Hiring other talented writers – among them Richard Ford, Colm Toibin, and Deborah Eisenberg – and sometimes getting to know them well during the process, made the headaches of the job seem more than worth it.

I also learned about how to raise money for the university. At my first meeting of the board of trustees, I met a graduate of the law school who was moved by my account of the importance of undergraduate teaching in the context of a major research university. We struck up a relationship – aided by the fact that we had both spent formative periods of our youth in the farming country of central Iowa – and he began to suggest he would make a significant gift to reward faculty for transformational teaching. As a dean, I was especially attuned to retaining promising junior faculty when they established their reputations for research and would begin to get offers from other universities where the cost of living was lower than in New York City. After a visit to Philadelphia, Gerry Lenfest offered to give us an endowment for unrestricted prize money to be presented each year to ten faculty. When I later phoned the winners of this prize – offering them each three years of payments of $25K with no strings attached – I felt like a quiz show host.

But there were headaches. One had to do with the relationship between the Arts and Sciences and Columbia College, and it had been troubled for years. In the summer of 1997 when I was in the process of moving to New York, *The New York Times* carried a story about a major administrative shake-up at Columbia. George Rupp, the president, had asked Austin Quigley, the Dean of the College, to step down from his position immediately at the recommendation of David Cohen. Cohen had become exasperated by the fact that the College Dean simply refused to report to him in any meaningful sense. He had been recruited to build up the scholarly profile of the departments, only to find himself at war with the College over issues like the teaching needs of the core curriculum. There had been years of tension between the Arts and Sciences and the College, dating back to the creation of the Arts and Sciences in 1982, expressing the deep-seated desire for autonomy and control on the part of the college faculty. The division of the Arts and Sciences was created in the first instance as an administrative entity to coordinate the hiring and administration of faculty who taught students in the graduate school as well as in Columbia College. While most faculty taught both undergraduates and graduate students, many had been hired in earlier days when there were separate faculties, with distinct administrative offices and budgets. The College no longer had a faculty of its own, but it still managed the teaching of the courses in Columbia's famed core curriculum and advocated for undergraduate education, while also controlling significant financial resources.

No sooner had Rupp fired Quigley, however, than he was besieged by prominent College alumni who saw Quigley's removal as a rejection of the university's commitment to undergraduate education, favoring graduate education and faculty research instead. Within several days, Rupp reversed his decision, and agreed to reinstate Quigley. As news of this reversal was printed in the Times on July 4th,[10] we had just put our possessions in a truck on its way to New York, and I called David in a panic. I was worried that he might resign, putting at risk all the commitments – many of them verbal ones – he had made about resources that were to be devoted to the rebuilding of the anthropology department.

David had in fact offered George his resignation, but Rupp worked hard to deflect criticism of the Arts and

---

[10] William H. Honan, "Bowing to Pressure, Columbia President Reinstates Dean," *New York Times*, July 4, 1997.

Sciences after the reversal and managed to keep David in his position along with Austin. The relationship between David and Austin never fully recovered, and there was often a stalemate between the College and the Arts and Sciences. While this had little impact on what I set out to do in anthropology, it was a major source of institutional tension, and damaged the administrative capacity of the departments as well as the College. It was also the discordant manifestation of the unresolved tension between teaching and research, a long-running problem that bedeviled universities as various as Harvard, Michigan, Chicago, and Berkeley. One of the first visits I made, upon taking on David's position in 2004, was to see Austin. I told him that we needed to find ways to work together without the friction that had marred his relationship with my predecessor and that could undermine both of our agendas.

I'm sure Austin was skeptical at first, though he was exceedingly polite and rather touched that I had made sure to have our first meeting on his turf in Hamilton Hall. He had reason to be skeptical; the anthropology department did not contribute much to teaching in the core, and during my six years as chair I had been much more focused on building the graduate program than on anything of direct concern to the Dean of the College. He took me at my word, however, and we built a partnership that surprised not just many of the prominent alums who were ready in turn to be suspicious about me but other senior administrators as well. Austin began to include me in key meetings of the College's advisory groups, and I sought his advice on how best to craft the priorities for the capital campaign in which the Arts and Sciences needed to play a much larger role than it had in previous fundraising efforts. Much to my son's annoyance, we also frequently met on Riverside Drive when I was either walking my son to school or taking him and our dog for a walk, invariably talking about university matters for what Ishan thought was an eternity.

In the spring of 2007, eleven years after a hunger strike that had been staged by students advocating for the introduction of ethnic studies, a group of students decided to camp out on the lawn and go without solid food again to press their new demands. Although my predecessor had successfully resolved the first strike – which had been in full swing during my recruitment to Columbia (David had received updates from that hunger strike at the restaurant when I was being wined and dined) – the students were right that all had not gone as planned. The historian of Asian American life who had been recruited from Cornell to direct the new Center for Ethnic Studies had never received a tenured appointment in the history department. The junior faculty – two of whom I had hired in the anthropology department – were either failing to get tenure or deciding to leave for other positions, and the lack of departmental status frustrated the initial efforts to install ethnic studies in a secure way in the Arts and Sciences. A group of five students declared that they would go on a hunger strike. They appointed another group of students to be their intermediaries with the administration. Austin and I began to meet with this group each evening, both to understand better what the demands of the strikers were, and to begin the process of negotiation.

At first, the demands were somewhat unfocused, ranging from establishing a full-blown department of ethnic studies to stopping the development of the new Columbia campus in Manhattanville, a mile to the north of the main campus. The first thing we did was to separate the different issues. The expansion project was still in early stages of development and not in my direct purview anyway. Instead, we agreed to take on the issue of ethnic studies. It helped that I had been one of the chairs who had been welcoming to the new initiative in ethnic studies ten years before, and that I understood and sympathized with the political aspirations of the students. I had to be clear, however, that I did not agree with them that a department was the only way to fix the problem. And I told them that most faculty would oppose the creation of a new department at that time. This led to a standoff for several days, though I continued to meet with the students each evening and began talking with Austin about how to raise funds for a senior position in the field that would allow us to garner greater academic standing for the kinds of faculty and programs the students wanted to secure.

At the start of the strike we let the students dictate the pace of negotiations, but as some students began to manifest the health effects of their exclusively liquid diet we knew we had to move more quickly. We negotiated that striking students needed to rotate, removing the immediate health pressures, but soon learned that another group of students was getting ready to protest the protestors. We ordered in extra supplies of pizza and soda and had several long night sessions, during which I kept reiterating that I had authorized three new positions in ethnic studies, no small commitment. This was something that in fact I had already decided to do to replace departing faculty, but which the students felt they needed to represent as a response to their demands. I added to this, however, that I would devote a new professorial chair – funded by the chair of the board at the urging of Austin – to this purpose and recruit a senior tenured faculty member to direct the Center. We worked together on developing new procedures to recruit junior faculty who would be more successful in their home departments. After close to two long weeks, the strike was called off.

In addition to their other concerns, the striking students had been deeply critical about the western and elite focus of the Columbia core curriculum, and its exclusion of the voices of people of color and experiences of marginalization that were key to ethnic studies. When I came to Columbia, I was also concerned about the ethnocentrism of the core, not surprisingly given that I had worked throughout my career to insert the study of Asia into mainstream curricula. But the issues were in fact more complicated. Columbia had developed canonic courses in non-western civilizations; I had used the "source books" for Chinese, Japanese, and Indian civilizations that had been developed at Columbia in the years after World War II in the courses I taught at Caltech and Michigan. These source books were compiled under the impetus of W. Theodore (Ted) de Bary, a scholar of neo-Confucianism who had introduced the teaching of Chinese civilization at Columbia in 1947. Soon after the end of World War II, when the US was taking on a new level of global power, Columbia incorporated a succession of non-western civilization classes, not to replace the western core, but to supplement it with a set of optional "distribution" courses. In subsequent years, a comparative civilization course was required, and in time this requirement was broadened to include a list of courses that were grouped under the rubric of "major cultures," no longer defined solely by a distinctly western "civilizational" standard, and inclusive of ethnic studies.

The fundamental elements of the core, however, were still decidedly western. During my years at Columbia, students in the college had to take two semesters of "Literature Humanities" – a course that started with Homer's *Iliad* (a copy of which was distributed to every incoming freshman during the summer before they started college), and then traversed a familiar canon of western texts from the Greeks and the Romans to Jane Austen. They also took two semesters of "Contemporary Civilization" – a course that covered western philosophy and the history of political as well as social theory. Two other core courses, one in music and the other in art history, were general introductions to western art and culture. Efforts were made to diversify the canon, but the limits were clear.

The core had its origins in a set of courses devised at the end of World War I, first on war, and then on peace. It evolved over the next two decades as these courses became the hallmark of Columbia's shared – "general" – curriculum. The core was an important part of Columbia's identity, and for a long time signified the priority given to studying western civilization while also retarding the development of discrete undergraduate majors (which only really developed in the 1950s). While changes were made, and reports were written, any major revision would have set off a tempest among alumni, administrators, and faculty. Not all students loved their core courses at the time they took them, but alumni tended to remember the core as the high point of their undergraduate intellectual lives. The fact that they all shared it in common also gave it a kind of meaning that only grew in strength over time as a kind of collective memory of undergraduate life. The texts were powerful, and powerfully important, whether students read Sophocles or Shakespeare, Hobbes or Hegel. Eric Foner, an American historian who taught for years at Columbia, noted that when he was an undergraduate in the early 1960s, the joke was that Columbia was a place where Jewish students studied Christian theology taught by atheist professors. And, in fact, one of the justifications for the core was that it gave students who had less "cultural capital" than students who went to Harvard, Yale, or Princeton (Columbia had significantly more Jewish students, and more students who went to public schools, than the other top Ivies) the kind of polish they needed to succeed in their careers when competing with graduates from more upper-crust backgrounds. Also, although I complained – like many departmental chairs – about the amount of time students spent on the core (and indeed as I criticized it for its reinstatement of the centrality of western civilization), there was also no doubt that it ensured a basic foundation for a college education that many faculty – myself included – appreciated when we taught upper class courses in the humanities and social sciences.[11]

David Denby, a long-time film critic for the *New Yorker*, decided to return to Columbia in 1991 to retake the core thirty years after he had studied it as an undergraduate, writing an entertaining memoir called *Great*

[11] For a broad and helpful account of the issues involved in the history of general education efforts in the US, see Menand, *Marketplace of Ideas*, pp. 23–57.

Books a few years later.[12] Denby had a wonderful time not only reliving the intellectual memories of younger years but enjoying the pedagogical gifts of some of Columbia's finest faculty. He wrote the memoir in part, however, because he understood "great books" courses were in the crosshairs of the culture wars – Allan Bloom's bestseller *The Closing of the American Mind* had been published just a few years before.[13] Denby hardly subscribed to Bloom's polemic, but he made an impassioned and intelligent defense of the classical content of the core, especially given the open, Socratic, methods of instruction in the courses he took. His book, a kind of reader's diary, illuminated how great texts were discussed and questioned by students who were invited to subject them to critiques of all kinds. He only briefly explored the tensions that had already begun to emerge for new generations of students, actively recruited to advance the diversity of the student body well beyond the many Jewish students from New York public schools, when they encountered the symbolic dominance of an enshrined western civilizational core. The two ethnic studies hunger strikes certainly raised those issues in a more urgent way than Denby could have seen at the time. But we still had to accept that the core made up the guard rails we had to use to negotiate student demands, and there was little the administration could do aside from reiterating that

[12] David Denby, *Great Books: My Adventures with Homer, Rousseau, Woolf and Other Indestructible Writers of the Western World* (New York: Simon & Schuster, 1996).
[13] Allan Bloom, *The Closing of the American Mind: How Higher Education Has Failed Democracy and Impoverished the Souls of Today's Students* (New York: Simon & Schuster, 1987).

ethnic studies courses, along with area studies, were part of a distribution list for what we called "major cultures," essentially a breadth requirement.

My own views on the core evolved during my time at Columbia. My father had taught "Contemporary Civilization" when he was doing his graduate work in philosophy in the mid-1940s. I still had his copy of the 1946 Source Book that had been compiled for that course on my bookshelf. When my wife became an assistant professor she, like most other junior faculty in the humanities, taught that same course for her first three years as a way of getting support for a full year of leave to finish her book. A historian of India, she came to relish teaching the core because of the sheer enjoyment she took from reading texts as various as the Hebrew Bible, Plato's *Republic*, Aristotle's *Nicomachean Ethics*, and Augustine's *City of God*. We were already well acquainted with basic works in the history of western political and social theory, from Locke, Burke, Marx, Freud, and DuBois, that made up the curriculum of the second term. And we knew these works were useful preparation for students when they went on to read contemporary critical theory – of great importance to debates in Indian history – whether Marx, Weber, Gramsci, or Foucault. But, like me, she understood that the core had a way of reaffirming the preeminence of the idea of western civilization that played out across the entirety of Columbia's curriculum.

Some years later, I decided to teach the second term of Contemporary Civilization myself, and I found it possible to mix and match texts, and authors, in a way that emphasized the constitutive role of European empire for the rise of modern western power. I taught the same authors that made up the standard CC class, but asked the students to read Edmund Burke's denunciation of Warren Hastings along with his screed on the French Revolution, to consider some of John Stuart Mill's paternalist writings on India along with his theory of liberty, to read Hegel on India and China alongside his idea of the "master–slave" dialectic, to encounter Marx on the 1857 rebellion in India as well as on capitalism, to contemplate Weber on the religions of India along with his work on the Protestant ethic, and to parse Gandhi's musings on the pitfalls of western civilization in his classic work on India's freedom struggle called *Hind Swaraj* at the same time they read Freud's *Civilization and Its Discontents*. I took this route, rather than simply teaching a course in Indian civilization as I had done before at both Caltech and Michigan, not so much to advocate for the idea of civilizational equivalence as to historicize the core – in this case in the context of the imperial past. Not only did this have the effect of casting a long historical shadow on western ideals, it also made clear that the naturalization of a narrative about western civilization was about more than just the inevitable triumph of superior texts and concepts. Yet I also enjoyed spending time with some of the authors that I, like Denby, had read when I was in college.

The core also had the curious effect of securing a significant place for the humanities in the undergraduate curriculum. Since the 1990s, and even more after the great recession of 2008–09, students across most colleges have been turning away from fields like English and history, not to mention anthropology, moving instead to economics, business, and computer science. They were told by their peers, parents, and prospective employers that they needed to focus their college studies on subjects that would land them well-paying jobs in banks or in technology. The fact that the core was baked into the Columbia curriculum, sustained as it was by its venerability as well as its strong alumni support, was a source of significant protection for a powerful "brand" of liberal arts education. It constituted a sequence of courses that were run as small seminars, focused on primary texts, with subjects that were shared across the student body in ways that encouraged conversation about classic texts and issues over dinners at the dining hall or while sitting out on the steps of Low Library on the first sunny days of spring. I was growing increasingly worried about the fragility of the model that had given me the kind of education I so valued. All things considered, the core looked better and better.[14]

At the same time, I devoted a good deal of my time working to increase opportunities for global education and experience, for reasons that were as tied to my own academic interests as they were to my sense of their importance for the university. I worked to strengthen the Area Centers, linking them as much to the relevant departments in the humanities and social sciences as to their original home in international studies. I helped build a cross-university "Committee on Global Thought" with the economist Joseph Stiglitz, using support from the president's office that was intended to generate new ideas for how to build global perspectives into disciplines,

[14] For a recent, moving account of the importance of the Columbia core for a first-generation student, see Roosevelt Montas, *Rescuing Socrates: How the Great Books Changed My Life and Why They Matter for a New Generation* (Princeton University Press, 2022).

schools, and programs well outside the usual provenance of area studies. And I worked with Lee Bollinger and other colleagues to develop plans for opening a suite of global centers in different parts of the world, starting with China and India. We designed these centers to serve the entire university, creating local offices to support faculty, staff, and students when traveling – whether collaborating on a project, doing research, studying a language, etc. – as well as to establish closer ties with alumni and other stakeholders based in other parts of the world. We opened centers in Beijing and Mumbai in 2008, following soon with centers in Amman, Paris, Istanbul, Nairobi, Santiago, and Rio de Janeiro. This was an effort to establish a more substantial global footprint for Columbia without building branch campuses as many other universities were doing at the time.

These initiatives allowed me to start traveling more frequently to India again, but I also began going to China for the first time. China was such a contrast to India, and yet for all the time I'd spent in Asia I had never been there. On my first trip to Beijing in 2007 I was astonished at the massive scale, the cleanliness and orderliness of the city, as also the architectural ambitions that were in full swing in preparation for the Olympics to be held there the next year. Despite all the economic growth that had taken place in India in the 1990s and early 2000s – which included dizzying urban expansion and building – India remained far more chaotic; the relative lack of control and order in urban and civic planning seemed in those years to be correlated with its political and intellectual openness and vitality. In between alumni receptions and meetings with senior administrators at Tsinghua and

Peking Universities, we went off on standard tourist out-
ings, to the Forbidden City just across from Tiananmen
Square, to the Tibetan temple on a hill not far away, to
the district made up of older and smaller houses (*hutang*)
that resembled old Beijing far more than the blocks of
tall apartment buildings that housed most of its current
inhabitants, and to a thriving art district – called 798 – on
the other end of the city. I gave talks at different universities and found a vital intellectual scene on these campuses
despite the difficulties of translation, becoming aware of
the scale of China's socio-economic transformation as
well as of its academic ambitions. I also saw that these
universities were keen to partner with Columbia and
other US universities in part because they sought to find
ways to replicate the success of the American university.

I was relieved that Lee had not wavered from his own
commitment to pursue a global agenda for Columbia,
and that he had given me a central role. This was despite
a major crisis he had lived through in the fall of 2007,
when his presidency might have come to an abrupt end.
He had already weathered less than flattering attention
from the press concerning his own responses to the campaign waged by the David Project. Now a controversy
emerged around the World Leaders' Forum, a project
Lee had launched to bring heads of state from around the
world to Columbia during their visits to New York each
fall for the General Assembly. The Dean of the School
of International and Public Affairs had invited Mahmood
Ahmadinejad, the President of Iran, to come to Columbia
and speak the spring before. At first, Lee rescinded the
invitation, only to revive it a bit later by placing it in
the Forum and saying that he would serve as the host.

As word got out about the invitation, the university came under increasing pressure to rescind it. Lee decided to honor the invitation but to do so by framing the event in a way that made clear Columbia did not intend to offer him a neutral platform. He began his introduction by saying that the president exhibited "all the signs of a petty and cruel dictator," and went on to admonish Ahmadinejad for reports that he had denied the holocaust by saying, "You are either brazenly provocative or astonishingly uneducated." When Ahmadinejad finally got up to speak, he sardonically noted that in Iran invited guests were treated much better, and not criticized before they had spoken. He also rejected the charge that he had denied the holocaust, insisting instead that he had merely asked what it had to do with the plight of the Palestinians. Press reports suggested that Bollinger's introduction played badly in at least part of the audience, giving rise once again to murmurs questioning his lifelong commitment to free speech and the First Amendment when it came to issues that touched on the Middle East.

In the end, few outside were happy either. Those who asked for the speech to be called off felt the introduction didn't go far enough, while others felt that he had used the bully pulpit too literally. Even Abraham Foxman, head of the Anti-Defamation League, called his remarks counter-productive. Others were harsher. It took some time for Lee to process what had happened, and between responding to death threats and having conversations with board members and other alumni who were critical, he seemed withdrawn and distracted. Soon thereafter, over 100 faculty issued a declaration stating that "President Bollinger has failed to make a vigorous defense of the core principles on which the university is founded, especially academic freedom." They went on to aver that his remarks "sullied the reputation of the University with its strident tone, and ... abetted a climate in which incendiary speech prevails over open debate." A faculty representative read out the declaration at the fall meeting of the Faculty of Arts and Sciences. I had met on several occasions with some key leaders of the faculty to dissuade them from calling for a vote of no confidence, the threat of which seemed quite real for several weeks in October. I was relieved when the reading of the declaration did not end with a formal censure or motion to vote. But it was clear that the faculty had registered their strong disapproval, not just of Lee's remarks, but also what they viewed as a disconnect around academic freedom. The crisis passed, and in time, Lee's position became secure. That was, however, when he stopped coming to his office in Low Library on a regular basis, and I began walking over to his presidential mansion on Morningside Drive for meetings rather than just down the hall from my office.

Lee had been a very public figure around the affirmative action debates of the 1990s when he had defended the University of Michigan's arguments in two cases that went to the Supreme Court, and I could feel his discomfort at being misunderstood and attacked even as he was doing what he could to protect freedom of speech and academic freedom around issues that took no prisoners. I only came to understand fully some years later when I was chancellor how difficult it is to withstand the kinds of pressures university leaders face when these kinds of crises take place. At the time, I was simply relieved that Lee made it through a difficult time. I was also aware that he was admonished by faculty groups for reasons that were as much about university finances as about politics. Lee had been taking a great deal of flak around his steadfast advocacy for a major campus expansion in "Manhattanville," a set of blocks that Columbia had purchased over the years north of 125th Street and west of Broadway. The faculty in the Arts and Sciences could not see what was in it for them, since they felt they were being told they had to wait for major investments in the main campus while money was raised and stored up for a major center in neuroscience, predominantly serving faculty from the medical school. The McKim, Mead and White buildings on the main campus still looked great from the outside, but the science labs were often shabby at best, and far from optimized for the scientific work taking place inside. Lee took the long view that a dramatic expansion both of space and of scope was necessary for Columbia's continued relevance in the twenty-first century, but it was not always a popular view among many of the faculty in my part of the university.

During the years I was VP Columbia was climbing steadily in the rankings while Columbia College was becoming increasingly popular for student applicants. But there was continuing concern that Columbia was not doing as well as it should in recruiting students who had also been admitted to Harvard, Yale, and Princeton. There were clearly several reasons for this, not least the traditional prestige of those colleges. We were aware, however, that they were offering more generous financial aid packages, no longer insisting on loans. Columbia, like most other colleges, included loans, and our admissions office told us that put us at a disadvantage. In the spring of 2008, just as Bear Stearns was collapsing, we spent hours meeting to devise a new level of financial commitment, allowing us to announce before the summer that we would no longer ask students to take out loans when they were given financial aid. Although in these discussions there were still occasional hints of earlier suspicions between the university and the College, there was a new and palpable level of trust, and a general sense that if it was good for the College – even when it was expensive – it was good for Columbia as a whole.

No sooner did we make this decision public, however, than the storm clouds of the financial crisis began to gather over the city – and the world. As students began to apply in record numbers to Columbia in the fall of 2008, Lehman Brothers closed its doors and the banks came close to losing all their liquidity, eviscerated by predatory and profligate lending practices and financial instruments connecting those practices with the entire financial system. The endowment crashed with the rest of the stock market, and our pledge to invest more in financial aid seemed to have been exceptionally badly timed. We had to freeze salaries and faculty hiring, cut departmental budgets, and look for other economies. It was a stressful time, though ironically the fact that Columbia was less dependent on endowment payouts than most of the other Ivies was in our favor, and we managed to make it through the difficult year without laying off any staff.

In time, the recession led to greater demand for some Master's programs that allowed people who had lost jobs in the financial services industry to gain credentials for new careers. This was a year, however, during which many of the more ambitious initiatives and projects that made the job such fun had to be put on hold. Meanwhile, Austin announced that he would step down from the deanship at the end of the year, and we embarked on a search for his successor. Alan Brinkley decided to step down as provost, and Lee began a search to replace him as well. Lee asked if I was interested in being considered for provost, though it was clear he really wanted me to stay on as VP and dean, a job that was both bigger and harder in many ways. Meanwhile, I commenced a national search for a Dean of the College. We recruited the first woman to hold the role, a philosopher from Cornell with a deep commitment to undergraduate education, who was also an African American. Lee decided to recruit Claude Steele, an eminent social psychologist from Stanford whose research on stereotype threat was a pathbreaking scientific defense of sustained diversity initiatives, as provost. He was the first African American in that role as well.

It was during these years that I began to get an increasing number of calls asking if I might be interested in college or university presidencies. At the time, I was uncertain about whether to consider leaving Columbia, as I had invested a great deal in its academic prominence, and my wife had secured an appointment in the history department. But the prospect of being able to think in new ways about the future of higher education was enticing, and while I hadn't taken on the VP role to advance further up the administrative ladder, I began to realize this was a real possibility. I had been approached earlier about an opening at Wesleyan, but despite my love for the institution decided it was too soon to make a move. When I was asked if I wished to consider replacing Bob Kerrey at the New School, I still could not overcome my residual ambivalence about leaving Columbia, not to mention my concern about the reliance of the New School – despite its glorious history as the university of exile that was itself created in part because of concerns regarding academic freedom at Columbia[15] – on the use of non-tenure track faculty. I was contacted about several prominent public universities, and by some in the United Kingdom, but was concerned about what it might mean to move to institutions where governance and structure were so different. Every time I got a call, however, I found my conversations intriguing and difficult to put out of my mind completely.

For the next few years there was nothing of interest, but then, just as I was beginning to plan to step down from my deanship, I got calls about Dartmouth and Berkeley. Jim Kim, a dynamic new leader for Dartmouth, had suddenly announced his early departure to lead the World Bank, and Bob Birgeneau, after trying to manage the drama around "Occupy" protests on campus in 2011 and running afoul of the university Regents because of his advocacy of a new governance model for Berkeley, announced that he would be stepping down as chancellor. I didn't know much about Dartmouth, but Lee encouraged me to consider it seriously (he had served as provost there before returning to Michigan as president). Dartmouth was interested in making substantial changes as they transitioned to increasingly greater stature in research while building further their

[15] For a thorough and spirited account of the history of the university, see Judith Friedlander, *A Light in Dark Times: The New School for Social Research and Its University in Exile* (New York: Columbia University Press, 2019).

strengths in undergraduate teaching. Berkeley, while a public institution, was, well, one of the finest universities in the world, and in a part of the world where Janaki and I always thought we might want to live. During the summer of 2012 I told Lee I would pursue both positions, and that if I stayed at Columbia I would step down in the summer of 2013 from my role to take on another position he had offered me that was exclusively devoted to global projects and initiatives.

Administration as Vocation

I always believed that I was honoring the same vocation that brought me into the university as a student and then as a professor in my role as administrator. I also believed that the vocation of the professor was not all that distinct from that of the administrator, although I had certainly recognized the shifts in perspective this entailed. More saliently, however, I realized that many of my faculty colleagues believed that I had abandoned the kind of intellectual purity they were able to hold onto by virtue of their steadfast commitment to the core values of their own political positions. I knew that moving into a presidency would only confirm their sense that I had left the world of political purity behind. At the same time, I had come to be increasingly skeptical of the refusal on the part of many tenured faculty to accept the manifold contradictions of university life, or to acknowledge their own implication in the decisions and interests of the senior administration.

Richard Hofstadter, an intellectual historian who taught at Columbia in the 1950s and 1960s, wrote about this conundrum in his classic work, *Anti-Intellectualism in*

American Life,[16] published in 1962. He framed his final chapter on intellectuals in contemporary America by referencing a set of essays that had been published in *Partisan Review* back in 1954, in which Irving Howe gave expression to a more general concern on the part of some left intellectuals about any association they might have with the establishment. As Howe wrote, whenever intellectuals "become absorbed into the accredited institutions of society they not only lose their traditional rebelliousness but to one extent or another they cease to function as intellectuals."[17] Noting that this would exclude all intellectuals who teach (leave aside administer) at universities, Hofstadter saw this as a more general symptom of a certain kind of American intellectual. He accepted that the intellectual "who has relinquished all thought of association with power understands well – almost too well – that his state of powerlessness is conducive to certain illuminations."[18] But he went on to say that "what he is prone to forget is that an access to power and involvement with its problems may provide other illuminations."

Hofstadter – who also wrote an entire book on academic freedom[19] – made an even stronger case for the wisdom that comes from acting in the world, rather than being merely a disengaged critic. He argued that "the characteristic intellectual failure of the critic of power is a lack of understanding of the limitations under which power is exercised. His characteristic moral failure lies in an excessive concern

[16] Richard Hofstadter, *Anti-Intellectualism in American Life* (New York: Knopf, 1962).
[17] Ibid., p. 397. [18] Ibid., p. 429.
[19] Richard Hofstadter and Walter Metzger, *Academic Freedom in the Age of the College* (New York: Routledge, 1996).

with his own purity; but *purity of a sort is easily had where responsibilities are not assumed.*"²⁰ Hofstadter was alluding to intellectuals who became active in government, but he was also aware that many faculty brought to their university appointments a hostility towards institutions – including universities – that was a continuation of this theme, heightened perhaps by the guilt they felt about their now comfortable life. The mythic status of the so-called "New York intellectuals" had been based in part on their freedom from institutional dependency, a myth that has survived largely intact despite revelations that some of the support they received for their journals, organizations, and travels during the postwar years actually came from the CIA. It is little surprise that intellectuals came increasingly to rely on university posts, though the contradictions flowing from that fact reverberated well beyond the small circle of writers and intellectuals associated with New York legends. In fact, many faculty feel some of the same ambivalence, clinging to the idea of their purity most strenuously when they are tenured and fully protected by the very institutions they routinely critique. And it is far too often the case that these same faculty are often largely ignorant or even contemptuous of the institutional realities governing their own places of work. How many times have I been told that criticizing the administration is a key faculty sport?

Over the years I have often returned to Hofstadter's chapter, seeing in it an astute diagnosis of the predicament of the modern professoriate. I had always assumed that the vocation of the university administrator had to be aligned with the vocation of the professor. I began,

²⁰ Hofstadter, *Anti-Intellectualism*, p. 429. Italics mine.

however, to see that this view was naïve. Administrators have to conduct the complex balancing act of negotiating competing interests, values, and choices in order to facilitate the smooth functioning of the university community, not always a recipe for either purity or harmony. Intellectuals may think purity is achievable, but it can easily become an alibi for abdicating responsibility for one's implication in institutional life. The desire for purity drives a wedge between many faculty and administrators. When talking about the university, the administrator attempts to explain institutional constraints, whereas most faculty tend to hold themselves aloof from their institutions while strongly criticizing them.[21]

While some administrators have complained that they don't have as much academic freedom as regular faculty, that is in some ways beside the point. It is understandably difficult for those both within and outside institutions to discern the difference between the statements made by administrators and the institutions they represent – and there is little doubt that too many administrative statements are both vapid and condescending. Administrators

---

[21] The critical disposition is in this way aligned both with how we make truth claims and how we express our relentless desire for purity from institutional entanglement. As Bruno Latour has written, caricaturing the critical theorist who never takes a positive position: "After arduous years of reading turgid prose, you will always be right, you will never be taken in anymore; no one, no matter how powerful, will be able to accuse you of naivete, that supreme sin, any longer. Better equipped than Zeus himself you rule alone, striking from above with the salvo of antifetishism in one hand and the solid causality of objectivity in the other." Latour, "Why Has Critique Run Out of Steam? From Matters of Fact and Matters of Concern," *Critical Inquiry*, 30/2 (Winter 2004), 225–48 (at p. 219). For a calmer but no less important re-evaluation of the place of critique in humanistic thinking, see Rita Felski, *The Limits of Critique* (University of Chicago Press, 2015).

are never genuinely neutral, or bereft of personal judgments, opinions, and views, nor would I suggest that they should be. Once I had a senior administrative position I had to learn to speak in a somewhat different way about matters that I saw as primarily institutional in nature. I sought to project – to the extent possible – an increasingly distinctive voice when asked about the values and priorities of the university.[22] Over time I came to see the ways in which this could create misunderstandings between me and many of my friends and colleagues on the faculty. Partly I had to contend with the perception that I never used my position *enough* to stay connected to those units or people in the university who deserved my attention (even as others always worried that I might use my position excessively in these areas rather than others). And partly I realized that many colleagues had an exaggerated sense of what I could do independently, given the extent to which institutional decisions had to be made in concert with many others and in deference to a host of different interests and values emanating from multiple constituencies (recall Hofstadter's statement about the "limitations under which power is exercised"). I had to forge a new language that reflected a different kind of responsibility, at the same time as I tried to ensure that I never used that responsibility as an alibi to do or say something that would violate my own sense of truth or fairness. I had, in other words, to fashion a different way of actively engaging the local politics of knowledge.

---

[22] For a recent, and to me persuasive, argument about how the performance of neutrality can actually create more fairness in institutional contexts, see K. Anthony Appiah, "Neutrality is a Fiction – But an Indispensable One," *The Atlantic*, April 20, 2023.

Faculty are hardly exempt from these politics. All faculty are routinely called upon to evaluate other colleagues for appointment, promotion, tenure, research support, etc. They judge their colleagues indirectly as well, through the ways they vote for new faculty lines, graduate student admissions, and the allocation of departmental funding. This is not work that best serves the purposes of purity, leave alone solidarity within the community, and the reality is that many bitter feuds and disagreements – often within departments – stem from these routine procedures. But administrators need to do this work across departments, programs, schools, and colleges, and as they do so they strive not just for the kind of "neutrality" I noted earlier but also to consider how to represent the best interests of the institution as a whole. Interests and values have to be translated into difficult decisions about which and how many faculty should be appointed and promoted. They also translate into financial decisions: how much of the budget should go for student financial aid (and how should financial aid be distributed), how much for faculty or staff salaries, how much for teaching support, how much for the library, how much for new research or graduate training, how much for constructing new buildings or maintaining old ones, and so on? When there are budget shortfalls, these decisions become increasingly difficult. And yet every decision is a compromise of some sort, hardly a singular manifesto about ultimate values.

Clark Kerr, among many others, observed that the most radical members of the professoriate are often the most institutionally conservative. There are some good reasons for this; universities have lasted longer than any other institution besides the church, and one of the primary goals of the university is to preserve knowledge and forms of engagement with knowledge that should not be determined primarily by contemporary political or economic forces. To be respectful of this more preservationist function of the university, however, we have to acknowledge the economic and political forces that affect the university and be willing to take on the task of defending and supporting the university through the banal tasks of administration that enable it to function. The desire to preserve what is best about the university requires us to think about change as well – sometimes radical change – if that is in fact what might allow the university to survive in changing times. This is hard for both faculty and administrators, and it is a question to which I will return.

I sought to maintain at least some balance between my commitment to the values of the intellectual life and my experience of working as a senior administrator. The university needed, in my view, to be more interdisciplinary; in fact, disciplinary loyalties and identities got in the way both of commitments to the university at large and of recognizing the need for change and innovation. I also believed that the university should be more global, although the global imperative should be carefully managed to keep it from merely serving global business interests. I wanted to make sure to preserve the spirit of a liberal arts education while adapting to new needs and conditions. I advocated for even more autonomy for faculty research and teaching and sought to find additional resources to support the intellectual life of the university. At the same time, I was deeply aware that the student debt load kept climbing, and that the effects of the great recession were still palpable. Universities needed to learn how to bend the cost curve while doing a better job of training students for new careers. Universities also had to do much better in attracting and then educating and supporting capable students who for structural reasons didn't usually go to top schools.

I had all sorts of ideas; but I also knew there were limits to which ideas I could act on in my administrative role, even if I was not always sure where I should best draw boundaries to demarcate those limits. As I talked about leadership positions, I developed the confidence – perhaps I should say hubris – first to think, and then to say, that I could make a difference, although I became steadily more aware that I would have to narrow the scope of what I might achieve. I ultimately decided to go to Berkeley because it was a public institution that had been hit much harder by the recession and subsequent defunding by the state than any of the Ivies. I would have had far more institutional scope at Dartmouth because it was a private institution with a supportive board, greater resources, and a more manageable scale. But Berkeley, representing as it did the best of what was possible in a public system of higher education, was in trouble. And I was doubtless attracted to the bigger stage.

Shortly after accepting an offer to be the next Chancellor of UC Berkeley, I was asked to do a videotaped interview to be released after the Regents voted on my appointment. Among many other questions, I was asked about my opinion on divestment around issues concerning Israel. Columbia faculty had been active in pressing for divestment, and there had been a time when I thought that was a reasonable strategy, though I had changed my mind when

I became a dean. I did not support the boycott movement for a variety of reasons, including my commitment to maintaining open scholarly exchange across borders even when there are significant political disagreements. As dean, I had felt the need to respond to student complaints about anti-Semitism at Columbia, even when those students were supported by an external political initiative. I had insisted on the preeminent role of faculty governance in adjudicating these complaints, committed as I was to principles of academic freedom that required faculty to play that role. I talked about all of this in an effort to reassure groups from different political positions that I had always attempted to be fair and neutral.

A week later, I was told that a group of faculty from the Middle East Department was going to denounce my statement in the Columbia student newspaper. This group included close friends, and a number of colleagues I had hired (many of them against the objections of other colleagues). They told me that instead of going along with what they felt was an egregious investigation around the charges of the David Project I should have simply said that the complaints were totally groundless and the result of a concerted effort on the part of Zionist forces to discredit them. I said that this was precisely the kind of statement that I could not make, that it would make it impossible for me to project the kind of administrative neutrality that had been critical for my success in making controversial appointments at Columbia. That did not satisfy them, and I learned that Roxie was right after all. I suspect that many of them had felt this way even back in my first year when I had managed this process, and when I took the department under receivership; despite the outcome they had resented my attempts to appear neutral from the start of the controversy. I was hurt, but I was also struck by the way the letter expressed a fundamental truth of my new life. I had begun to speak a new language, and much was lost in translation. Including some friendships.

Still, being a dean – especially a dean of faculty – kept me much closer to faculty life than moving to become a president or a chancellor, especially at a large research university. I was about to experience a completely new kind of life in Berkeley. I often wonder whether I would have made the decision to take on that role if I had had a better idea of what it was. As important as public universities are, and as outstanding as the university system in California is, they carry with them a culture of deep suspicion about university administrators, from politicians, journalists, the public, and the faculty. They have in recent years entered a new phase of crisis that has threatened their survival as the kinds of institutions they were originally created to be, while making them increasingly ungovernable, as I found out the hard way. As Clark Kerr discovered in his time as well, Berkeley was always a hot button issue in California politics. It is a great place to be on the faculty, even if the crises around funding and public support are steadily disruptive. But administrative life there is uniquely challenged by multiple and overlapping constraints. Despite, or perhaps because of, its storied history, it is a university that crystallizes some of the larger challenges facing the entire system of higher education today.

3
Chancellor Tales

~

"The university president in the United States is expected to be a friend of the students, a colleague of the faculty, a good fellow with the alumni, a sound administrator with the trustees, a good speaker with the public, an astute bargainer with the foundations and the federal agencies, a politician with the state legislature, a friend of industry, labor, and agriculture, a persuasive diplomat with donors, a champion of education generally, a supporter of the professions (particularly law and medicine), a spokesman to the press, a scholar in his own right, a public servant at the state and national levels, a devotee of opera and football equally, a decent human being ..."[1]

Clark Kerr

Berkeley Beckons

It was an odd interview. I had flown out to San Francisco in early October 2012 to meet with the search committee. Escorted to one of the unmarked meeting rooms of a hotel just outside the airport where the committee was gathered, I was told they were about halfway through seeing a slate of candidates. The actual decider, Mark Yudof, President of the University of California system, was recovering from an ankle injury and was there on Skype, peering at me through a laptop computer perched on the table to my right with a shifting camera angle that rarely allowed me to see his face. The committee asked the usual round of questions, but focused on two major

---

[1] Kerr, *Uses of the University*, p. 22.

issues, the first around governance, the second concerning student protest.

On governance, I was asked by the alumni representative if it might be possible to create greater institutional autonomy for Berkeley. He said that he thought the cost of state interference was greater than the amount of the state's contribution, and that Berkeley could prosper if it were set free from governmental control. I suspected that this was a trap, though I wasn't aware at the time of the extent to which the current chancellor had alienated the president and the Regents by already proposing a greater level of autonomy. I spoke generically about the necessity of finding adequate ways to support the flagship campus of the system given its extraordinary academic excellence. I did not have to flatter Berkeley – it had more top-ten-ranked departments than any university other than Harvard, and it was routinely ranked not just as the top public university in the country but as one of a handful of the most distinguished research universities in the world. But I knew that it had suffered from severe budget cuts. By that time, however, I assumed that California, now that it was beginning to recover from the most severe effects of the recession, would restore its funding. The alum said he doubted that would happen and recommended I consider other structural changes to ensure Berkeley's continued preeminence. I looked as agreeable as I could without wishing to worry Yudof in turn (really wishing I could see his face), though I did mention that as someone from a private university I was open to exploring different relationships with the system and the state, while also extolling the mission of a public university.

We spent rather longer talking about student protest. Asked if I had any experience of this, I noted that

Columbia was a place that shared a history with Berkeley of being a center for student activism (I quipped that it was Berkeley on the Hudson). I spoke about how I had handled the hunger strike for ethnic studies, and how we had come to a successful resolution despite the tensions of the standoff.

I had read about the history of the Free Speech Movement back in the early 1960s, and knew that Berkeley's reputation for student radicalism over many years was well deserved. Only during the interview, however, did I begin to understand how much this still weighed on Berkeley, unlike Columbia that had largely left that kind of activism behind after the Vietnam war era. Berkeley had witnessed major occupations and protests on the campus in 2009 around tuition hikes caused by the recession and in 2011 in association with the Occupy movement. I established good rapport with the two students on the search committee – both of whom were in some ways the most engaged of my interviewers – after I confessed that I had once upon a time occupied a president's office myself as a student protestor. I also learned that Bob Birgeneau had announced he was stepping down not long after he had been criticized for his handling of major protests on campus in 2011. In short, I was asked about the two issues that had been most troubling to my predecessor in recent years.

The two previous chancellors, Bob Berdahl and Bob Birgeneau – both of whom had been university presidents before coming to Berkeley – had also been outsiders. When they had run into difficulties around issues such as ethnic studies, governance, and protest, they didn't have a wealth of local networks they could rely upon. Indeed, it might have seemed natural at this point for Berkeley to appoint an internal candidate. All of the internal candidates, however, had major detractors on the committee, which decided to go again with an outsider. Unfortunately, that did not mean that the campus was fully ready to welcome another "outsider."

Even as Berkeley beckoned, it was clearly still in a fragile condition after the great recession. Buried in the briefing materials was a draft paper (soon to be published under the title, "Time is Not on Our Side") by John Wilton, the Vice Chancellor for Administration and Finance, demonstrating that without significant increases in state funding or tuition dollars Berkeley would have a structural deficit of $150 million in the space of the next two to three years.[2] But I was reassured by everyone I spoke with that things would soon get better.

Berkeley had been a university in which departments such as history, English, and political science were as highly ranked as computer science, chemistry, and physics. It was where the great educational leader Clark Kerr had worked with Governor Pat Brown to develop the Master Plan for higher education, the bargain that stipulated that Berkeley would have the resources to rival the best private universities in the world in terms of research and faculty quality. It was also, however, where Kerr got caught between the rise of the 1960s student movement around free speech and the emerging political reaction against universities. Fired in early 1967 by the Regents just after Reagan took office, Kerr – who quipped that

---

[2] John Wilton, "Time is Not on Our Side," Berkeley Administration and Finance, November 29, 2013.

he left as he came, "fired with enthusiasm" – could at least take satisfaction in the way in which the Master Plan endured through his entire life (he died in 2003).

Well after the 1960s, however, Berkeley continued to be a political lightning rod. And yet, I did not anticipate the extent to which the role of chancellor would thrust me into a highly public role. Berkeley's history should have provided some clues. In 1919, it was the first university where the faculty revolted against the administration to establish its fabled faculty senate, in what became a hallmark for a new level of faculty governance across many universities in subsequent years. In 1949 Berkeley was at the center of the storm around academic freedom precipitated by the requirement that faculty swear their loyalty to the US constitution, anticipating the red-baiting years of McCarthyism that began in earnest in 1950. In 1964 it saw the rise of the Free Speech Movement, led by students who wished to recruit supporters for civil rights and engage in political speech on campus. In 1969 it was the scene of violent encounters with the police over the conduct of the war in Vietnam, coming to a head on a university property that became dubbed thereafter as "People's Park" where two protestors had died in the melee. Ronald Reagan had run his campaign for Governor of California in 1966 around his promise to "clean up the mess at Berkeley," and arguably his entire political career – leading to the neoliberal restructuring of the US economy during his presidency in the 1980s – was premised on Berkeley's utility as a potent political symbol for student radicalism run amuck.

None of this made me think, however, that Berkeley would continue to be at the center of one political storm after another, certainly not in 2012 with Obama safely re-elected, the great recession in the rear-view mirror, and a general sense of optimism across the country. And yet, as I discovered, events at Berkeley continued to anticipate the major political storms of the coming years, even as it was to be the first to earn Donald Trump's ire when he tweeted that Berkeley should stop receiving federal funds. But I am getting ahead of my story.

I agreed that I would come out for the Regents' meeting in late November 2012 to be present when my appointment would be formally approved. On my way I got a call from Governor Jerry Brown. He said he was happy enough about my appointment (the governor serves ex officio on the Board of Regents) but was concerned that I was going to be paid slightly more than my predecessor (though less than my salary as dean at Columbia) and wanted me to give the "raise" back. I said I looked forward to meeting him, though I didn't think it was appropriate to reopen the terms of my contract after I had already signed an agreement. At the Regents' meeting Brown voted against my compensation package. That evening, as I met with an alumni advisory group for the first time in the large conference room adjacent to the chancellor's office, we got a call that the governor had come to pay me a visit. I left the meeting and met with him in the chancellor's office, where he was reading a memo on Birgeneau's desk and exclaiming about the need to bend the cost curve of higher education. We sat and talked for an hour.

Jerry had done his homework on me. He had read my book on caste and wanted to tell me why he thought I was fundamentally wrong. He believed that caste was a good system because of its acknowledgement of the necessity of hierarchy as a religious value. I knew that he had traveled to India as a young man and had practiced Buddhist meditation but was surprised he had read my book. I was more surprised that he sought to defend caste, a social system not unlike race, and I said as much. He shifted to the subject of the university, telling me that I had to figure out how to significantly lower the cost of higher education, to introduce austerity measures for the good of the university and the state, beginning with a refusal to take the "extra" salary. He said that all the administrators and faculty should understand that they received "psychic income" from being associated with the great university. I countered by saying that if Berkeley was to remain a great university it would have to be able to compete – financially as well as psychically – with Harvard (and other great universities including Stanford and Columbia) to keep its world-class faculty. He told me that competition of that kind was a product of rampant capitalism, that the university should be seen as a calling rather than as a business. I knew he had trained in his early years to be a Jesuit, but now I saw the curious blending of Jesuit and politician. His critique of capitalism – one that as governor he used only when it suited him – was meant to suggest that the university should be seen as a public entity, like government, not as a business. But it also invoked his reverence for the monastery. This was a utopian idea of the university, though as a canny politician, Brown hardly governed as a Marxist. I told him that when I was back in the Bay Area I'd like to meet and talk further, but that now I had to go to a dinner being put on for us at the chancellor's residence.

As we walked from the office to the dinner at University House I heard the sounds of a helicopter directly overhead. There was a student protest on campus and at first

I thought it might be about me. That would come later. This one turned out to be about funding by the Vice Chancellor for Equity and Inclusion for a student group on campus – seven students had chained themselves to the door of an office and refused to leave. The alum with whom I was walking told me that he had been on campus back in the days of the protest at People's Park, when helicopters overhead sprayed teargas down on protestors. This, he said, was mild by comparison. The dinner was pleasant, though the police helicopter hovered for the full first course. When my wife and I returned to the hotel after what had been a very long day, I commented that the two issues that had come up in my interviews surfaced powerfully on our first day on campus. A governor with arcane views was meddling in university affairs, and students were protesting over one line item in a university budget. After another day of introductions and meetings, however, we were sent off to have dinner at Chez Panisse, Alice Waters' classic farm-to-table restaurant in Berkeley that had been one of the first to use locally sourced ingredients. Alice was an enthusiastic Berkeley alum, and treated us to a delicious dinner that reminded us of the charms of California.

I stayed in touch with Brown, and shortly after moving to the Bay Area we had brunch in San Francisco. He was warm, intellectually curious, and keen to talk about ideas. He repeated his earlier view that I had used too much jargon in my book on caste and didn't sufficiently appreciate the way caste embodied a critique of the individualism of the west. He reiterated that he was serious about how I needed to find a radically different way to run the university. As we were sitting on a restaurant patio having our meal, a woman walked up to him and told him what a great job he was doing as governor. Jerry introduced me as the new chancellor and then said: "I want you to know that I am pledging that I will not allow any tuition increases for the University during my time as Governor." Although I had heard Jerry talk before about his desire to "bend the cost curve" for higher education, this came as a total surprise and a genuine shock. Bob Birgeneau and his budget chief John Wilton had reiterated a few days before that without a series of substantial increases in tuition the university would be confronting a yearly deficit of $150 million in three years. Now, what once was a distant possibility seemed a palpable reality. At first, I thought perhaps he was engaged in political posturing, but I soon learned he was serious.

Although it was initially amusing to spar with Jerry about matters ranging from India to politics, I never felt that he wanted to have a serious conversation about how he envisioned Berkeley might maintain its extraordinary quality without the kind of funding I believed necessary (leave alone about India and caste). When Brown would say in meetings of the university Regents that he didn't understand why UC should compete with Harvard and Yale, I understood his concerns about an educational arms race, though I assumed he was still serious about preserving Berkeley's comparative excellence. But he also complained about the fact that "normal" people could no longer get into Berkeley, suggesting once that the UC should model itself on Chipotle, offering just a few items (courses, programs, tacos, whatever) to keep costs low.[3] Hearing a progressive and intellectually minded governor

[3] See *Sacramento Bee*, May 31, 2018.

talk like this about the University of California made me feel I had entered an alternative universe.

At the time of my brunch with the governor, I was waiting to hear who the new President of the system would be. In January of 2013, not long after I had accepted the job, Mark Yudof announced he would be stepping down at the end of the summer. Mark had had a long and distinguished administrative career, starting as the Dean of the Law School at the University of Texas, then as President of the University of Minnesota, then back to Texas as President of the system. He was still waiting for the five-year mark in his tenure at the university but was clearly more than ready to retire. He told me that the last thing he wanted to have finished was appointing a new chancellor for Berkeley, and now that was done.

Throughout his tenure in California, he had been attacked for tuition increases – necessary to make up some of the lost revenue after the deep cuts from the state – and just about everything else too. He had to move from one house to another to avoid having protestors outside his residence on a regular basis, and at one point he ran through a mall (he was not a sprinter) to avoid being overtaken by a group of self-proclaimed anarchists. He had presided over a meeting of the Regents that had effectively been blockaded by protestors, and the Occupy movement had targeted him for being "the Man" who was corporatizing the university and making it inaccessible to the people of California. I was upset that he was leaving just as I was about to arrive, though soon came to understand that he had fallen out of love with the job after what he had been through. Several days after he stepped down, he was rushed to the hospital for bypass heart surgery, an ironic justification of his decision to quit.

A month after I moved to Berkeley, I heard that the Regents had decided to appoint Janet Napolitano, the Secretary of Homeland Security, former Democratic Governor of Arizona. It was an unconventional pick. She was an accomplished politician, but neither an academic nor experienced in the ways of university administration. Apparently, the Regents felt that they needed someone who understood politics and political life, given the actual nature of the job. But they didn't consult the chancellors about their choice.

Orientation

On my first day in office, I had a meeting with the chief of university police, Margo Bennett, along with some of her top officers, to discuss personal security arrangements. When I went to hang my coat earlier that morning, I had discovered that an old bullet-proof vest was hanging in the closet. I brought it out to show Margo with a puzzled look on my face; she said that they would get me a new one if I wanted. I began to hear about how the police thought about the dangers of the job. I hadn't moved into the chancellor's residence yet, though was told that they had assigned 24/7 police coverage to the house after an incident the previous November when the back door and entry way had been defaced with human feces. Police had originally been assigned to guard the house at night in late 2011, when a group of protestors had attacked the house after Birgeneau had gone to sleep, throwing pots and breaking windows while trying to knock down the front door. Margo said I would be introduced later to the other security measures in the house, where there were a number of panic buttons that would immediately alert campus police in the event of a threat, and where the wardrobe closet in the master bedroom could be converted into a safe room.

When Chancellor Tien and his wife lived in the house in the 1990s, I learned later, a woman had broken in with a machete with the intent to attack them while they were sleeping, only to be shot and killed by the police when she went into the master bedroom and hid in the closet (Tien and his wife were sleeping in a different bedroom because some repairs were being done at the time). They were serious about security. When Janaki moved into her office in the history department, the police insisted on installing a panic button there too, giving her a mobile panic alert to carry with her at all times. My new colleagues seemed to relish telling me stories about protests and attacks on the chancellor's house. I told Margo that I didn't want to have a conspicuous police presence, concerned that I not be seen as hiding behind protection. But Janaki was shaken by the succession of revelations about real physical danger. She was shown the safe room in the house and told what to do if someone broke into the house and threatened her with violence, while being given the unwelcome code name Mrs. CRX. It was more than a little jarring to be told we had targets on our backs, not to mention being called "Mrs." for the first time in her married life.

Still, the first few months on the Berkeley campus were exhilarating. It is a beautiful campus with breathtaking views of the Bay, old groves of redwoods, and stunning buildings designed by John Galen Howard, Bernard Maybeck, and Julia Morgan. The marching band greeted me outside California Hall on my first day, and I was introduced to my new cabinet, the deans and chairs, key faculty and staff, while being taken around to a succession of events and meetings to welcome me. I saw for myself the scientific and academic distinction of the university, legendary for its extraordinary accomplishments across virtually every field and discipline. I was asked about my vision for the university. I congratulated Berkeley for weathering the storm and promised that there were better days ahead, as I was assured I could. I allocated significant funds for a new neuroscience initiative that took full advantage of Berkeley's extraordinary engineering faculty as they were designing new ways to take images of the brain, and I began to plan for an undergraduate initiative to focus on the education and life of undergraduate students on the research-intensive campus. I also began to convene groups to talk about how Berkeley might establish a more ambitious global footprint, feeling fortunate that the university had not committed itself to any particular strategy before my arrival.

Meanwhile, I was lobbied by biologists who wanted to create a College of Biology to sit alongside the College of Chemistry, and by computer scientists who told me about the thousands of Berkeley students they could not accommodate in their classes despite overwhelming interest in studying computation and data analysis. Although I didn't feel there was sufficient support to engage in another reshuffling of biology departments, I did learn of the extensive reorganization work that in the 1980s and 1990s created a much more productive environment for the most cutting-edge biologists, and noted that such work was difficult, if often overdue, at Berkeley. Meanwhile, I reassured humanists and social scientists that I would not forget them, as they reported having felt systematically neglected despite the critical role they played in teaching undergraduates and tending top departments even with minimal resources; they noted that although there were many shiny new buildings and facilities on campus, none had been built for them.

And then, just a few months into my time in office, I was told that the football team had posted a 45 percent graduation rate. Football at Berkeley was a fraught affair. When referring to football, and sports in general, Berkeley went by the name *Cal*, a sign of a basic schizophrenia in the institution, the residue of the fault line between its academic identity and strong history of student activism on the one hand and its collegiate identity for many of its alumni, donors, and students on the other. Berkeley was hardly known for its football team, but as a member of the Pac 12, one of the power five athletic conferences, the university was known for its prowess in Olympic sports, and for some Cal's success in football was as important as its academic reputation. My predecessor had spent a lot of time thinking about football, and now I realized I would too. Prodded by the Regents to do something about the seismic dangers of a football stadium perched right on top of the Hayward fault, Birgeneau had invested over $400 million in a renovation project that not only secured the stands but also built a suite of boxes and club spaces overhanging the western wing of the stadium.[4] He had to borrow most of this money and developed a financial plan that assumed that loyal fans would buy lifetime

<hr>

[4] See Rachel Bachman, "Cal Football-Stadium Gamble," *Wall Street Journal*, April 18, 2012; Nanette Asimov, "Cal Scrambling to Cover Stadium Bill," *SFGate*, June 16, 2013.

access to the clubs and seats, for a football team that had a long tradition of losing despite launching stars like Aaron Rodgers and Marshawn Lynch into the NFL. Suffice to say this budget decision hung over the university during my tenure given escalating costs of the loans and far less in the way of revenue than had been projected.

In one of his last major executive decisions as chancellor, Bob had fired the previous coach, Ted Tedford, replacing him with Sonny Dykes, a coach from Louisiana Tech. Even as Dykes was fielding his first team, we learned the extent to which Tedford had allowed the graduation rate of the football team to fall as he focused on recruiting players who could win football games against Oregon, USC, and Stanford.[5] Now I had to reaffirm the importance of academics in Cal football. I convened a committee made up of alumni, faculty, staff, and student athletes to evaluate the problems around academic achievement in our athletics programs. Meanwhile, alumni who did not like the athletic director, Sandy Barbour, used the crisis as a reason to suggest it was time to hire someone new in that role as well. It turned out there were many alumni and fans who had not yet forgiven the university for developing plans to close a number of major sports programs during the budget crisis because of their drain on the financial resources of the campus, and some of them blamed Sandy in particular.

It didn't help that Cal had a 1–11 record that first year; Sonny Dykes had brought a great offensive strategy with him from Louisiana and Texas, but apparently

[5] See Seung Y. Lee, "Despite Improvement in Mind, Cal Football's Graduation Rates Fell to National Lows," *Daily Californian*, October 28, 2013.

had neglected to think about defense. The chancellor's stadium "box" was stunning – even serving sushi along with hot dogs – though I soon learned that football games were for schmoozing with alums, not for watching the game. That spring, a member of the football team died during practice, leading to multiple investigations and additional concern about the football program. While I worked with the athletics committee to reform procedures around admissions and increase resources for the academic resource program, I began to think there was something fundamentally wrong when universities like Berkeley had to spend so many resources on an enterprise that seemed orthogonal to the main mission of the city of intellect. Track and field, tennis, gymnastics, and crew were sports in which Cal excelled, and where standards related to academic performance were undiminished. Football and basketball – the revenue sports – were different, not just because they helped fund those other programs, but also because they brought much-needed diversity to the student body. But the contradictions here were as easily apparent as any possible solutions seemed out of reach. I pledged to emphasize the academic priorities of the university, and reworked the admissions procedures for athletics recruits, ensuring that a faculty committee reviewed all athletics admissions and that the old system of "tagging" student prospects (in which coaches would mark those prospects for expedited admission) would no longer be abused, as clearly it had been.

I also began to hear that some students were extremely angry at Berkeley for having mishandled their complaints about sexual assault. Each case was different and there were multiple stories about some of the incidents, but I learned that the Title IX office had been slow in its investigations and that on some occasions it had failed to follow through in informing complainants about its conclusions. We needed to invest more resources into that office and streamline the process there as well, and I worked closely with the associate chancellor in my office in charge of Title IX to do so. When I met with some of the students, including one who was working with a filmmaker to shoot a documentary called *The Hunting Ground*, I heard a lot of pain. I gave my assurance we would do everything we could to address the growing issue of sexual assault among students. Later that year, we held a conference at Berkeley – bringing together some major university leaders to talk about new measures and best practices to combat this critical issue. But this was only the beginning.

Despite all these immediate and pressing issues, I was working to develop an academic vision that I believed would match the excellence and ambition of this great university. I worked hard on my inauguration speech in which I outlined the signal significance of Berkeley, how it embodied the utopian aspirations of a country that, however imperfect, had created extraordinary institutions in its magnificent public universities. I held that Berkeley was well positioned to "re-build public faith in the value of education." As I laid out my plans for Berkeley, I spoke of the need to "re-envision the great American university," acknowledging all the while that our "utopian ideals are about the values that we profess and act upon rather than the realities of institutional life that will always and inevitably be flawed."

For the undergraduate initiative, I set up a committee that began meeting soon after the inauguration.

Despite and in some respects because of the fact I had spent so much time and effort at Columbia working on the relationship between the undergraduate college and the rest of the university, I was aware that Berkeley had a similar problem. For years the graduate programs had dominated the undergraduate experience, and I thought that a rebalancing might help provide not just more support but a more lasting kind of identity for the college years. I began to advocate for repositioning at least some of the major units of undergraduate instruction to give Berkeley students some of what was best about Columbia College, without creating the kind of competitive tension between undergraduate and graduate programs that was invariably counterproductive.

My new colleagues at Berkeley did not always see things this way. They agreed that we had to do more for undergraduates but could not agree about anything that entailed major structural change. Most of them were understandably more concerned about maintaining the traditional strengths of departments in the aftermath of the budgetary pressures of the previous years; what this often meant, however, was more attention to graduate than to undergraduate programs. Besides, I was told repeatedly that Berkeley was suffering from "change fatigue." Having just arrived, and aware as I was that Berkeley was at a critical moment in its history, I assumed that with the right ideas we could energize enough people to make changes that would make not just for happier and more fulfilled undergraduates but also more supportive alumni in the years ahead. As these meetings dragged on, however, they were often overtaken by entrenched arguments, positions, and long-standing antagonisms.

I was also surprised to learn about the restrictions placed on college life by the UC system. For majors that were over-enrolled, students had in effect to declare their major when they applied to college. I thought this put too much of a burden on high-school-level applicants; I also learned that students from many high schools lacked the course work needed for immediate admission to competitive programs in engineering or economics. Additionally, we were not allowed to accept letters of recommendation for students as part of the application process. Napolitano told us that she thought such letters were "arcane," even as I believed they could help us identify students whose grades or test scores did not tell the full story. In the end, the most I could do was to appoint a former vice provost to be the first Vice Chancellor for Undergraduate Education with a mandate to expand our efforts to improve undergraduate life.

I made more progress with an initiative to explore how data science might be taught across multiple departments well beyond the Department of Computer Science (EECS). Students were flocking in huge numbers to computer science courses, both out of interest and because they felt they had to gain some advanced training in coding and related data analytics to get jobs in the burgeoning tech industry in California (or for that matter to get jobs at all). Computer science faculty responded to the surge in interest with requests to double the size of their department. I appointed a committee that was composed of faculty in computer science and statistics, as well as from math, physics, history, and a variety of other departments and professional schools. A small group of faculty led this initiative, and although I met regularly with this core group, I stayed away from the committee meetings over the next months. That turned out to be a good plan, since my presence seemed to be distracting. My chief of staff, a Berkeley-trained historian who was specifically interested in expanding the reach of training in data analytics across the curriculum, served as a facilitator. The committee not only met productively but came up with recommendations within the specified timeline. Not that all was smooth here either, since there was a rift between faculty who wanted to set up a new department or school and those who wanted to preserve existing administrative structures. We found agreement when we proposed establishing a pilot course in data analytics, linking this course with a variety of other courses across the curriculum that would provide the actual data to be analyzed by students as they developed their skills.

I also convened workshops around ways to expand Berkeley's global footprint. Faculty were also enthusiastic here, at least at first, but again I encountered some distinctly territorial reactions. The Dean of Public Policy wanted to expand international studies and therefore thought any new initiative should be housed within his school, while other offices – from the Institute for International Studies to the regional centers – had competing views about how to move forward. Initially I proposed that we might follow Columbia's model by setting up global offices in key cities across the world, but we didn't have funding and I soon decided it would be better to find a new model for Berkeley based on its distinctive strengths and mission.

Meanwhile, I learned that an agreement between the university and the Lawrence Berkeley National Laboratory – a national lab perched on the hills above the campus and funded by the Department of Energy – to secure national funding for a new expansion had fallen through. The project was to have been located on a stretch of land in Richmond, ten miles north, that the campus had acquired after the war. Over the years it had been cleaned up from pollution left behind by munitions factories and other industries. It was a beautiful location – 134 acres of land by the bay with some marshes, a large eucalyptus grove, and just a few buildings that had been used to build a "shake table" to measure responses to an earthquake, to test some of the first autonomous vehicles in California, and to store overflow books from the Berkeley library.

As I thought about how to use this land, I came to think we could build a global campus right there. My idea was to attract universities from around the world to put up buildings and set up programs in association with Berkeley – and with the general ecosystem of the Bay Area – on a jointly built campus, bringing the world to California in a way that would befit the model of a state-funded public university. Berkeley itself would build new global programs, while developing relationships with the local Bay Area start-up culture in areas ranging from new technology to the biomedical sciences, while also establishing a genuinely multi-campus college for advanced study. The college would stress issues like global governance, cross-national and cultural collaboration, and ethical approaches to the major global challenges in the twenty-first century (e.g., climate change, global health, inequality, genetic engineering, and the impact of artificial intelligence, robotics, and machine learning). The campus was to reflect this vision, developing as part of a "mutualist" approach to collaboration with other universities. Rather than sallying forth to spread our footprint across the world through the establishment of branch campuses, we would establish a genuinely global network of research activities, public–private partnerships, and educational projects, drawing the resources and talents of people and institutions from around the world. We called it the Berkeley Global Campus.

When I announced the idea, we initially heard only positive reactions. Universities from around the world began to approach us to ask how they could get involved. Meanwhile, I'd been speaking regularly with the President of Tsinghua University. He quickly grasped the idea and was keen to join us, both because of the research opportunities at Berkeley and because of his interest in connecting with the Bay Area culture of entrepreneurship. He had another reason, which he told me about in private, to provide a space of open academic engagment for his faculty and students. I was also in regular touch with Leszek Borysiewicz, the Vice Chancellor of Cambridge University, and Chor Chuan Tan, President of the National University of Singapore (at that point the top-ranked university in Asia, though it was soon to be outpaced by Tsinghua). Both wanted to create an alliance with Berkeley around the global campus idea, a first for Cambridge, and a reversal of NUS' previous model of only supporting projects that would attract partners to Singapore. We established an alliance to pursue plans for the campus and began the process of working out an agreement with each other as well as with our respective faculties.

I spoke about the idea at Davos, where I went with a group of Berkeley faculty to showcase their research, in January of 2015, and began to interest private donors and potential corporate sponsors. We received several gifts to begin making plans for how to use the Richmond campus, designing it as an innovative, energy-efficient campus of mixed-use facilities and public as well as natural spaces meant to preserve the beauty of the place while housing a wide range of global activities. We also began to meet with leaders and groups in Richmond to assure them that any plans we made would be developed in concert with the city and with the goal of bringing as much benefit to local stakeholders as to the University of California. Not long after, one of the faculty we had brought to Davos, Bob Knight, invited us to lunch at his home with the Richmond Mayor, Tom Butt, who was hugely enthusiastic about the project, pledging his support.

Many of the faculty with whom I discussed this idea were enthusiastic too, including an eminent Chinese historian who had been advising the administration on relationships with China, and a broad cross-section of engineering faculty, social scientists, and members of professional schools such as public health. Although I knew there were pockets of genuine concern, I encountered a fundamental suspicion about any administrative initiative. Some were worried that the project would siphon off much-needed resources, and no matter how many times I emphasized that we were going to use the project to attract new funds that would benefit the main campus as well, it was hard to get past this. Faculty wanted me to raise money for them, or for deferred maintenance of buildings as well as units, but didn't accept that it would be easier to raise money for new, big ideas, which then would make more funding available for existing needs. I was also told that the administration should not be seen as developing any curricular programs, since they belonged exclusively to the faculty. Although I convened several faculty committees to commence discussions of educational options for the campus, some faculty complained about what they saw as administrative overreach. And when faculty were not part of a committee or advisory group, they proclaimed that since they had not been consulted, it was evidence of a failure on the part of the administration to take faculty views seriously.

At the same time, despite the support of many local leaders in Richmond, we began to be lobbied by unions as well as by other interests that wanted us to sign binding agreements before even beginning to build on the Richmond campus. We weren't in a position yet to build anything, since we were still in fundraising and development phases, but already I realized how difficult it would be to pull off this project even if we had all the money in the world. I had watched Lee Bollinger face similar skepticism about the Columbia move to the new Manhattanville campus, and while I anticipated skepticism, I also felt I knew what needed to be done to surmount opposition and create a sense of real and broad participation in the process. But I soon began to see the downside of not having a Berkeley-focused board of trustees to watch my back while trying to do something that ambitious.

During my first year, I was fortunate to recruit Claude Steele as my new Executive Vice Chancellor and Provost. He had returned to Stanford as Dean of their Graduate School of Education after leaving the provost position at Columbia. When I discovered that Claude would be willing to move to Berkeley and take on the provost role again, I brought his name to the committee, and found it to be as enthusiastic as I was. One of the leading social psychologists in the world, Claude had convincingly demonstrated the way "stereotype threat" worked not just to discourage minorities but to lower their academic performance, even on standardized tests. To recruit a leading scholar who had shown in his work the critical importance of diversity would make a statement, while providing a powerful role model as an African American scholar and senior administrator. I already knew how well I could work with Claude given our experience together at Columbia. We had been through some interesting times there, and had learned both to figure things out together, and to find ways to laugh at the peculiar challenges of the administrative life. He had the best sense of humor of anyone I had ever worked with.

I would need to delegate a great deal of budgetary and institutional authority to the provost if I was to be successful in fundraising and developing the kinds of big ideas Berkeley needed to thrive in its current environment. What I did not realize at the time, however, was that the Berkeley chancellor was a much more "inward facing" role than that of the President of Columbia – Berkeley faculty and students looked to the chancellor for almost every major decision on campus. This appointment also meant that my "outsider" image was underlined, since now both senior administrators were from outside Berkeley.

In the fall of 2014, we celebrated the fiftieth anniversary of the Free Speech Movement. That movement had been a signal moment in Berkeley's history and more generally in the history of student activism on American college campuses in the late twentieth century. Sparked in the fall of 1964 by the realization that the desks set up by students to recruit others to participate in civil rights activities were on university property, the controversy that ensued was over the policy of political neutrality on UC campuses. Students, led by the charismatic Mario Savio, insisted that First Amendment rights should extend to the campus, while Clark Kerr, the President of UC, maintained a policy that restricted political activity on campus. The Berkeley chancellor at the time, Edward Strong, was even more intransigent, treating student demands as a problem of campus discipline. There were sit-ins and occupations, but also inspiring oratory from Savio, a philosophy major who quoted Diogenes and other classical thinkers when he championed the importance of free expression. His was the enlightened, passionate as well as elegant voice of the movement.

In the end, Berkeley faculty sided – after numerous protests, sit-ins, and occupations – with the activists, and Kerr, after initial resistance, backed them as well. Kerr forced the Berkeley chancellor to step down, and Berkeley led the way for all public universities to be required to host free speech on their campuses. That the conflict had occasioned serious friction between students and the administration was not quickly forgotten, but fifty years later the veterans of the movement, including Lynn Savio – Mario's widow – were pleased to work with us to co-sponsor a variety of commemorative activities. This seemed quite natural to most people on campus, who often collected their coffee and sandwiches from the Free Speech Movement café in Moffitt, the undergraduate library, just next to the chancellor's office in California Hall. Even so, when we held a wine and cheese reception for movement veterans in the café that fall, one woman came up to me and, realizing who I was, demanded an apology, arguing that she had never heard a formal apology from "the" chancellor.

Each fall I was told that I needed to send a campus-wide memo reiterating "community principles." These principles had been developed and accepted by a broad group of faculty, staff, and administrators and stress the importance of civility. Civility in this context meant a respectful commitment to hearing and engaging diverse opinions on contested issues. I decided to spice up the dry administrative language of the memo and include a comment about the importance of honoring Berkeley's history of promoting free speech. In the spirit of invoking "community principles," I noted that free speech on campus was best exercised through civil exchanges of ideas so that we could genuinely hear and engage views that occasioned discord and disagreement. We put finishing touches on the memo and I signed off on it as I was on my way to the airport to fly to Taiwan for a fundraising trip. No sooner did I arrive in Taiwan, however, than I realized there was a firestorm back on campus. Some faculty and students took my memo to suggest that I didn't fully embrace the value of free speech, that I wasn't respecting the history of activism and political expression that should not be constrained by the polite demands of civility.

Although I was suggesting that civil exchanges of contested views might be more productive than a shouting match, I was by no means saying that speech in the context of protest was not also fully protected and highly valued. I worked with a few trusted friends on campus, including the critical theorist Judith Butler, to write a follow-up memo to make clear what I meant, and to enunciate my robust defense of free speech and academic freedom. This follow-up did nothing to deter critics from off campus, however, that included such disparate voices as another old friend, Joan Scott (retired professor of history and social science from the Institute for Advanced Study), Greg Lukianoff, the director of FIRE, an organization tracking free speech and academic freedom on college campuses, and Larry Summers, who had his own concerns about any limits on speech from his time as President of Harvard.

I soon learned that one reason for the firestorm was because my memo coincided with a decision made by the Chancellor of the University of Illinois about the appointment of a faculty member who had been accused of making anti-Semitic comments on his Twitter feed. Stephen Salaita's appointment to a tenured position in ethnic studies at UIUC had been stopped at the last moment when the Regents of the university caught wind of the controversy and put pressure on the chancellor to block final approval. This brought back controversies I had faced at Columbia, where I had always been adamant not to use political speech outside the classroom as the basis on which academic decisions were made. I was dismayed to see my own administrative words affiliated with a very different position than one I had always practiced, both at Columbia and Berkeley. At the same time, over the next few years, this local controversy came to seem strangely ironic. I would soon realize that faculty views about free speech were far more nuanced – and deeply conflicted – than they had been back in the 1960s.

In the short term, however, I learned from this experience that any message I sent around to campus could be read, or misread, in extravagantly unpredictable ways and, given Berkeley's iconic status, could possibly be disseminated nationally. I also learned that each message set expectations about subsequent ones, as I was regularly petitioned to send messages out on behalf of different campus constituencies about a wide range of issues, some related to actions on campus and some of more general political relevance. The politics of administrative statements were fraught, and it was hard to balance the need to make important statements with the sense that I should only speak out on issues when they impacted the campus community directly.

I knew that the best forms of communication took place in person, when there were opportunities for genuine exchange and patient elaboration. From the time I went to Berkeley I had asked my staff to arrange as many in-person events for faculty, students, and staff as possible to facilitate greater understanding between the administration and different campus groups. I asked to have regular fireside chats in University House with student groups. I was informed that I should not follow the Columbia model where students were chosen at random, but rather work with the elected student body representatives to invite groups around specific themes. What this meant was that I met with groups that were for the most part made up of student activists for one cause or another. I also asked the Vice Provost for Faculty to devise lists of faculty from across the university to come to the official residence for regular dinners. And I organized a variety of different ways to engage staff, from fireside chats to town hall meetings to interactive interviews beamed across campus on video.

These events crowded an already busy schedule, but I saw them as critical for opening up lines of communication, especially important as one who came to Berkeley from elsewhere. And yet I also learned that there were multiple interpretations of what I was doing. Some faculty found elegant dinners at the chancellor's house to be irritating reminders of the shabbiness of their departmental offices or of the houses they had difficulty affording in the Bay Area, a special challenge for many junior faculty who were largely priced out of the local market. Students came as members of discrete interest groups with lists of demands they felt I should be ready to respond to immediately. I found myself sympathizing with student concerns but unable to provide the resources that were requested, leaving these meetings with vague unsatisfactory promises. Staff members were concerned with a host of issues, from the effects of campus shared services as they had been introduced over the past several years on their own work lives and routines, to the bullying they sometimes experienced from senior faculty, to continuing issues around campus culture more generally. I came away from these events feeling frustrated that I was not able to do more to respond to all the issues I heard about.

It had seemed exciting to move into the chancellor's residence, a Mediterranean-style villa that had been built on the north side of campus in 1911 for the President of the University. From the 1960s it became the home of the university chancellor (the first Chancellor of Berkeley started in the role in 1952). It was a grand mansion, on three floors, with an extensive ground and garden, and for many years the presidents – and later the chancellors – lived in the house, eating in the wood-paneled dining room on the main floor, next to a cavernous catering kitchen. In later decades a small kitchen was built on the second floor, where a quasi-independent residence was created to separate what became the private quarters of the chancellor's family from the public rooms on the lower floors. Even that was not completely private, however, as it was only separated by an open staircase, and on several occasions we found guests wandering around the upstairs when they came to the house for a reception or event. The house was the only residential quarter of any kind on the campus, and it was viewed with a measure of awe, envy, and disapproval. Chancellors were required to live there.

Although it was seen as a perk, it quickly became a burden. Not only was it a visible symbol of the chancellor's position, it was a regular destination for protests, mostly peaceful, though on occasion entailing – or at least threatening – violence. It was also a regular source of snark for the gossip columns of the *San Francisco Chronicle*. We spent an enormous amount of effort trying to ensure that the staff who tended the public parts of the house were not performing what might be considered "personal services" for us – whether that might mean opening a door to let our dogs into the house from the garden or bringing deliveries to us upstairs. Learning that such services needed to be rigidly accounted for, we asked that we receive none. The artwork on the walls downstairs, extraordinary works from the Berkeley Art Museum including paintings by Diebenkorn and Romare Bearden, were inspiring, but increasingly we felt that we were not only living in a fishbowl on the outside, but that it was a fishbowl on the inside as well.

Stormy Weather

Despite these worries, the new life I led was fulfilling, and I embraced my role. I knew, however, that we were headed to a fiscal cliff if we didn't receive more support from the state or discretion over tuition from the Regents. I also knew I was not in possession of many of the levers to control our finances that I had been used to during my time at Columbia. Meanwhile, I couldn't forget the governor's pledge to hold tuition flat while using his state budgetary authority to impose an austerity regime on the University of California. Even though I resisted the complaint that Berkeley suffered from "change fatigue," I did know it suffered from budget crisis fatigue, and I wanted to do everything possible to bring new resources to the university to restore a sense of genuine optimism about Berkeley's future prospects. During my first year at Berkeley, this began to look much more difficult than I had initially assumed. My new provost, who started in April of 2014, soon realized that the provost's "discretionary" funds had been spent down significantly before he took up his position, and I came to realize that we had very little debt capacity given the amount of building that had been done in previous years. Our only hope was to combine massively successful fundraising with a political strategy that would outflank Jerry Brown's austerity platform. I began encouraging Janet Napolitano to find a way to persuade the Regents that we needed a series of regular if moderate tuition increases to provide funding for what was still the finest public university system in America.

During her first year in the role, Janet spent a lot of time with the chancellors trying to get up to speed. We met periodically for dinner to talk about how best to confront the particular challenges of the University of California. If university administration was new to her, state-level politics was new to me. Although we talked about novels we had enjoyed, I also realized how foreign the actual world of the university was to her. She was an intensely private person, who had devoted herself entirely to politics, a testimony doubtless in part to her fortitude as a woman seeking public office. We spoke candidly about our sense of Jerry Brown and the political struggles ahead. I enjoyed hearing about her experiences working with Obama and his administration. I explained Berkeley's financial challenges and tried to persuade her that we needed to take serious action if we were going to preserve its academic excellence.

She listened carefully and began to discuss a plan with other chancellors to initiate a regular set of tuition increases while ensuring that resources for financial aid awards would also increase to mitigate any impact on students who qualified for aid. In autumn of 2014 she worked with the Regents to gain support, showing her considerable political savvy and skill. By the November Regents' meeting, she felt confident enough to introduce the plan, having arranged for key Regents to voice their public support. No sooner, however, did she and others say the word "tuition," than student groups began to protest very loudly, both on campuses and at the Regents' meeting where students had arranged for buses to bring protestors from nearby campuses in Santa Cruz and Davis as well as from Berkeley.

Napolitano had encountered major protests when she first arrived in California, driven in large part by the fact that despite her authorship of Deferred Action for Childhood Arrivals she had been responsible for a larger number of deportations than any previous Secretary of Homeland Security. The first major protest I dealt with at Berkeley was on the occasion of her first visit to campus, and a few weeks later my own inauguration ceremony was briefly disrupted as well by protests about her participation. At the bi-monthly Regents' meetings, deliberations were routinely disrupted by protestors who shut down the meetings for hours at a time, at one meeting charging from the gallery to the rows where the chancellors sat (this was well behind the central round table where the Regents sat with Napolitano), only to be tackled (literally) there by the university police.

Once the word "tuition" began circulating again, I found myself to be the object of protest. On one occasion, when a group of students was loudly denouncing tuition increases outside my office, I went out to talk, against the advice of staff colleagues who had lived through earlier protests. I tried to explain that this would have no effect on any students receiving financial aid. Some students used their megaphones – some pointed right at my face – to denounce me, asking me to give a simple yes or no answer to the question: do you want to charge students more? I talked about the fact that the university required more income, and that some of it would have to come either from state allocations or from students who could pay more. The meeting was tense, since the students had come to protest and not to listen. At least not to me. None of what I said had any impact, as many of them seemed to assume – in part on the basis of having heard Jerry Brown talk about my salary – that if I (and my administrative colleagues) worked for free that would take care of the financial issues of the university. I suggested that they join the administration in lobbying Sacramento for more state funds. They understood that to mean that I was encouraging them to protest the next Regents' meeting.

Brown wasn't happy either. He complained loudly that he had been sandbagged by not being told well ahead of the meeting of the plan for tuition increases. He had just been re-elected as governor and was especially unhappy that the first new thing to happen was to hear that the university wanted him to renege on his commitment to hold tuition flat. He spoke about his ongoing commitment to reducing the cost of education during his time as governor, and said, with some real anger in his voice, that he would block increases in state allocations if the Regents approved any change in tuition levels. Complaining about what he called the spiraling cost curve of higher education, he reiterated his views on psychic income, the need for real austerity, and the lack of courage on the part of the assembled Regents and chancellors in tackling the big issues. Some of the Regents looked nervous, and those who had been through the earlier tuition wars seemed especially reluctant to pick up arms again, even as they conceded in private the need for serious financial measures.

It was clear to us at Berkeley that five years of 5 percent tuition increases would significantly help to address our budget shortfall without affecting any students on financial aid, since the formulae for aid would have been adjusted to compensate for any increases to them. I assumed that the state, newly flush with budget surpluses, could also contribute far more to its premier university system. I had come from a private university that routinely increased tuition by 3–4 percent to keep up with expenses, but which also kept raising levels of financial aid for students. I was not yet aware how any mention of tuition would elicit protest, indeed how the word "tuition" seemed to imply a full-throated neoliberal commitment to the privatization of the university. As some predicted, the protests at the Regents' meeting were loud and disruptive, giving pause to everyone. Regents and chancellors had to be escorted by university police through to the loading dock, where we were brought to the meeting room in the freight elevator. On the second morning of the meeting I'd been delayed by traffic crossing the Bay Bridge on my way into San Francisco, and it took me an hour to find police who could figure out how to gain entrance for me to the building. When Brown called for a committee to study the issue, Napolitano hastily agreed. Soon we were told that the committee would consist solely of Jerry and Janet, the committee of two. They announced that the Regents would defer any further consideration of tuition hikes until the committee had met with different groups and reported back.

From that time onward we didn't hear much. Janet gave the chancellors general updates at our monthly meetings, telling us a bit about the people and groups who had been invited to attend meetings on specific subjects. For the most part, Janet and Jerry kept their own counsel, making the "committee of two (CO_2)" seem altogether too literal.

In May, six months later, I received a call from the CFO of the university system. He had previously served at Berkeley as the Executive Vice Chancellor for Administration and Finance, and he understood the specific budget challenges we were facing. When he called, however, he seemed to be reading from a script. He told me that the plan agreed to by Brown and Napolitano should come as welcome news and bring long-term financial relief to the campus. We were then told by Napolitano's chief of staff – a lawyer Janet had brought with her from Homeland Security who seemed to relish his role of doling out difficult news – that our job was to disseminate the plan as a victory for the university.

In fact, the plan was woefully inadequate, certainly for Berkeley. While the governor had promised four years of 4 percent increases in the state allocation, these increases were only on a base of the budget that came from the state, an amount that only constituted 12 percent of our revenue. When my predecessor had started as chancellor in 2004, the state provided close to 34 percent of the university's funding, but this, as noted earlier, had been radically cut after the recession of 2008–09. Now, the modest increase in state funding – at levels still far below where they had been a full decade before – was in exchange for a pledge to hold tuition constant, among many other conditions that clearly had been introduced by Brown, including measuring the cost of different fields of study (not bad in itself, but potentially a prelude to cutting certain fields on financial grounds), changing the pension system from defined benefit to defined contribution (putting all the risk of retirement on employees), increasing transfers from California community colleges, and controlling the number of out-of-state students (who paid considerably more than in-state students). The state-funded increase was not even enough to cover increases in salaries that had already been negotiated by the office of the president with unions for represented staff, at least on the Berkeley campus. I felt disheartened, not just by the recognition that we were soon going to have to deal with a massive deficit, but also by the sense that the political process governing the university was not well suited for dealing with the fiscal challenges Berkeley was confronting. I was two years into the job and had many plans for the university. Now I knew that we were heading into crisis territory, even without the excuse – and political protection – of a major external crisis like the great recession of 2008–09. The next meeting of the chancellors was a sullen affair. It was then that I saw that some of the staff at the office of the president seemed more concerned with protecting Napolitano's reputation – and future political prospects – than many of the academic issues we were facing on the university's campuses. I felt an increasing disconnect between the world of politics and that of the university. I wasn't simply concerned about the academic side of the house. Berkeley's excellence was all the more important because it had been achieved with far greater access for students from diverse backgrounds than its peer universities – most of which were private, much smaller, and far better endowed. Now a new question emerged. Was that excellence sustainable? What were the costs of that excellence? Indeed, was that excellence even defensible, leave alone affordable, when it was no longer fully subsidized by the state? These were existential questions for Berkeley – the iconic institution that made clear how academically excellent a public university could be.

In a new ranking of universities commenced by *The New York Times* in 2015, meant to measure access as well as excellence, the University of California captured six of the top ten slots, catapulted to the top because of the unique combination of research and educational quality on the one hand and high percentages of Pell-Grant-eligible students on the other. Pell Grants were available to students from low-income families, and they were the easiest way to measure "access" across different colleges and universities. If one factored in the many transfer students who entered Berkeley, mostly from California community colleges, about one third of our students were in that category, double the percentage of the highest Ivy League college. In fact, one of my standard lines in the speeches I gave was that Berkeley alone had more Pell Grant students than the entire Ivy League combined. I later learned that these numbers fluctuated and weren't quite true any longer, but they captured the essence of the comparison. Berkeley and UCLA combined did in fact have more than the top fifteen private universities (including the Ivy League as well as Stanford, Chicago, Duke, and others). This was a remarkable achievement, but it was especially remarkable because we didn't sacrifice academic excellence to attain those numbers. Berkeley's academic excellence was remarkable, and important, precisely because of those numbers. I wanted desperately to be able to protect this achievement.

I became worried that our financial difficulties would begin to erode our academic quality. Having worked as a dean at Columbia who had tried to recruit Berkeley faculty, I knew that they were for the most part fiercely loyal to the institution, and not just because the Bay Area was such a pleasant place to live, nor because the defined benefits pension system rewarded full career faculty (and staff) with secure retirement income. They liked working at the university because of the quality of their colleagues, departments, and academic environment. They were genuinely moved by the diversity of the student body, and many were fully committed to teaching not just the students who could have been at the top of Harvard's classes but others who were from backgrounds that included being undocumented, formerly incarcerated, from foster care, and having grown up in areas with substandard schools and at best difficult family and community circumstances. At the same time, highly ranked departments were the real key to recruiting and retaining top faculty. They could train superb graduate students and work with some of the best scholars and researchers in their respective fields. The high cost of housing in the Bay Area had already begun to erode the financial competitiveness of their salaries and benefits, especially for junior faculty who had no housing equity, even as some of our campus buildings, when not seismically unsound, were getting steadily shabbier, and other kinds of investments in the quality of faculty and student life seemed to be endlessly deferred. I knew that universities only lost their academic edge slowly, but I also knew it was much easier to fall than it was to rise. I felt the weight of responsibility to ensure Berkeley's survival as a preeminent university.

As we began to plan for how to respond to the impending financial challenges, I spent hours that spring and summer talking with Claude about what we should do. We compared notes on what we had learned about the university since we arrived, which programs and schools needed special protection, and whether there were units that were both overextended and underperforming. Every university is good at creating new programs, and Berkeley excelled in this regard. No university, however, is good at ending programs when they have either served their purpose or stopped being as good as they once were. Berkeley was no exception. All programs had boosters and defenders, who knew how to mobilize public opinion to ensure that the administration could not close them down even when circumstances warranted. Preliminary discussions about program closure could occasion protests, articles in the local newspapers written by reporters with an axe to grind against the university, and the mobilization of multiple stakeholders who feared for similar administrative decisions regarding their own special interests. Our staff began to give us white papers from earlier administrations with long disquisitions on why this school or that department needed serious reform, downsizing, or even mergers of some kind or another. And we began to hear directly from senate leaders on the faculty that this was an opportunity to clean house in a way that was long overdue for Berkeley.

Many of the programs that had been funded by ample state monies in earlier years had shifted their budgets to general university support, including extremely worthy programs such as offering pre-medical training for students from underprivileged backgrounds, as well as what had become vanity centers that provided faculty with administrative support for their regular academic activities. These programs did little to look for new revenues beyond the yearly allocations from the central administration, but kept asking for additional funding. Now that state funding had been so reduced, this put a huge strain on Berkeley's regular budget. Some schools had large PhD programs because of their research aspirations, but could neither fund the programs well enough to provide necessary support for research nor mobilize support to create new Master's programs, even in obvious fields such as teacher training. These were programs that could both earn revenues and provide quicker – and often more usable – degrees for students seeking skills and credentials for better careers.

As we refined our budgetary projections, we convened a series of all-day retreats for the cabinet to begin to develop a plan. My chief of staff had spent time working as a consultant after completing his doctoral work and had a good sense of how to think about using future scenarios for planning; he crafted some that helped us imagine a break with many current practices. Many of the senior administrators in my cabinet had served with Birgeneau, and they had gone through similar deliberations in the wake of the financial crisis just six years before. That period of time had been well documented in Fredrick Wiseman's long documentary *At Berkeley* that was released just after my arrival. Watching the film again later that summer I realized that these retreats brought to mind Yogi Berra's adage that it was deja vu all over again for those who were still there.

Although we knew we had to borrow from what worked before, we thought that this time was different. We worried that we could not simply cut across the board – even though that had been the Berkeley way, which treated all units equally (despite vastly different internal resources and reputations). We came to believe that the only way to address a long-term structural deficit would be to reorganize some key components of the university. We needed to make decisions that would allow Berkeley to prosper at a time when we finally understood that the state was not going to restore pre-recession levels of funding. If we could reimagine Berkeley's basic organizational structures in ways that were both more streamlined and more efficient, we might be able to ensure long-term excellence despite the strained relationship with the state and the university. We also knew that we had to protect some units and departments from cuts that would damage their excellence and their mission, even as there were other units that could not only withstand cuts but also be redirected to more financially feasible activities, in some cases using existing resources to develop new degree programs for which there was demand. To be sure, I was deeply intrigued by discussions we had that also aligned with my own predisposition to look for interdisciplinary opportunities for different units to make better connections between and among them. Berkeley could be a test case for innovation while responding to budget necessities. But I was reluctant to authorize any particular changes until we had extensive consultation with the faculty.

We reprised earlier discussions about whether we could claw back greater autonomy for Berkeley, revisiting proposals that Birgeneau had made a few years before, wondering if political circumstances would ever allow changing the terms of Berkeley's relationship with the system. It became clear to us, however, that the bulk of faculty and staff would oppose such a move, as would Napolitano. Many faculty believed in Berkeley's special flagship status, but they were also – understandably – deeply hailed by the idea of being in a public university, despite the fact that when you only received 12 percent of your budget from the state the meaning of being public had surely changed. And Napolitano came to the university with centralizing tendencies, well-honed by her time as Governor of Arizona and Secretary of Homeland Security. She had made abundantly clear that she was against campus autonomy – which she had already significantly reduced since taking office.

As we talked among ourselves and with faculty representatives, we wondered how to roll out the news about the deficit, at what point we should provide details about the impending crisis. Some argued that we needed to make sure not to damage morale, especially at a time when we knew other universities were doing fine and seeking to hire some of our best faculty. Others argued that we needed to be transparent, but that we first had to prepare at least the outlines of a plan to address the crisis. And others felt that we needed to broadcast the problem before developing any plans at all. I briefed Janet regularly, for we needed her help and support. Although she said that she would not stand by to see Berkeley's quality eroded, she also channeled a pervasive feeling in the system-wide office that Berkeley was entitled and that it was long past time to bring it more in line with the other campuses.

She also encouraged us to hire a crisis management communications firm to help us prepare for the roll-out during the next year. This became increasingly critical since we were not just talking about possible cuts or mergers for academic programs, but the possible need to downsize our athletics program. Berkeley had thirty intercollegiate sports teams and all but football and men's basketball either lost money or were barely sustained year by year through alumni contributions. Birgeneau had announced some years before that he would cut some sports teams only to generate a vast outcry from alumni and other interested parties. Although we didn't yet have specific plans, we knew that if we didn't talk about cutting sports, some faculty would rebel. And if we did talk about cutting sports, many alumni would be up in arms. There were only a few degrees of freedom for making serious decisions.

Although we continued planning for the Berkeley Global Campus, we realized that we had to be especially careful about making any commitments there. This had produced great anxiety on the part of different constituencies in Richmond, who were anxious for us to sign agreements with them about the exclusive use of local labor, the hiring of local construction firms, and the creation of new jobs. Students who no longer protested about tuition hikes began to protest against our exploitation of the people of Richmond for not signing agreements. One evening Claude and I were asked by a student group, the Berkeley Forum, to appear for a debate about questions concerning the future of public universities. As soon as we took our seats on the stage of International House, we were shouted down by students, some upset at Claude for a tenure decision he had made about an African American member of the faculty, others angry at me for my alleged failures to advance the Richmond campus in the public interest, and still others outraged in general because we were allegedly corporatizing the university (by which they meant that we were emphasizing fundraising and revenue growth). After half an hour of shouting, we left the stage without being allowed to speak. Those protestors concerned about Richmond were unable to understand that we hadn't yet raised money for the Berkeley Global Campus; we had pledged to the faculty that we would wait to do so before making any commitments.

University House became a scene of regular protests, often taking place late in the evenings. The protests seemed to be staged deliberately to disrupt our evenings and sometimes our sleep. Janaki began to be extremely nervous about staying in the house when I was traveling, despite the continuation of the police presence from Birgeneau's time in the house. In response, the campus police developed plans to fence the entire property both to make it more secure and to reduce the expense of paying for police protection – as had been the case for years – around the clock and throughout the entire week. Initial plans for the fence would save money after only one year and reduce the police presence on campus.

A full perimeter fence seemed a necessary decision when later in the year negotiations between the university system and a number of unions broke down and students took up the cause of represented workers on campus. One Sunday morning I heard noise outside and saw about 120 people approaching the house, chanting, "Dirks Dirks you can't hide, we can see your greedy side," a chant that had begun when Brown had publicly rebuked me for my salary. The protestors banged loudly on the door and sprayed angry (and obscene) graffiti over the front of the house, vandalizing the front steps and windows. Only after the crowd dispersed did I realize that the front door had been seriously damaged by some protestors who were clearly trying to break into the house. I began to be accosted as I walked around campus; I was once approached by a student protestor with her phone's video camera trained on me as I was buying groceries at the Berkeley Bowl on a Sunday afternoon asking – yes or no – if I could commit to a living wage for workers, my unsuccessful effort to purchase Cheerios recorded on video. The mood was tense, and we hadn't even begun to make serious cuts.

This was a time when we were in fact ramping up fundraising in significant ways. We had begun a thorough review of our "development" operations since we suffered not just from multiple inefficiencies but also outright competition between and among different units on campus. I asked Claude to direct this review since it would require the full support of the deans. We managed to reform the organization of the fundraising teams while facilitating much better collaboration, and our fundraising results reflected this. Finally, Berkeley had a fundraising and development operation that could rival major private universities. During my third year we outpaced all previous records and came close to raising half a billion dollars for the first time in our history. I spent a great deal of time with donors (or prospective donors), speaking about the importance of supporting Berkeley to alumni groups and other gatherings. I started days with breakfast meetings and ended them with official dinners, working through weekends even when there wasn't a home football game; the pace of life combined with the prevailing worry over the budget was relentless. But even as we were raising unprecedented amounts of funding, we knew how far short we were in funding our basic operations.

For the remainder of the fall, we worked to develop plans for a suite of strategic initiatives by identifying areas we might cut or reconfigure as well as units that might be able to raise more revenue. We also began to prepare for the roll-out. The crisis firm worked with us and other members of the senior administration and the faculty to prepare us. They didn't just do cosmetic work. They challenged us to clarify our message and prepare answers for questions that were sure to come. What was the cause of the deficit? What specific actions had led to such a spiraling shortfall of funding? Was it our fault; that of the preceding administration; of the office of the president; of the governor and the state of California? We knew that the answers were complex, that there was no single actor or set of decisions that had led to this outcome. We also knew we had to be careful if we were to cast blame on the university system or the state's political leaders.

I knew I had inherited a precarious situation, and I had done my best to persuade the president and Regents to take a different course of action, an approach from which they had now retreated. If we were to succeed in addressing some of the resulting issues we had to recruit the university community to work together. We knew it would not be easy. On weekends we worked on endless drafts of different messages and memos. Claude and I took the lead, working closely with our chiefs of staff, the vice provosts, our communications team, and the leadership of the academic senate. We were told we had to run all our communications through the office of the president, unprecedented overreach further complicating our job. By February 10th, when we finally made the announcement, we had probably written twenty-five different versions of the main message we finally decided to send.

Claude and I had also begun to meet on a regular basis with Janet and her senior team in Oakland to talk about the budget crisis. In January, I tried to slow down some of the planning that had been taking place, concerned as I was that we were trying to do too much too quickly. When I told this to Janet, giving voice to our worries about the possible obstacles and political pitfalls ahead of us, she lost her temper, shouting at us for being indecisive. I had never been yelled at like this in a professional situation before, and I found it disconcerting to say the least.

I knew that the prospects ahead were genuinely daunting, and I wanted to be cautious. I also realized that when people – whether colleagues in the administration, faculty on senate committees, or Napolitano and her associates in her office – were encouraging me to take bold action, they were also clear that I would take full responsibility for whatever happened next. Fortunately, after that meeting, she apologized, and began to think about how her office could be helpful, including providing lines of credit to give us more time and runway for the work we needed to do. But it felt tense.

In my February memo, I announced a campus-wide initiative to address our "new normal" of limited state funding and flat tuition. I said that we would examine every part of our budget, from our human resource policies to our research funding processes, from our schools, colleges, and departments to our broader educational portfolios. "Some of the changes we will undergo will be painful," I admitted, but I insisted that nothing we did would constitute "an abandonment of our commitment to a public mission." Instead, we would make "a fundamental defense of the concept of the public university, a concept that we must reinvent in order to preserve." I wanted to break through the anodyne rhetoric of most administrative messages without alarming the larger community. At the advice of the leaders of the academic senate with whom we had been working so closely, we underplayed the possible role of academic restructuring, especially since I had already begun to see how much resistance there would be. Ironically, faculty leaders of the senate and in the administration – long-time members of the faculty who had much more understanding of the wasteful redundancy of university structures – had been trying to persuade us to be far more aggressive in academic reorganization than

I thought either prudent or possible. Some colleagues advocated that we close the PhD program in the School of Education, while others trained their critical gaze on the School of Social Welfare or on Journalism, citing both academic concerns and long-term worries about financial viability. While there was a growing list of good ideas for the modest reorganization of units and programs that would save money and effort, I began to push back against the more aggressive proposals, as well as against my Vice Chancellor for Administration and Finance who wanted me to defend the "shared service" mechanisms he had introduced, while also agreeing that I would put everything on the table for discussion and evaluation. I did not announce any concrete top-down initiatives, for there were none to announce.

In the run-up to the announcement, I did a media blitz, talking to reporters at local papers as well as *The New York Times*, appearing on national radio programs, and followed up with a set of town halls and interviews on campus as well as an open conversation with Berkeley alumni. We met with the newly created board of visitors I had formed precisely to give me counsel on matters like this. I was unable to communicate directly with the Regents, since they worked through Napolitano, who as it turned out had not given them an update about our situation until the news was out.

At first the responses were mostly positive, both from some departmental chairs and senate leaders: at last, we were told, we were trying to address in serious ways the problems Berkeley had faced for some years rather than kicking the can down the road by doing across-the-board cuts. As Claude began doing the rounds of different colleges and schools, however, we began to hear a more negative refrain. We had intended to begin a serious conversation with the faculty, but even this muted message set in motion the wrong conversations. Some people reacted to the announcement by spreading false rumors that we intended to close the College of Chemistry, which housed the number-one-ranked department of chemistry in the country,[6] while some faculty from the College of Natural Resources reacted to ideas that had been floated to consolidate some programs – connecting discrete economics programs, for example, or linking separate pre-med programs – as examples of administrative overreach. Increasingly, we weren't so much rolling out a planning process as denying rumors, insisting that we had made no decisions in advance, countering Tea Party-like rhetoric within the university about the Obamacare death panels we were allegedly establishing.

At a roundtable meeting with faculty and staff in March, I repeated that "we won't do anything without extensive consultation." We had precipitated a feeling of panic, the outpouring of years of pent-up worry about the future of this great public university. Coming to Berkeley from Columbia, I was perhaps unable to sense the pervasive anxiety and even trauma about budget cuts that had stemmed from years of financial crisis, but I also found myself weirdly cast as an administrator who was out of

---

[6] This was a total misrepresentation; the status of chemistry at Berkeley was one we routinely celebrated for its paramount academic excellence and I planned only to support it; the sole question I heard anyone discuss regarding chemistry was whether it should be in a stand-alone college with the Department of Chemical Engineering or housed instead alongside the Department of Physics – also a number-one-rated department – in the Division of Mathematics and Physical Sciences.

touch with the real Berkeley. Since the leaders of the academic senate didn't step up to talk about their role in our deliberations, the charge that we had already begun a top-down administrative process began to stick despite the reality of the situation and the constant reassurances we gave. This was where being "newcomers" to Berkeley was decidedly a problem, as not only were we repeatedly called "outsiders," we didn't have close faculty colleagues to whom we could back-channel our commitment to develop robust planning processes and no easy ways to counter the rumors that started circulating. And this is also where we began to pay for resentment against earlier administrative decisions. The introduction of "campus shared services" had gone badly, along with an associated program called "operational excellence" that tracked savings from administrative efficiencies in earlier years. Our new Office of Strategic Initiatives was seen as another version of that, and the fact that the administrator who was leading this effort was still in my cabinet made this seem plausible even though he had not been responsible for previous breakdowns and was incredibly careful about seeking advice and consultation from the faculty.

Convergent Crises

In mid-March of 2016, just as we were dealing with growing anxiety on the part of faculty about how any possible academic restructuring might affect them, there were new headlines about sexual harassment. The executive assistant of the new Dean of the Law School had filed a suit against the university, claiming that she was unsatisfied with the resolution of a grievance she had filed a year before about harassment from the dean. This had been handled in the provost's office the previous summer, and although I'd been kept out of the decision – given my role as ultimate arbiter of faculty disciplinary hearings – I was also told that the resolution was done according to precedent and had been acceptable to all parties. Now I learned that the whole case had not only fallen apart but was doing so in full view of the world. I received an angry call from Napolitano telling me not only that she should have been told about this, but that I should have simply rejected early policies in which these decisions were delegated to the provost's office. I understood her anger; I too was confronting the eruption of years of anger about inadequate provisions and procedures about sexual harassment on campus. We had already encountered significant blowback about an earlier effort to prevent a prominent astronomer, Geoff Marcy, from engaging in further sexual harassment, in which the administration had been hampered by existing rules about statutes of limitation and procedural protections for tenured faculty. Both cases had been adjudicated according to precedent; now it was clear that the public in general, and a growing percentage of faculty and students, no longer believed the rules were sufficient. Neither did I. It was clear that they had been drafted to protect faculty and we had to revise them accordingly.

Claude told me that the Law School case was complex and that he had tried to balance different issues with a settlement that would be agreeable to the different parties, but that he had relied on advice from those in his office who knew the system and protocols much better than he did and had made such decisions before. Now a rumor started that suggested that he had given the dean favorable treatment because Claude was getting an appointment in the Law School as part of his "step down" agreement. This was preposterous, since I was the one who had proposed that he have a partial appointment in Law when he was first appointed, and the faculty there had leapt at the chance to have him teach there when he ceased being provost. Napolitano summarily preempted local campus authority by ordering the dean to leave the campus in a public letter designed to show that she was taking charge, converting a local crisis into a political statement as she responded with a quick acceptance of insistent student demands that the dean's presence on campus made them feel unsafe. As I watched her throw normal rules aside, I also came to realize my own reticence to seize political issues and take control of them; I was clearly too circumspect in deferring to existing procedures and trying to understand the details of any given situation. Meanwhile, some faculty started suggesting that Claude step down from being provost.

Claude had been my partner in everything I'd done at Berkeley, and in the rush to judgment some Berkeley colleagues were quick to believe rumors that were not only manifestly untrue, but outright betrayals of Berkeley's progressive credentials. We witnessed a new mentality overtake the campus, leading Claude himself to wonder what was really behind the groundswell of denunciation. Meanwhile, he had been virtually absent from home for the previous six months as we worked on the budget crisis, despite the fact that his wife, Dorothy, was fighting a losing battle against cancer. I sat with him as he wrestled with the situation, finally deciding to step down, if only because he didn't want to fight for his own future

148

as provost in a hostile environment while trying to care for his wife. In retrospect, I should have refused to accept his resignation and begged him to stay. I also knew he had struggled with the decision about the Law School Dean and later came out to say publicly that he wished he had done it differently (e.g., dismissing the dean from his position); that only later had he come to understand that following the rulebook around sanctions was no longer justified. If I too had fully understood the level of residual outrage I would not have allowed Claude to make this decision on his own. For me, losing Claude at that point, in that way, was not just a huge blow, it compromised everything I had been seeking to accomplish at Berkeley.

Just a few days before his resignation, we had sat through a special senate meeting about the strategic plan for restructuring the university. One faculty member after the next walked up to the open mic to talk about how long they had worked at Berkeley, how much they loved being there, and how pernicious it was that the administration was clearly unaware that its job was to protect the university as it was, not to change it. We heard outrage about the clumsy roll-out of campus shared services by the previous administration and a parodic account of the office that we had set up to manage the strategic planning process. A former chair of the academic senate, a friend who had been a great supporter of the undergraduate initiative, denounced me for not bringing in more money from the state to ensure there would be no layoffs on campus, despite knowing full well that we had tried and found it impossible to budge the governor. The senate ultimately voted to instruct us that we were not to merge, close, or change any academic unit on campus without the express permission of the faculty within those units. At no point in the meeting did the leadership of the senate admit how closely they had been working with us to think about how we might introduce changes to make Berkeley more resilient for the longer term. Indeed, the most dramatic ideas for academic restructuring had been suggested by long-time Berkeley faculty, not by either Claude or me.

When I finally spoke to the spring faculty meeting later in the spring I said that I had listened to faculty concerns and taken their advice, dissolving the Office of Strategic Initiatives, and also beginning the process of unraveling the long unpopular campus shared services to make for a more localized approach. I reiterated that we would make no decisions without full faculty participation. By then, I had, at the recommendation of the deans, appointed a former provost, and more recently Smith College President, Carol Christ, as the interim provost. Her presence was reassuring to deans and faculty with whom she had been colleagues, since she had first joined the department of English in 1970. I was grateful to Carol for stepping in so quickly, and I knew that her long experience at Berkeley would be helpful as we worked to devise better procedures for handling sexual harassment cases while also trying to balance the budget.

But I was also aware that many of my initiatives had to be put on hold. Most painfully, I realized I had to step back from my signature program to develop the Berkeley Global Campus. Although we had invested no campus funds in the project, were receiving more and more interest from other universities, potential corporate partners, and individual donors, and had already developed stunning plans for the Richmond campus that otherwise would continue to be largely empty, I hit the brakes. That news was devastating to the political leadership of Richmond who had supported us from the beginning of the project. It was also a major disappointment for the leaders of Cambridge University, the National University of Singapore, and Tsinghua, undoing all the work of the previous years for a new kind of global university collaboration. And I had to call a number of prospective donors who had wanted to contribute to the project to say it was off.

The faculty meeting had quelled palpable discontent. Nevertheless, none of our budget problems went away, and there were still sore feelings among some who believed – based on still persistent rumors – that they had been unfairly targeted for cuts. I gave up on pursuing any significant structural changes in university organization. Even so, a few faculty were still antagonistic. The two leaders of the Berkeley Faculty Association (an independent faculty body, not the duly elected faculty senate) were against the administration on principle, one believing that we should do no fundraising, the other that all administrative work should be conducted by a rotating faculty committee. They were quoted in every news story even though they had views that were by any measure on the fringe of faculty sentiment. Some of the other vocal faculty had been among the old guard that worried they were losing their privileged access to positions of authority in the university (including one I had reprimanded for drinking too much at university functions). A few of them called the local newspaper, complaining about the expenditure involved in constructing a fence around the official residence as well as the cost of renovations on the public parts of the house where fundraising events took place.

That summer, after the tumult of the spring had died down, I read an article in the student newspaper that I was building an "escape hatch" in my office. I had no idea what this was about, but the next day a television crew had come to campus to try to take video footage of this new symbol of my alleged preoccupation with personal safety. The escape hatch turned out to be a door, in the process of being installed to allow the staff in my wider office to have a back exit from their office on occasions when students – or others – had occupied the office. The office had been occupied several times that spring, and some of the staff had been deeply frightened; they had requested both protection and a second way to exit the building. The door was not for me – I had neither asked for it nor did I need it. When my communications officer told me that it was the most tweeted story about Berkeley that summer, I laughed at first. But there had been other stories – exaggerated and misrepresented as with the escape hatch, along with spurious and ultimately dismissed lawsuits and complaints – that had made me realize how I had been made not just to "own" but also to embody the budgetary chasm at the heart of Berkeley's predicament. I saw how a complex story about the disinvestment of the state in a public university could be translated into an unrecognizable narrative about the administration, and ultimately about me.

I had staked my chancellorship on trying to encourage the university to rethink its identity in the wake of recurrent and deeply threatening financial challenges. There was widespread agreement that this was an important thing to do, but the collective resolve to do so was a much different matter. I asked the university to confront extremely difficult questions. As phrased by Bill Kirby, the former Dean of the Faculty of Arts and Sciences at Harvard, in a case study he wrote about Berkeley:

What did it mean to be a 'public' institution, when the vast majority of institutional funding came from private sources? What were Berkeley's obligations to the citizens, taxpayers, and children of the state of California, which no longer funded it in a sustainable fashion? Could Berkeley meet these regional expectations while remaining one of the best universities in the world? Finally, had one of Berkeley's historic strengths, faculty governance, made it impossible to face inevitably difficult choices?

After long discussions with Janaki – who herself had been criticized in the press for refurbishing a public bathroom and changing the carpeting in the formal reception area of the house for fundraising purposes – I decided to announce that I would step down from my position after the next academic year. We both felt there had been too much tension – and downright nastiness – to continue for longer than that, leave alone focus either on what I had tried to begin in the first place or on what needed urgent attention now. I turned my attention instead to the enormous budgetary issues rather than defending my record. As Kirby put it, "In doing so, this Berkeley outsider honored one of Berkeley's oldest traditions: Daniel Gilman, the second UC president and one of Berkeley's most influential early leaders, also ended his term ... 'beset by financial difficulties and political harassment.' Dirks's two immediate predecessors, both, like him, recruited from the outside, had left office after some measure of faculty discontent as well." I had been attacked for Berkeley's dismal finances, and then in turn disempowered by the strictures placed on Berkeley by the UC system, whose president had repeatedly intervened in internal Berkeley affairs. Now, my sole intent was to leave Berkeley better off than when I arrived.

Trumpism and the Attack on the University

When I announced that I would step down at the end of the next academic year, I outlined a plan to reduce Berkeley's deficit by $85m during the same timetable. I knew that while some of the actions I would have to take in the months ahead would be deeply unpopular, it would be easier to do so now that I was leaving. I did not know, however, that the year would also be a test of our capacity to deal with the cataclysmic election of Donald Trump as president and the associated assaults on the university, using Berkeley's canonic commitment to free speech as the weapon of first choice. As I set about dealing with Berkeley's budget woes, I wondered who among the political figures in my orbit might be headed to Washington to join the new Clinton administration. Instead, I should have begun thinking about how Berkeley's iconically "left" political profile would put the university back at the center of the coming political maelstrom, right where it had been in the turbulent sixties.

The night of the election Janaki and I had gone to a reception in San Francisco being put on by Richard Blum, long-standing Regent of the university and the husband of Senator Dianne Feinstein, for what we thought would be a celebration. We milled around with Richard and Dianne, then Lieutenant Governor Gavin Newsom, Janet

Napolitano, and other major political figures, speculating about who would get cabinet positions in the Clinton administration. As CNN began to report Trump's victories in Florida and other states, we realized the polls were wrong and that a man who was not only unqualified for the office but with a background of being corrupt, racist, and totally unprincipled would likely be the next president.

We boarded the train back to Berkeley, and I went to Sproul Plaza, where a large TV screen had been set up for students. I took my two Labrador retrievers with me – they needed their nighttime walk – and they happily served as comfort animals for students who couldn't believe what they were witnessing. Almost immediately we began to worry about the survival of the DACA program for undocumented students, and about a host of other issues Trump's election might raise for higher education in general and public higher education in particular. I slept only a few hours before writing a statement for the university that I sent out early the next morning. It seemed unusual to be writing a message that could easily be interpreted as partisan (although I phrased it in a way that was defensible even on that score), but the feeling of threat across many communities on campus was palpable and turned out to be appropriate given much of what transpired over the course of Trump's term. I wasn't the only university leader writing such a message, as many of us felt the need to provide assurances about the values of the university at a time when it seemed likely they would be under increasingly greater attack.

Shortly after the election, I began to hear news that the Breitbart provocateur, Milo Yiannopoulos, was coming to campus. Milo, a Cambridge dropout who despite identifying as gay was a raunchy critic of what he considered the political liberalism of American college campuses, was coming to Berkeley to speak as part of his year-long "dangerous faggot" tour. He was promising to insult students who were transgender, undocumented, Muslim, feminist, or simply (and misleadingly) "politically correct" (this was before "woke" came to substitute for and displace that term). Milo had been invited by the Berkeley College Republicans, who were following the playbook of other college Republican groups that had invited Milo for a nationwide college tour. We had watched while his campus visits had on occasion turned nasty and violent. At the University of Wisconsin, Milwaukee, Milo had mocked (and identified) a trans student who had protested the UWM locker room policy. At the University of California, Davis, protests became so intense the campus police called off the event. And at the University of Washington in Seattle, there had been a shooting, in which a demonstrator protesting against Milo had been shot and seriously injured. In the wake of all this unsettling news, a significant group of faculty and an even larger group of students called on me to cancel the event. There were real reasons to be concerned about public safety. We were receiving threats from some on the right who said they were coming to campus to ensure Milo's appearance, and from others on the left who promised to come to shut it down, both promising to use whatever means might be necessary.

As I met with student and faculty groups, I witnessed the real turmoil that Milo's prospective visit was causing. Some faculty said to me in threatening tones that if anything bad happened I would have blood on my hands. Students wept in fear of what the visit would unleash or mean to them. I thought back to the tumult that had resulted from the memo I wrote about civility, how just two years before I had been charged with insufficiently defending free speech on a campus that was synonymous with that principle. As a public university Berkeley was obligated to host speakers invited by legitimate campus groups regardless of political opinions. The juridical "heckler's veto" sets a high bar for preemptive cancellation of these invitations on the basis of generalized threats. If we called this event off, we would be widely criticized – by alums and public figures as well as by Fox – for showing that we only believed in free speech when it was speech of which we approved. Berkeley's outsized political reputation seemed at stake. And yet, to be honest, I was extremely worried that the event would be accompanied by violence, and possible physical injuries.

Two years earlier, I had resisted calls to cancel an invitation made to Bill Maher, on the initial recommendation of a student committee, to speak at our December commencement. Just before coming to Berkeley he made some comments about Islam that were both offensive and wrongheaded. Remembering the legacy of the Free Speech Movement, I did not see how I could cancel that invitation; he came, gave a commencement address that had a spirited defense of free speech, and was quietly protested against by students. I felt the same when Milo had been invited by a legitimate student group, even if I understood the objections. Many faculty and students correctly believed that these speakers were at odds with the stated values of the university community. A growing number of students and faculty came to hold the view that unequal power relations made the noble idea of free speech impossible in reality and therefore not a value worth defending under the circumstances when speakers were likely to spout "hate speech." But I thought a little history was salutary. In the 1960s the right had objected to the campus visits of Stokely Carmichael and even Robert Kennedy on similar grounds. I could hardly defend the academic or intellectual value of a troll and provocateur like Milo, nor would Bill Maher have been my choice for a graduation speaker, but who should be empowered to make decisions to cancel invitations, and what lasting damage would that cause to the campus? Now, I believed that I had to protect the right to invite controversial speakers to campus, despite my strong distaste for Milo. Milo had been invited precisely because he was a provocateur – to expose the hypocrisy of liberal Berkeley. We worked closely with the campus police department to recruit back-up support from other UC campuses and drew from a well-honed strategy to deal with protests of the sort to which Berkeley had become accustomed over the years. We developed a tactical plan that we believed would avoid violence and protect the safety both of protestors and of students who wanted to hear Milo speak.

Shortly after darkness fell on the California winter evening of February 1st, 2017, 150 activists, dressed in black – wearing masks, hats, and donning backpacks – coalesced and marched up Bancroft Avenue towards Sproul Plaza. Sproul was the original scene of campus protest over free speech back in 1964, and the space abutting the student union where Milo was due to speak two hours later.

Loosely named "antifa,"[7] the anonymous "black bloc" group set a fire in the middle of the street before entering the plaza, quickly dispersing into the crowd of students and others, some of whom were shouting and chanting but all of whom were protesting peacefully. Within minutes, the antifa activists, as if on command, began firing explosive fireworks as they broke through the barricades, using them to smash open the tall glass windows of the student union, while setting fire to a propane-powered lamp that had been installed to light up the plaza. We had more than 100 police on duty but given that we did not want to further incite violence, they seemed unable to prevent the antifa protestors from charging the student union. We watched in horror as an anonymous anarchist group succeeded brilliantly in its mission to shut down the event. At the first sign of violence, Yiannopoulos had to be escorted out of the student union to ensure his safety, and the police began to disperse the crowd in an effort to prevent physical harm to anyone in the building or the plaza. As soon as Yiannopoulos returned to his hotel, he started sending out videos in which he falsely asserted that he was kept from speaking by the Berkeley students and administration.

The melee caused major physical damage to the campus, costing the university over $100,000 for repairs, with the group causing even more damage to banks and other buildings, including a Starbucks, in the neighboring city

---

[7] This was a term some participants in the protest, as well as students who supported them, used at the time, though in subsequent years the term (like "woke" and others) has acquired a phantasmatic meaning for the right wing who have made these words meaningless except as slurs and labels to evoke fear and terror.

of Berkeley. As the fire burned out and the black bloc group finally dispersed, I was enormously relieved that no one was seriously hurt. We thought that there were few if any Berkeley students in the group since at one point they had declared they were going to march to the chancellor's house but didn't seem to know where it was. My staff and the police tried frantically to arrange to evacuate me from the house when they heard the crowd might be coming, only to realize that I could finally go to sleep, exhausted, in my own bed. I nevertheless woke the following morning to see a tweet from Trump, accusing Berkeley of suppressing free speech, and threatening the loss of all federal funds. "If U.C. Berkeley does not allow free speech and practices violence on innocent people with a different point of view – NO FEDERAL FUNDS?" In truth, we woke up to a new reality more generally, as we witnessed the close connection between Breitbart News and Trump's tweets, realizing that the antifa had played right into Milo's campaign to troll Berkeley, while Milo elevated himself as a new symbol of free speech under attack.

The tweet seemed benign at the time, though in fact universities across the country began to worry about how Trump might use the power of the federal purse to mount a more widespread campaign against university life, including the research enterprise. Social media and cable TV were ablaze with attacks on Berkeley – and by implication the American university – for its alleged failure to ensure that speakers like Milo Yiannopoulos had their free speech rights protected, no matter what the disruption, regardless of the cost, leave aside questions about the academic legitimacy of these speakers. Ann Coulter announced on Fox – and her own website – that she was going to speak on campus later in April, so we geared up our preparations for providing security despite the fact that no formal arrangements had been made to secure a venue and appropriate permissions for the event. Threats from the right – many of them anonymous and conveyed over social media – promised that groups including the Proud Boys would come to campus with arms to make sure that the event would take place, while declarations from others who appeared to be sympathizers of the antifa promised once again to shut down the event. I wrote to the campus community: "This is a university, not a battlefield. We must make every effort to hold events at a time and location that maximize the chances that First Amendment rights can be successfully exercised and that community members can be protected." In the end, Coulter, who refused to adjust her schedule to speak at a time and place that would have allowed us to offer necessary security, did not come, claiming at one point that her visit had been called off by the administration. We still had to anticipate protests around her possible visit, however, costing us well in excess of $300,000 to pay for extra policing and barricades.[8]

Although Coulter's visit was, in the end, a "non-event," Fox News and social media proclaimed that once again Berkeley had cancelled a conservative voice. Janaki and I began to get death threats, one – against her – specific enough to require a police investigation. The media frenzy presaged a succession of nasty altercations at Berkeley later that spring and over the summer, mostly in the city park where there were "free speech" rallies organized by

---

[8] www.nytimes.com/2017/04/26/us/ann-coulter-berkeley-speech
.html?smid=url-share

figures identified both with the alt-right movement and with various neo-Nazi groups. The heat that built up at Berkeley expressed itself in deadly fashion later in the summer in Charlottesville, where a neo-Nazi rally was held on the University of Virginia campus, and a rallygoer subsequently rammed his car into a crowd of protestors, killing one and injuring many more. While a national debate about the place of Nazi rhetoric and political action in the country ensued, Berkeley was left spending millions of dollars to keep the peace both when Ben Shapiro came in the fall of 2017 and when Milo shortly thereafter popped onto the campus for a deranged fifteen-minute monologue before decamping again. Berkeley had been at the center of a concerted effort to weaponize the First Amendment not to introduce meaningful conversations about controversial ideas on a political campus identified with left politics but rather to target the university itself.

Our complaint, however, was not helped by the conspicuous and violent visit by the antifa back in February. Leaving aside the use of spurious allegations about the antifa by Trump and others on the far right, Berkeley demonstrated some of the contradictions of the current political moment. I grappled directly with these contradictions in the form of students and faculty who exemplified some of the ideological rigidity that critics – from Jonathan Haidt to Charles Murray – had been complaining about for some time. After all, Claude and I had not been allowed to speak at the Berkeley Forum, in what still rankles as a moment when questions around free speech, diversity of viewpoint, and openness to opposing perspectives and points of view on campus, were left decidedly unanswered. Even though the assault on the university from the right was of a different character, the left closed ranks in a way that exposed the full vulnerability of the dramatically changed character of campus discourse about free speech and "civility." Trump's election exacerbated the situation and upended the balance between those who believed in the importance of free speech and those for whom free speech was seen as impossible. On the one hand, the campus newspaper carried multiple opinion columns from students congratulating the antifa anarchists for closing down the event, while the administration and I were admonished for not listening to the warnings of students and faculty that violence would be the inevitable fallout of invitations to Yiannopoulos, Coulter, and Shapiro. On the other hand, Trump's tweet licensed an escalating assault on the university for being the home of left-wing extremism no matter how egregious the right wing was in its disregard either for debate or for dialogue.

If the political whirlwind associated with the 2016 election dominated the headlines for my final year as chancellor and the budget struggles around the deficit dominated my quotidian administrative life, it was in other respects a very good year for Berkeley. In September, we celebrated the launch of the Chan Zuckerberg Initiative "Biohub," a $600m investment in scientific research conducted by scientists at Berkeley, Stanford, and UCSF. I had been working throughout my time as chancellor to develop much closer ties with UCSF – despite being part of the same UC system the two campuses had not worked well together on a number of projects. When Sam Hawgood started as chancellor of UCSF not long after I did, we pledged to figure out a different approach. The philanthropist Sandy Weill was working at the time on a major gift for an integrated neuroscience building at UCSF, while beginning to talk with me about a major gift for Berkeley, provided we could collaborate with UCSF. For the CZI project, the Berkeley biologist Robert Tjian, who had been President of the Howard Hughes Medical Institute for some years, helped formulate the plan for a joint project, and I talked extensively both with Sam and with John Hennessy, the President of Stanford. The Biohub was established with the ambitious agenda of eradicating disease in the twenty-first century (Silicon Valley is not known for its rhetorical humility), but its most immediate effect was to demonstrate that large biomedical research projects were best done by multiple scientific institutions working together. I was also especially gratified that Berkeley and Stanford – traditional football, and sometimes academic, rivals – were able to find such a great way to collaborate as well.

We made significant progress on our data science initiative that year as well. We had launched a pilot course the year before that had been a spectacular success, recruiting students from across the university to learn the basics of data analytics while working with data sets from their own specific areas of study. It was the hot new course on campus and students were requesting that we use it as the basis for developing a major program. Now we were considering the recommendations of the committee I had convened to propose where to house the data science initiative. I had thought early on that we should convert the School of Information (formerly the Library School, now colloquially called the I-School) into a new entity that would manage the undergraduate program while expanding the reach of its graduate offerings (building on its already strong programs in data science). The I-School only had eleven faculty members, and it seemed obvious that it should grow. The dean, urban theorist Anna Lee Saxenian, was originally in favor of the idea, though she got pushback from her faculty who believed – correctly – they would lose control of what was at that point a boutique school. I knew from prior experience that if we wanted to succeed we needed to move more slowly than I would like, but we appointed a founding Dean of the Data Science Division with the hope that this new dean would be able to broker a solution with the School. The final work on this was done after I stepped down, but I was relieved that in a matter of two years a permanent dean was hired to run the Data Science Division out of the I-School as I had originally hoped, and as this book goes to press a new College of Data Science was approved by the Regents, the happy culmination of what I had set in motion years before.

We also revamped procedures for dealing with sexual harassment on campus during that last year. I had appointed a senior administrator to advise us on sexual harassment, and she oversaw a committee that made a set of recommendations that significantly changed how we dealt with grievances, especially those involving faculty. First and foremost, we agreed that the chancellor had to be informed at the outset of any investigation, no longer insulating me or my office from the process. But we also put in place a checklist of procedures that brought greater coordination between the work of the Title IX office and the work of the provost's office around faculty affairs. The academic senate was part of all these deliberations and approved the same recommendations we did, to ensure that faculty rights were maintained while we also streamlined the process not just for investigations but also for disciplinary action. We coordinated the work we did with that of the office of the president, but importantly this work now had the full buy-in of campus constituencies, all of whom had been dissatisfied with the way we had overseen this process in previous years. Given the amount of turmoil around sexual harassment during my time as chancellor – from the early cases I followed around student sexual assault to the much-publicized cases concerning Marcy and Chaudhuri – I felt it was urgent that we complete this process before I left office.

Finally, we made even more progress on addressing our budget problems than I first thought we could. We had made the decision to explain the depth of our difficulties, even as I abandoned the strategic planning process. But, as my successor knew better than me, Berkeley had plenty of experience of across-the-board cuts and accepted their necessity, albeit fretfully, and with uneven impact given the relative wealth of resources on certain corners of the campus. By the time I stepped down, we had substantially reduced the deficit, with concrete plans to erase it in full in the next year or two. Much of the longer-term progress depended on realizing gains in revenues that would come from new and expanded Master's programs and other revenue-generating activities that units embraced once they realized they would either have to do them or cut their own budgets proportionately. Still, while we moved forward to address the immediate financial crisis we were facing, I had come to believe that by not acting in more focused ways we were abdicating the task of facing up to some long-term structural issues. I worried that the campus would continue to be vulnerable to future crises that were bound to come, as they inevitably have.

On July 1st, the day I stepped down as chancellor, Janaki and I boarded a flight to Wyoming to visit friends. We spent several days hiking in the Grand Tetons soaking in the beauty of the mountains and chatting about the future of the university. Although we met a few recent Cal alums on the trails (some of whom recognized me and asked for selfies), I was happily anonymous. Still, it was a bittersweet week. For the first time in years, I felt a huge weight lift off my shoulders. And yet, my experience had been massively destabilizing. I was unsure what to do next. I had spent the last fifteen years of my life working on behalf of two universities whose causes I had made my own to the virtual exclusion not just of much else, but of continuing the scholarly work of my previous life. I'd been in college or universities – as undergraduate, graduate student, instructor, assistant, associate, full professor, dean, EVP, and chancellor – since I was 17.

During my senior administrative stints, I did what I could to serve what I thought were the best interests of the university, but I began to review every decision I'd made, as well as what had really motivated me to take on these roles. What did I miss? And what was I happy to leave behind? Did I have regrets, large or small? What might I have done differently? I had doubtless been too ambitious in the agendas I tried to introduce in my early years at Berkeley, and then perhaps too quick to assume that an open conversation about strategic priorities at a time of budget crisis would be genuinely productive. Whatever else, I came to believe that Berkeley needed to acknowledge the changed conditions under which it operated as a leading public university, and to commence a process of rigorous evaluation of its academic programs.

Now I realized that the university was not ready for a strategic exercise in which targeted cuts might be on the table. Whatever else, it would have to figure out a path forward on its own, with its administrative leadership drawn primarily from within its own ranks for the foreseeable future. Even so, I know that it is too easy for faculty to blame administrators for their ills, and that no one would have an easy time of it, especially if they too wished to advocate for major changes.

Although, having come from outside the university as chancellor, I was not sure what it might mean to go "back to the faculty," as the saying goes, I also knew that I had never left behind my fundamental identity and interests as an academic, and for that matter as a historian and anthropologist who had come to treat all social experience as usable. I already had decided that I would write up my "fieldwork"[9] in university administration, and that I would use my experiences to reflect more broadly on how even great universities arrived at the present impasse. Increasingly, however, I also thought I might make some recommendations about where they might – or should – go in the future. It is to these larger undertakings I now turn.

---

[9] I use the term fieldwork here in a guarded way, as I was certainly no outsider to the university, and I was a participant who played a major role in what I was observing. I had been part of a generation of anthropological thinkers, however, who had called both for reflexivity in the work of the anthropologist and for an ethnographic sensibility that might apply equally to the institutions within which one worked as to the societies and cultures where one went to study. See, for example, James Clifford and George Marcus, *Writing Culture: The Poetics and Politics of Ethnography* (Berkeley: University of California Press, 1986); Clifford Geertz, *Works and Lives: The Anthropologist as Author* (Stanford University Press, 1988).

PART II
A HISTORY OF THE FUTURE

≈

4
Genealogies of the University

~

"By far the best thing about America is its universities. Not Harvard, Yale *e tutti quanti*: though marvelous, they are not distinctively American – their roots reach across the ocean to Oxford, Heidelberg, and beyond. Nowhere else in the world, however, can boast such public universities. You drive for miles across a godforsaken midwestern scrubscape, pockmarked by billboards, Motel 6s, and a military parade of food chains, when – like some pedagogical mirage dreamed up by nineteenth-century English gentlemen – there appears... a library! And not just any library: at Bloomington, the University of Indiana boasts a 7.8 million volume collection in more than nine hundred languages, housed in a magnificent double-towered mausoleum of Indiana limestone."[1]

Tony Judt

Histories

Most origin stories of the university begin in Bologna and Paris, where small groups of students and faculty settled respectively (c. 1100 and c. 1200) in learning communities that, however circuitously, grew over time into what came to be called universities. Oxford and then Cambridge figure prominently in these stories as well, beginning as local enclaves as early as c. 1165 in Oxford when a group of English-speaking scholars were expelled from Paris, before another beleaguered group moved on to Cambridge. These early communities were laicized

---

[1] Tony Judt, "America: My New-Found-Land," *The New York Review of Books*, May 27, 2010.

versions of monastic institutions, focusing at the beginning on fields such as philosophy, theology, medicine, and law. Oxford colleges, initially self-governing residences for scholars, date back at least to the thirteenth century, while Cambridge only really emerged as a major center of scholarship in both the humanities and natural sciences from the fifteenth century on.[2]

During the fourteenth century the Italian humanists, led by Petrarch, emphasized the cultivation of broad forms of humanist learning rather than any profession or trade, commencing what has been a long-standing balancing act between the competing pull of what today we call general and professional training. Thanks to the contribution of the humanists, and the advocacy on behalf of civic learning by figures such as Machiavelli and Erasmus, universities in Europe became associated during the sixteenth century with ideas of civic virtue, another lasting legacy of those fledgling academic institutions.

Harvard was first established in 1636 as an effort by mostly Cambridge-educated members of the Massachusetts Bay Colony to create an English college on the banks of the River Charles, in what then was called Newtowne, just north of Boston (the university town was renamed Cambridge two years later). Soon, other colleges were founded across the east coast, an array of denominationally affiliated Protestant colleges to serve the new colony, some of which later became grouped together in a sports conference called the Ivy League.

---

[2] For a useful synoptic account of the university's early origins and its connections to medieval humanism, see Ronald Musto, *The Attack on Higher Education: The Dissolution of the American University* (Cambridge University Press, 2021), pp. 21–32.

American puritanism had a significant influence on these early colleges, which taught Latin grammar and philology as well as scripture and rhetoric. English humanism was translated into a specifically colonial idiom in the effort to educate "Christian gentlemen" who were to be leaders of the new world. In those early days, the colleges stayed small, and their connections to the church kept the study of scripture and Christian values at the forefront of the educational mission. They were governed by strong boards of trustees who in turn hired presidents to make virtually all decisions, from the hiring of faculty to the admission of students, the setting of rules for student behavior, and the fundamental features of the curriculum. After some famous legal disputes over college ownership at Dartmouth in the early nineteenth century, the Supreme Court ruled to secure college charters, and private universities became corporations that could operate outside of state control.

The first genuinely secular university in the US was built by Thomas Jefferson, in 1819, as the University of Virginia. He established the university after his unsuccessful efforts at reform at the College of William and Mary, his alma mater. The new university was a temple to civic learning, inscribed as much in the neoclassical architecture of the campus as in its lofty educational purpose. As it became a kind of early model for a public university, it was established from the start, befitting its secular philosophy, as a comprehensive university. It also borrowed from the Oxbridge model by building student and faculty residences into the heart of what Jefferson called the "academical village." For many years, American colleges and universities were a motley assortment of church-sponsored institutions, often stark at best, while the older and better endowed institutions – including Harvard, Yale, and Columbia (first named King's College) – grew slowly not just to take on more students, but to expand the liberal arts curricula to include some directed instruction in professions such as medicine and law, though not engineering. Two major factors became the driving forces for change during the second half of the century. The first was the massive expansion of federal and state funding for higher education in the Morrill Act. The second was the influence of the German research university of Humboldtian fame.[3]

On July 2, 1862, Abraham Lincoln signed the Land Grant Act, giving individual states 30,000 acres of federal land for each of their Congressional representatives and senators, to be used to establish an endowment supporting new colleges in each state with a mandate "to promote the liberal and practical education of the industrial classes on the several pursuits and professions in life."[4] Authored by Vermont Congressman Justin Smith Morrill, the Land Grant Act established or expanded sixty-nine colleges across the country. In envisioning a comprehensive system of colleges for the industrial class – the "thousand willing and expecting to work their way through the world by the sweat of their brow" – Morrill sought to elevate the practical vocations of agriculture and mechanics

---

[3] For more, see Roger Geiger, *A History of American Higher Education: Learning and Culture from the Founding to World War II* (Princeton University Press, 2015).

[4] Act of July 2, 1862 (Morrill Act), Public Law 37–108, which established land-grant colleges, enrolled Acts and Resolutions of Congress, 1789–1996, General Records of the United States Government, National Archives.

to the same social standing as the liberal arts and sciences, welding schools of agriculture and mining to more traditional colleges, elevating a broader cross-section of students as well as subjects of study.

Universities in states such as Wisconsin and Minnesota were established before the Morrill Act, but used its funding to expand significantly. The University of California took the land-grant funding it received and grafted it onto a small liberal arts college in Oakland, moving to a new plot of land in Berkeley and starting as a university in 1868. Its founding president, Henry Durant, sought to build a "comprehensive" university, recruiting Daniel Coit Gilman, from Yale's "scientific school," to come west as president. Gilman was clear that the university focus on more than just practical subjects. As he proclaimed in his inaugural address in 1872, California had committed to building a "university":

not a high-school, nor a college, nor an academy of sciences, nor an industrial-school ... Some of the features may, indeed, be included in or developed with the University; but the University means more than any or all of them. The University is the most comprehensive term which can be employed to indicate a foundation for the promotion and diffusion of knowledge – a group of agencies organized to advance the arts and sciences of every sort.[5]

Gilman only lasted three years, frustrated and obstructed as he was by the California legislature and political interest groups that opposed the comprehensive

---

[5] Daniel Coit Gilman, *The Building of the University: An Inaugural Address Delivered at Oakland*, November 7th, 1872 (San Francisco: John H. Carmany, 1872).

idea and what they saw as the elitism of the east. It was not that he resisted programs in agriculture and mining, but rather that he held on to the idea that both the liberal arts and a comprehensive ideal were important, a commitment that mobilized his political opponents, who sought to undermine him at every point. He left to go to Baltimore, where he became the first President of Johns Hopkins University. Beginning with graduate studies and advanced research, Hopkins established a new American model that drew heavily on the German university. Hopkins not only had enormous influence on the subsequent evolution of universities in the US but encouraged other individuals of means to consider establishing and endowing universities of their own.

It was in fact the German university that in many respects shaped the new American university of the late nineteenth century rather than the first colonial colleges that had been modeled far more on Oxford and Cambridge.[6] Many of the founders and leaders of newly formed departments and graduate programs had completed their education in German universities, where they imbibed the Humboldtian idea of research as a critical feature. The gold standard was the University of Berlin, founded in 1810, that advocated for a unity of teaching and research, and in supporting serious research began to set the expectation that faculty would have advanced degrees. Although German universities experienced the same tensions between general and professional training

---

[6] For an excellent recent account of the history of the German research university and its influence on universities in the US, see William C. Kirby, *Empires of Ideas: Creating the Modern University from Germany to America to China* (Cambridge, MA: Harvard University Press, 2022).

as later characterized US institutions, they developed new characteristics that included departmental divisions, more rigorous standards for scholarship, and the salience of the advanced seminar for graduate training. Leopold von Ranke was the architect of a new form of rigorous empiricism for historical studies, inspiring several generations of American historians as they, along with other humanists and social scientists, began to put together the protocols and institutional building blocks of the professional guilds that congealed into the disciplines as we still know them today.

Increasingly, universities – new and old – were seen as critical for the nation's moral and material progress, centers of teaching and learning that powered industry, business, medicine, and government: institutional bulwarks for American prosperity, competitiveness, and well-being. Universities across the land grew in scale and ambition, establishing new research programs with graduate departments and professional schools alongside larger and larger undergraduate student bodies. In 1885, the railroad tycoon Leland Stanford established a university in Palo Alto, California, in honor of his son, who died at the age of fifteen. In 1890, the oil tycoon John D. Rockefeller used his wealth to create a new university in Chicago. While Stanford started small – only becoming a major research university after World War II[7] – Chicago quickly became an academic powerhouse, competing with the state universities in Illinois and neighboring

---

[7] For an important account of Stanford's strategic use of the Cold War to catapult itself to the top ranks of research universities, see Rebecca S. Lowen, *Creating the Cold War University: The Transformation of Stanford* (Berkeley: University of California Press, 1997).

Wisconsin and Michigan as well as with more established universities on the east coast. The University of California – with a constitutionally authorized board of governing Regents established in reaction to Gilman's hasty departure – expanded and became not just the leading flagship university on the west coast but also a growing center of scientific research during the first decades of the twentieth century.

As the basic model for American universities emerged in the late nineteenth and early twentieth centuries, however, the seeds of their vulnerability were planted alongside those that led to their greatness. As Laurence Veysey argued in his classic work, *The Emergence of the American University*, the new American university was inherently incoherent. It was "the product of a working combination of values which the university could uniquely promise to realize. The combination of interests worked, it might further be hazarded, because the various participants were sufficiently unaware of the logic of the total situation in which they found themselves."[8] Veysey wrote that students went to college to satisfy the ambitions of their parents often because they were seduced by the "romantically gregarious tone of undergraduate life." Professors were able to endure social neglect because of their control over an insulated world of overblown self-regard and "stylized… courtesy." Administrators were "shielded by a hypnotic mode of ritualistic idealism." Overall – "each academic group normally refrained from too rude or brutal an unmasking of the rest."[9] As Veysey put it in caustic

---

[8] Laurence R. Veysey, *The Emergence of the American University* (University of Chicago Press, 1965), p. 337.
[9] Ibid.

terms, "the university throve on the patterned isolation of its component parts, and this isolation required that people continually talk past each other, failing to listen to what others were actually saying."[10] He was at pains to explain why faculty too seemed so unaware of their lack of institutional understanding, when he went on to note that "This lack of comprehension, which safeguards one's privacy and one's illusions, doubtless occurs in many groups, but it may be of special importance in explaining the otherwise unfathomable behavior of a society's most intelligent members."[11]

Veysey's sympathies were with the occasional faculty member who was out of step with the profession, as he himself – an early recruit to the experimental Santa Cruz campus of the University of California – clearly was. He provides, however, an uncannily accurate diagnosis of the fundamental instability of an institution in which the interests, expectations, and understandings of its different constituents were at such odds with each other from the beginning. He recognized the extraordinary research that was produced by universities – an accomplishment that he saw as confirming the successful implantation of the German model on American soil. But he was especially critical of university administrators, suggesting that the main task for the administration by the first two decades of the twentieth century became one of maintenance, "or at most continued construction along duplicatory lines."[12] Universities lost their freedom, and certainly their independent drive, during these years, seeking mostly to compete with peer universities by trying to recruit the same

[10] Ibid., p. 338. [11] Ibid. [12] Ibid.

kinds of students, hire the same kinds of faculty, and raise the same levels of funds. He noted that a new breed of more professional administrators were keen to collect star faculty so that they could boast about them even as their own sympathies were with the football crowds – students and alums – that thronged college towns on autumn Saturdays.

Even the universities that had been created anew with genuine promise to change the landscape had to adjust to the mean in order to survive. The one college president who stood out for him was Harvard's Charles Eliot, who at the end of his long presidency responded to a compliment from William James by thanking him

for including in the list of my serviceable qualities 'devotion to ideals.' I have privately supposed myself to have been pursuing certain educational ideals; but so many excellent persons have described the fruits of the past twenty-five years as lands, buildings, collections, money and thousands of students, that I have sometimes feared that to the next generation I should appear as nothing but a successful Philistine.[13]

While university presidents are still routinely judged by their fundraising prowess and the number of new buildings they erected, Veysey appreciated the direct role Eliot played in diversifying the intellectual foundations of the Harvard College curriculum.

Even if, as Veysey suggests, the American university "had assumed its stable twentieth-century form" by 1910,[14] it was slow to expand to accommodate more than just a small percentage of the American population as

---

[13] Ibid., p. 438.   [14] Ibid., p. 338.

students until the Second World War and its aftermath. Nevertheless, the percentage of college-age students going to college increased from 5 to 15 percent between 1910 and 1940. As college became more popular, many students, as Veysey suggested, went more for the social status, the parties, athletic activities, and networking that were critical components in the creation of an American "elite" than for serious academic pursuits. While the most prestigious colleges and universities began to be better endowed by gifts during those same years, the large state and land-grant schools did the major job of preparing substantial cadres of students for professional roles in more fields than the most elite private schools, which conferred pedigree but for the most part resisted investing in practical fields like engineering. Ivy League universities, with the exception of Harvard, Columbia, and Cornell, tended not just to remain more intellectually conservative, but to maintain the preeminence of their undergraduate colleges over graduate programs and professional schools well into the twentieth century.

Daniel Coit Gilman, who had abandoned a public university precisely because of his frustration about what he saw as the necessary compromises around academic breadth and excellence, became convinced later in life that public higher education was too important to be left to individual states, with their parochial political interests and populist sensibilities. At the Columbian Exposition in Chicago in 1893, he advocated for the establishment of a new national university that would set scholarly standards for education and research at the highest levels. When he stepped down as President of Johns Hopkins in 1902 he took on the presidency of the Carnegie Endowment, using his perch there to call for his dream of a central public research university. Although he seemed initially to have prevailed, other university presidents, including Charles Eliot of Harvard, lobbied against the idea, doubtless in part because of the competition it might pose for their own institutions. Carnegie himself had been keen on establishing libraries across the country, with the idea that mass readership might be more consequential in American life than a central educational and research facility. Faced with resistance to Gilman's idea, he soon abandoned the idea of a central university. Gilman, who had used the power and relative autonomy of philanthropic support at Johns Hopkins to counter the political pressures he had endured at Berkeley, lost the last major argument in his long and distinguished career.[15] By 1920, states such as California could finally refute Gilman's worries and boast of the development of universities that were every bit as good as any national university might have been. Still, the public universities that competed favorably with the privates tended to be located well away from the eastern seaboard, where top private universities – especially those in the Ivy League – continued to dominate the world of higher education in prestige and influence.

If college began to be seen as a pathway for the "American dream" during the early decades of the twentieth century, it became *the* pathway once the war ended and the GI Bill was authorized. The Serviceman's Readjustment Act of 1944 funded nearly 2 million veterans for college and university study by 1950, and college enrollment soared

---

[15] Emily Levine, *Allies and Rivals: German-American Exchange and the Rise of the Modern Research University* (University of Chicago Press, 2021), pp. 130–34.

during the 1950s and 1960s. By 1970 college enrollments were at 8 million, more than a fivefold increase since 1940. During those same years, universities benefitted enormously from federal investment in research through Vannevar Bush's proposal for the creation of the National Science Foundation. As Bush wrote in his famous report of 1945, entitled *Science, the Endless Frontier*, science would be critical for the "war against disease," for "continuous additions to knowledge of the laws of nature, and the application of that knowledge to practical purposes," as well as for "new and improved weapons." The university was critical in this effort, both in educating scientists, and as "centers of basic research." Although Bush argued for the practical purposes of science, he also understood that "the creation of new scientific knowledge" was best done in institutions that would be "least under pressure for immediate, tangible results."[16]

Universities that took full advantage of this new federal funding did especially well during the postwar years, including Stanford, Berkeley, Caltech, and MIT, and public as well as private universities with extensive programs in science and engineering. They benefitted from the recognition that the US was now a global power, specifically in the context of the competitive climate created by the cold war, prodded further by the Soviet Union's launch of Sputnik in 1957.

During these same decades – the period of the most sustained growth in American higher education – Clark Kerr, who was Chancellor of Berkeley from 1952 to

[16] Vannevar Bush, *Science, the Endless Frontier: A Report to the President*, July 1945, reprinted by the National Science Foundation, Washington, DC, in 2020.

1958, and then President of the system until January of 1967, was by all accounts a visionary leader. He not only propelled the expansion and raised the academic quality of Berkeley, he improved the entire network of campuses that made up the system of the University of California, while designing innovative new campuses in San Diego, Irvine, and Santa Cruz. Perhaps Kerr's greatest accomplishment as President of the University, however, was the agreement he engineered in 1960 called the Master Plan for Higher Education.[17] The plan formalized an interdependent system of postsecondary education that gave specific roles to each sector, reserving graduate training for the PhD and advanced research for the UC campuses rather than allowing this to spread to California state colleges. It did this in exchange for stipulating a set of agreements about how California students would have access to the university system, either if they applied from the top 12 percent of high school classes or, as transfer students two years later, from California community colleges. Under the banner of a system that captured the stated ideals of a meritocracy, it provided the basis for the support of elite higher education: the foundation on which Berkeley could be the peer of Harvard, or indeed any other great university, private or public, while being far more accessible to the middle class. Perhaps most important, and of relevance well beyond the actual terms of the Master Plan, it legitimated the idea that public higher education needed to occupy multiple levels in the hierarchy of research and education, including the very

[17] For a thorough and learned account of the history and politics around the Master Plan, see John Aubrey Douglass, *The California Idea and American Higher Education* (Stanford University Press, 2000).

top, precisely to fulfill its original purpose of offering the best possible university for the public.

While the Master Plan did not concede any additional authority to the governor or the state legislature around academic policy, it was a specific, and for a time very successful, political bargain, an effort to recruit significant political support for a variety of undertakings that promised both access and academic excellence: using the full California system of higher education to help with the question of access (if of a heavily tiered kind) while also expanding and supporting advanced research. Kerr's strategic alliance with California's governor, Pat Brown, was critical to the acceptance of the plan, both because it encountered a great deal of resistance from legislators in the many districts where California state universities and community colleges were located, and because there was general skepticism about the idea that the top tier of the university system should not only be better funded but also accorded a monopoly for high-level research and graduate training.

On the other side, some Berkeley faculty and administrators had argued that there should be an even greater divide between the top UC research universities and the rest; they proposed that Berkeley take its undergraduates only as transfer students for their final two years, at the point in other words when the top students would switch from general education to studying for their majors, when they would effectively work alongside the talented graduate students who would be at the center of the research university. The compromise reached by Kerr and Brown was to insist that one third of UC's students should be transfers from community colleges, with the idea that this mechanism would ensure access for socially disadvantaged or late-blooming students to the top research university. This compromise worked to defend against the charge of elitism, a charge that has always been close to the surface in public higher education unless, as for some years was the case for example in the City University of New York, public colleges had completely open admissions.

The Master Plan was a compromise that revealed the perpetually unsettled relationship between access and excellence in public higher education. This is an old story. In 1892, the National Education Association constituted the "Committee of Ten," made up mostly of college presidents, to advise about the curricular design of public schools. The Committee came out against the tracking of different students, on the grounds that all students deserved the same academic opportunities, whether or not (and at that point it was mostly not) they would go on to college. But this commitment to equality hardly conveyed the full story, and not only because many of the institutions represented on the Committee took a preponderance of their students from elite private schools. In fact, tracking at every level of public education soon became the norm, both because of a concern that bright students would be held back if they weren't grouped with similarly talented students, and because of the strong pressures to maintain some level of parity between public and private institutions. And yet, there have been political pressures against tracking of any kind for as long as there has been public support for education.

As Kerr put the final touches on the Master Plan, he felt that he had secured a permanent basis on which Berkeley – at the apex of the other campuses in the University of

California system – could thrive as an elite center of public higher education, competing not just with Stanford down the road but Harvard and MIT on the east coast. While the Master Plan provided the basis for Berkeley's continued success, however, it also showed how fragile public support often was. John Aubrey Douglass has shown how the plan was at some level an effort simply to confirm and lock in the status quo that had developed during the 1950s, one that was already being strongly contested by the political process in California. Despite its great success, the plan began to erode almost as soon as it was enacted.

The problems that ensued were the direct consequence of the contradictions embedded in public higher education. It was difficult to maintain flagship universities that could compete with the best private institutions both in research and in the quality of educational offerings. Massive state funding to support graduate training programs and advanced research in fields ranging from microeconomics to particle physics was required, along with the faculty who had to be recruited from much wealthier universities and supported far better than the norm at most public universities. At the same time, flagships had to maintain a credible public commitment to educating a broad swath of the resident population of states and providing local benefits to those who paid taxes for these specialized institutions even as their children frequently could not gain admission into them. And flagships invariably provoked envy and competition from other state universities that, especially in a system like California's that had other top universities, were reluctant to concede full flagship status to any one campus.

For a time, however, public universities continued to be ranked among the best universities in the country, especially with the advantage granted by scale in their research activities. Rankings of universities had begun early in the twentieth century, and by 1925 seven of the top twenty were public institutions, with Wisconsin, Michigan, and California ranked in the top ten. By mid-century, Berkeley moved to the top slot for all publics and ranked alongside Harvard. Michigan, Wisconsin, and Illinois continued to be ranked among the top ten until the late 1980s, when the first real funding crises for public institutions commenced. Until then, however, the great public universities were the real success story of American higher education, representing the institutional nexus in which commitments to high academic quality – in the liberal arts and sciences, professional education, graduate training, and advanced research – could widely be seen as compatible with large-scale access for the middle class to a college degree.

In the 1960s, growing political turmoil around the civil rights movement and the war in Vietnam began to undermine the broad base of public enthusiasm for funding universities. The Free Speech Movement of 1964 had convulsed the Berkeley campus, broadcasting the new power of student activism and pitting students against faculty, faculty against the administration, and the administration against the Regents and state-level politicians. Kerr, who had become Berkeley's first chancellor twelve years earlier in large part because of his successful negotiation of the political crisis around the state-imposed "loyalty oath" of 1949, was less adept in the early stages of the Free Speech Movement. He held on to his conviction that the campus should be a neutral political space, standing back while Chancellor Strong held firm against Mario Savio and other student leaders. When faculty began to side with the students – a process that came to a head in their endorsement of the demand for free speech on campus at a senate meeting on December 8th 1964 – Kerr changed his position and became more sympathetic to the students, ultimately shepherding their demands into new university policies and forcing the Berkeley chancellor out by making him the scapegoat for the crisis. In so doing he survived in the short term, though he also handed Ronald Reagan an issue that became the centerpiece for his fledgling political career.

Berkeley was a convenient target for Reagan's rhetoric, as he repeatedly asked whether "we" should "allow a great university to be brought to its knees by a noisy, dissident minority? Will we meet their neurotic vulgarities with vacillation and weakness?"[18] He not only went after students, but faculty and the administration as well, asking rhetorically whether he should "tell those entrusted with administering the university [that] we expect them to enforce a code based on decency, common sense, and dedication to the high and noble purpose of the university?"

In part because of Reagan's continuous invocations of Berkeley's left politics and licentious cultural and social life as he campaigned for governor – during the very years it had established itself as Harvard's equal – Berkeley became synonymous with student unrest and

---

[18] Seth Rosenfeld, *Subversives: The FBI's War on Student Radicals, and Reagan's Rise to Power* (New York: Farrar, Straus and Giroux, 2012), p. 302.

excess, a convenient foil for the early assault on public institutions. As student protest geared up around the war in Vietnam in subsequent years, the university became a hive of unrest again. This time, however, it was not the only campus to see disruption. By the spring of 1968, it was being eclipsed by other universities, most conspicuously Columbia and Cornell.

Columbia had also prospered in the years after the war, though it had already been a major center of intellectual and academic life earlier in the century. While it could not court the level of research support that went along with massive investments in big science and engineering, it built up its basic science departments, and took full advantage of New York's global centrality. Columbia attracted many of the most creative and influential academics during years when Harvard was seen as too provincial, and Yale as well as Princeton devoted more to undergraduate teaching than graduate-level training and research.[19] But its proximity to Harlem had led it to retreat further within its gated neoclassical campus, venturing out only on rare occasions, as it did when it announced its plan to build a community gym in Morningside Park in 1968. This plan was the spark for both student and neighborhood unrest, which began in earnest in April of that fateful year – a few weeks after the assassination of Martin Luther King, Jr. – when a group of African American students occupied Hamilton Hall, the central classroom and administration building for Columbia College.

---

[19] For a valuable institutional history of Columbia, see Robert McCaughey, *Stand, Columbia: A History of Columbia University* (New York: Columbia University Press, 2003).

White students (many of them members of Students for a Democratic Society) had demonstrated along with black students but were asked to allow the occupation to proceed without them. They continued, however, to organize protests, occupying several other campus buildings, including Low Library and the president's office. The student leaders, led by Mark Rudd, insisted not just on scrapping the plan to build the gym, but also the end of any agreements to conduct classified research for the government, among a longer list of demands. On April 30th, the administration called the NYC police onto campus to end the occupations and break up the protests. In the violent encounters that ensued, over 100 protestors were injured, with close to 700 arrests. Cornell saw similar kinds of protests, memorialized most saliently in a widely circulated photograph of a black student standing at a window with a rifle and ammunition belts. At both Columbia and Cornell, there was a sense of panic and loss of control, with both of their presidents stepping down (despite having taken different positions on student conduct), a sense that the students had taken over, and growing tensions between different political factions on and off campus. For years, Columbia suffered in the aftermath, as it lost the support of many alumni on both sides of the conflict and became a less attractive destination for college students and star academics alike.

Many other campuses saw significant protests during the spring of 1968, including Berkeley. But the most violent confrontation in Berkeley's history took place the next year, in May of 1969, when students, who had been protesting plans by the administration to build a sports field on a park it owned not far from the main campus, declared it to be a free speech zone.[20] Reagan, and California Attorney General Ed Meese, sent in the National Guard at the invitation of Berkeley's Republican mayor to clear the park. One bystander was shot and killed, another blinded, and multiple injuries were incurred after the police began firing buckshot into the crowd to disperse it. Helicopters overhead sprayed tear gas, and Berkeley became a war zone. Once again, Reagan used the events to gain further political capital for himself, even as the university, whose students and faculty overwhelmingly supported the protest, was further branded as a haven for left-wing agitators.

Berkeley did not, however, suffer as much as Columbia – Berkeley continued to receive ample state funds while Columbia suffered from loss of support from alumni as New York City veered towards bankruptcy – even when student protests waned after Nixon finally began to withdraw troops from Vietnam. Both campuses did become potent political symbols. In a way, they also represented a new reality for universities in the United States. In the short term, the numbers of students enrolling in college stopped increasing, and university systems no longer expanded at the rate they had in the first two decades after the war. Academic jobs in many fields in the humanities and social sciences became suddenly much more difficult to find, as I was soon myself to

---

[20] This plot of land was subsequently named "People's Park," and though it has devolved into a barren place inhabited mostly by homeless residents and itinerant drug addicts, is still at the center of Berkeley's culture of protest, which currently is devoted to ensuring that the land not be used by the university to build housing for students as well as unhoused residents.

discover. Universities were still engines for social mobility and economic advancement, even as they were magnets for politicized college students like me who also had intellectual ambitions, but just as they seemed to reach a saturation point, they had become sources of widening political polarization, with devastating long-term consequences. On the political right, all but a few universities were seen as politically hostile, while right-wing figures – including John M. Olin and Charles Koch – inaugurated a wide range of efforts to infiltrate campuses with more conservative views and voices. As Jane Mayer has demonstrated in her book *Dark Money*,[21] they used a long-term strategy, ranging from the strategic use of university donations on different campuses to the formation of independent think tanks outside the university system. The confrontations at Cornell might be said to have led directly to the writing of the 1987 bestseller, *The Closing of the American Mind*, by Allan Bloom, a classicist who had himself become deeply politicized (on the right) as a faculty member at Cornell in 1968.

Connections

I went to college in the autumn of 1968 during these upheavals. During the spring of my freshman year, I protested against military recruitment on campus, joining a group of fellow students in visiting the president's office without his express invitation. It was a polite affair; President Etherington talked with us about some of the

[21] Jane Mayer, *Dark Money: The Hidden History of the Billionaires behind the Rise of the Radical Right* (New York: Doubleday, 2016).

complexities of the issue from his point of view, and then ordered pizza (there were around twenty-five or so of us who had assembled) as he went off to New York for a meeting he told us he had to attend. He asked us to clear up the office when we left, which we did a few hours later, after getting our photographs taken for the local newspaper. But things became more tense on campus in the spring of 1970, when Wesleyan joined a nationwide strike over the bombings in Cambodia, protesting the escalation of the war as well the National Guard shootings at Kent State. Still, compared to Columbia and Berkeley, Wesleyan exuded peace and calm. We did have some political standoffs in our classes, most notably when one of my small cohort of students in the African and Asian studies program challenged a developmental economist as being a hired gun for corporate interests. For the most part, however, we had civil exchanges with our professors and a quiet perch from which to lament the continuing violence in Southeast Asia.

By the time I went to the University of Chicago for graduate school in 1972, university life on most campuses had calmed down, though scars remained. As I went on to join faculty ranks, academic politics were steadily transposed into more academic registers. At Chicago we accused Cambridge historians of writing about India in ways that appeared to be an apology for colonial rule, while some of my professors claimed the moral high ground for perspectives on India by claiming that they took "the native point of view," arguing against the putative ethnocentrism of the west. As I went to Caltech, and then Michigan, I became more and more interested in the politics of knowledge, assuming that theoretical positions influenced by Marx or Foucault, feminism or critical race theory, had huge political stakes – long before some of these positions had serious impact outside the confines of strictly academic debate. Humanists and social scientists talked about politics incessantly, but in retrospect we didn't seem to be nearly self-critical enough about the limited scope of our academic activism, or for that matter about the limits of the audiences we reached. Meanwhile, until I moved to Michigan in 1987, I didn't even think that much about the university as a political institution, given my overweening preoccupation both with establishing my own scholarly reputation and with securing tenure.

When I did make the journey from Caltech to Michigan, my new university had mostly recovered from its own political struggles in the sixties and early seventies, though there were significant echoes still. It too had been an important center for the politics of Students for a Democratic Society, and the faculty there had famously launched a series of teach-ins to disseminate their critiques of the war and the ills gripping US society at the time. Now, however, it was reeling far more from its first major funding cut in the early 1980s (well, and from losing in football to Ohio State), when the state had been in the grip of a serious recession and the fortunes of the automobile industry began to be reflected in the state's public universities. At the time, I didn't learn much about the general budgetary environment of the university, only feeling slightly disgruntled because I had to take a cut in salary when I moved there from the richer Caltech: it was still a great university – especially in the disciplines that mattered to me – and that is what was most important to faculty at the time. I came to understand later that Michigan quickly began to adopt a set of measures to change its financial circumstances, accepting a growing number of out-of-state students (who would pay higher rates of tuition), launching a serious fundraising operation, and diversifying its sources of revenue. By the early 1990s, it was well on the road to recovery, only losing senior faculty because of the pull of the coasts. When David Hollinger, a colleague and friend in the history department, moved to Berkeley in the early 1990s, he told me that he justified leaving because many top faculty left Michigan for greener pastures after their children grew up and finished school; he predicted that I too would leave in the next five years or so, which turned out to be true. Michigan's great strength, however, was that it recruited terrific junior faculty, quickly replenishing its intellectual capital as soon as the empty nesters departed for warmer climes, bigger cities, or Ivy League marquees.

The 1990s was a prosperous decade for many universities, benefitting as they did from a growing economy and a steady increase in wealth that propelled fundraising operations, especially in private institutions. By then, Michigan too was behaving much like a private institution. Other public universities, however, were beginning to struggle. The University of California had its first major funding crisis in the early 1990s, when it devised a program for early retirement that led some of its most eminent faculty to leave as a means for balancing budgets. Public universities began to drop in the rankings, while private universities saw their endowments grow to the point that they became major forces in financial markets. Since the funding crisis for public higher education began

in the eighties and nineties, Berkeley steadily declined
from the 5–7 range to 20; Michigan went from 7th or
8th to the mid 20s; Wisconsin and Illinois dropped from
around 10th to positions in the 30s or 40s. We know all
the pitfalls in correlating rankings with actual quality, but
this represented a sea change from the situation that had
obtained in the US since the late nineteenth century. The
great recession of 2008–09 further exacerbated the divide
between the publics and the privates. While private universities suffered losses from their endowments and had
to make quick adjustments to their budgets, public universities lost significant levels of state funding. Berkeley
lost more than half its state funding, and even more than
a decade later received far less in real dollars than it did
before the recession.

During my years at Columbia, the university was a beneficiary not only of the financial prosperity of the 1990s
but of the associated good fortunes of New York City.[22]
The university had begun to recover its sterling academic
reputation in the late 1980s, despite continuing concerns
about safety on and near campus. When I first started
visiting Columbia in the early nineties, memories of 1968
had begun to dim, but I was still told by colleagues living in Columbia apartments on Riverside Drive not to go
into the park after dark, that their cars were frequently
vandalized, so much so that they had removed radios, tape
players, and other easily stolen accessories. There had
been conspicuous incidents of violence in Morningside
Heights for decades, though by the early 1990s violent
crime had begun to lessen significantly. By the time we

[22] See McCaughey, *Stand, Columbia*.

moved to Riverside Drive in 1997, however, New York was transformed and Columbia benefitted enormously. The College became the new hot Ivy in part because of its location, taking over the buzz from Brown that had been the "go-to" place a decade before. Columbia changed its logo to include "in the City of New York" in its title, and various new academic initiatives – including the one that brought me to Columbia to chair anthropology – conferred a sense of palpable momentum.

Meanwhile, NYU was also making major strides, recruiting star faculty in fields from law to philosophy from top universities across the US and elsewhere, soon developing an innovative global network of campuses; instead of diminishing Columbia, this had the effect of making New York compete with Boston as the most desirable college town in America. When I became the VP at Columbia, I spent my first years building departments that had either fallen on hard times or had suffered from ongoing political squabbles, but I was able to do this since there was more money to go around and there was a new sense of excitement across the campus and the city. I was able to build new interdisciplinary programs, recruit senior as well as junior faculty, and launch a wide range of global activities. I took immense pleasure in competing with other universities over faculty, students, initiatives, and, yes, rankings.

It was not a time – despite the political registers of academic debates in which I was an active participant – when I was rethinking higher education in broader societal terms. I thought I was pushing "the envelope" as much as I could. When I became a dean, I tried to broaden the scope of departments through initiatives like the

Committee on Global Thought, opening global centers in China and India and elsewhere around the world, or finding ways to bring the undergraduate and graduate programs into greater alignment with each other while pursuing fundraising opportunities to make possible expansion into new areas. I was especially interested in the hiring of more faculty, including faculty who would have an impact on the university well beyond their own specialized fields. I wanted to extend the kinds of institutional work I had done before I was a dean, building interdepartmental programs like the joint Anthropology and History program at Michigan, creating more flexible appointments for faculty as I had done in the anthropology department at Columbia, or featuring and supporting the innovative work done in fields like area studies where interdisciplinary collaboration was remarkably good and unremarkably commonplace.

We were still, however, primarily focused on making departments and schools more competitive. And when we worked to enhance financial aid for Columbia College students we were thinking as much about Harvard, Yale, Stanford, and Princeton as we were about larger questions of social responsibility or mission. We increased the numbers of students in the College on Pell Grants, which meant that they came from low-income families, and we also made real strides in increasing the percentage of African American students in each College class. We also worked hard to raise funds for the School of General Studies, which recruited "non-traditional" students to Columbia. But despite a general commitment to diversity both in hiring faculty and recruiting students, it was really only in the aftermath of the great recession of

2008–09 that I began for the first time to think differently about larger questions of who was benefitting from all this competition.

What, I began to ask myself, are the obligations of universities not just to faculty, students, and alumni, but to the larger society? Was it sufficient just to think about academic quality, or for that matter the need to provide a broader education for the elite even if also seeking to diversify it? I became increasingly enamored by the role of Columbia's School of General Studies, which accepted students after a break in their studies, sometimes because of career choices – including ballet dancing and military service – and other times because of hard luck, whether driven by socio-economic or medical issues or other personal setbacks. I took satisfaction in the fact that General Studies students had been completely mainstreamed into the university (when it was created it had a separate faculty and the students were kept separate from Columbia College students) and was especially pleased when I heard from faculty about how good they found some of these students to be.

I had also begun to think about what it would take to break down some of the boundaries between the university and the world outside. Columbia had always been a university that drew faculty because of its location in New York, a city that had not just a vibrant cultural life but also had boasted of its own distinctive "city-brand" intellectuals over many decades. Columbia had more than the usual share of public-facing intellectuals on its faculty and a higher tolerance than many universities for colleagues who published for a broader reading public. But there were limits. I had regular conversations with two donors who wanted to endow a chair in the philosophy department named after the legendary Columbia philosopher Sidney Morgenbesser. They wanted to do more than honor him, however, as they offered us a chair for a philosopher who was as much a public intellectual as a leading academic. The department agreed in principle, but it turned out to be hard to satisfy both the donors and the department given their very different conceptions of what being a public intellectual entailed. And when I sat in on tenure reviews, I only rarely heard faculty say that being a public intellectual was a positive. Instead, faculty would suggest either that public writings should not be counted, or at the very least not held against faculty when evaluating their scholarship.

As I began a research project about the history of area studies in American universities, grappling with the realization that the very programs that had spawned my own entry into the academy emerged originally out of the intelligence services in the Office of Strategic Services during the Second World War, I also began to re-evaluate my own critical refrain about the mutual entailments of knowledge and power. I did not recant earlier critiques so much as acknowledge them in real time. It seemed necessary to hold that instrumental origins – and ends – neither overdetermined their ultimate meaning and importance nor undermined the academic integrity of a field or the knowledge that emerged as a result.[23] All knowledge was

[23] I found Bruno Latour's reflections on his own interventions in the field of science studies, when faced by the extent to which climate change was being contested by political figures who sought to use the idea that science itself was "unsettled," enormously helpful. See Latour, "Why Has Critique Run Out of Steam?"

embroiled in context, propelled as much by political contingency as by what came to be called "knowledge for its own sake." At the same time, it seemed increasingly useful to be able to tell donors, whether individuals or institutions, that academic work was significant not just because it advanced an academic field, as important as that was, but because it might serve broader social (or for that matter economic or cultural) interests. Would it really compromise academic seriousness to claim that humanistic fields were also critical because they could enhance imagination and creativity, or for that matter entrepreneurial and business savvy as well?

Paradoxically, as I thought more broadly about the social impact of universities and the education they offered, I felt more in touch with how I had thought about the political and social obligations of educational institutions when I first went to college, at a time when politics outside the university's gates dominated my academic experience. As a student I could never accept that the university was not part of the "military-industrial" complex, and like many in my generation I advocated for universities to be more "relevant" – even if we defined relevance somewhat differently at the time – and for that matter less elite. I was also, not least perhaps because of my own religious background, aware that the university was positioned at a slight angle to the world (or at least at an angle that allowed it to be a time of reflection, even contemplation, about matters of the soul). In both contexts, I believed that addressing larger societal questions was part of a mission that demanded that universities have an explicit moral and ethical relationship to the world.

It was Berkeley, however, that moved me to imagine broader kinds of institutional responsibilities that might both be possible and necessary. As I began to speak about Berkeley's distinction, I came to see that the excellence of the university was irrevocably connected not just to its academic success but also its deep set of commitments to the public good and mission. Historically, even as it became one of the world's leading centers of research, the university articulated this mission in a range of its institutes, outreach programs, and research priorities, even as it proved that a public university could be both academically excellent and far more accessible to different kinds of students than smaller private universities. However, excellence and access were expensive, especially when combined. On the one hand, Berkeley's academic rankings of departments and programs continued to be the envy of most other universities. On the other, Berkeley had become increasingly diverse in recent decades despite the loss of state funding – I was aware of this not just through the reported demographics of the student body but because I met so frequently with groups of students who represented different identity groups (from Asian and Pacific Islanders to African American and Latinx students), as well as students who were "Dreamers," formerly incarcerated (often members of a campus organization called Underground Scholars), from foster homes, and who had grown up homeless, among many other groups and backgrounds. And although Berkeley – along with other public universities in California – had been set back by the 1996 proposition that banned the use of affirmative action, we were able to launch an African American initiative to increase applications and financial support for students we were trying to recruit. It was also at Berkeley that I confronted the full force of the issues that began to collide on university campuses across the country in the wake of the financial crisis. Before moving west, I had not realized the continuing hold of the widely shared conviction that public universities should not charge tuition, the extent to which tuition as a category was still seen as fundamentally at odds with the idea of public higher education. I understood the growing concerns about cost, but I had long ago given up hope that states would return to the early postwar years and provide full funding for students. From my vantage point, there was a pressing need to fund students by building up financial aid, while recognizing that those who could pay more should expect that the university would use that money to support students who could not. While I argued that higher education was a public good, I had also come to accept that it was critical for personal growth and advancement whether or not it was free. I was ready to join the fight to press for more state funding, but at the same time I had more trouble with the heightened debate over the residual value of college degrees, the escalating disinterest in or outright rejection of the humanities and the liberal arts, and the growing force of the right-wing critique of universities and the expertise, elitism, and liberal ideas associated with them. I also found myself surprised to see how quickly core commitments to free speech began to give way to the arguments of those for whom any real commitment to free speech was merely seen as an alibi for ignoring the vastly unequal power relations of the speakers.

While the right hammered away at every example of the radical "snowflake" culture of wokeness on campus, I sympathized with impassioned pleas to do more to address the predicament of underrepresented minorities and marginal communities on campus, many of whom were actively recruited and then left on their own as soon as they entered college. But I hesitated when I was urged to create safe spaces and new mechanisms for reparative justice, in response to the rising call to upend old hierarchies and values, and then to change fundamental commitments to free speech and academic freedom.[24] I found both the regular protests that became part of my daily life, and the recurrent skepticism about the administration on the part of faculty, the public, the media, including mainstream journalists, as well as the political leaders across California, vexing at best. Berkeley was not alone in this, as controversies erupted across universities as various as Yale, Middlebury, Evergreen, to mention just a few. Although there were seeds of all these controversies and debates stretching back years, they had not only intensified markedly after the financial crisis and its political aftershocks but begun to take on completely new registers of political meaning. All this was before, if hardly unrelated to, the election of Donald Trump. And everything was more intense at Berkeley.

The situation became steadily more challenging because of our growing financial distress. When I realized

[24] For a superb discussion of how an interest in safe spaces can co-exist with a commitment to freedom of speech and inquiry, see Michael Roth, *Safe Enough Spaces: A Pragmatist's Approach to Inclusion, Free Speech, and Political Correctness on College Campuses*. New Haven, CT: Yale University Press, 2019.

that all the assumptions and assurances that significant new revenue would be found had run aground against the political exigencies of California, I knew that we were headed towards a genuine crisis, and not just in the obvious financial sense. Berkeley was already exhausted by the turmoil that had followed the financial crisis of 2008–09, when the system responded to the shortfall in state support (reducing its funding of Berkeley by more than 50 percent) by almost doubling tuition rates, from $5,790 (in 2007) to $11,160 (in 2011). During those years, there had been regular and serious protests, contests that had linked up with the Bay Area Occupy movement and led to tense and sometimes combative clashes not just on Berkeley's campus but across other UC campuses as well. Oakland police had confronted peaceful protestors on Berkeley's campus. A group associated with BAMN (By Any Means Necessary) had surrounded the chancellor's residence and thrown potted plants and rocks through the second-floor windows when Bob Birgeneau and his wife were asleep. And the new Chancellor of UC Davis was engulfed almost as soon as she arrived in California from the University of Illinois over a controversy having to do with the use of pepper spray by the police against protestors on her campus.

Life as chancellor seemed to follow a schizophrenic pattern. On the one hand, Berkeley's research work was better than ever, in fields ranging from brain imaging, artificial intelligence, and the understanding of RNA (most spectacularly in the discovery by Jennifer Doudna and her colleagues of the capacity of CRISPR CAS-9 to "edit" genes) to scholarship in the humanities and social sciences (among much else). Much of the work was also uniquely attuned to pressing contemporary social, cultural, political, and economic issues. Students repeatedly told me how their time at Berkeley had been transformational, and I saw example after example of how students who had come from difficult backgrounds found themselves unexpectedly in an elite college where they quickly began to excel in their academic achievements. They were poised not just for great careers but to make a tangible impact on the world awaiting them once they left Berkeley. And yet there was a steady drumbeat of crises, many of them the residue of years of neglect or inattention, sometimes by the state, and other times by the university itself, while others were the distillate of growing contradictions and tensions in the life of a great public university during the tumultuous second decade of the twenty-first century.

Because of my experience at Berkeley, I had to ask whether – or at least to what extent – the various ideas that had animated the university since its "modern" institutionalization in the late nineteenth and early twentieth centuries still applied. What should or could be preserved? And what might be either jettisoned or significantly redesigned and reworked, to transform the institution we know as the university into a more workable, effective, responsive, accessible, attractive, and efficient entity? How might the university not just survive but thrive in the years ahead, and that too at a time when it is battling critics from within and without?

Any answers, however speculative, depended then, as they still do now, on what we see as critical to the idea of the university. Does the university have a fundamentally moral purpose, whether to cultivate character, furnish the mind with critical values, or to advance the public good? Does the university exist to advance knowledge across as many fields as possible, with the hope that students will both learn from that continuing research enterprise and, in time, contribute to it? Should this knowledge be defined by disciplinary units that have increasingly insulated themselves as discrete professional communities or by some other set of means or metrics? Or does the university have more limited ends, only to impart skills that are directly relevant for careers, whether in agriculture, mining, or metallurgy as was the case at the time of the origins of the research university, or in the domains of healthcare, business, or technology that are more dominant today? Clearly, we need to train individuals to be prepared not just for life but for careers. But that hardly seems a sufficient goal for a great university.

And yet these questions only generate more, specifically about who the university is for? Should every young person be expected to go, and if so, should the educational opportunities they are offered be similar, and for the same price? Assuming that there should be a multiplicity of institutions, how might one justify the fact that quality will vary enormously, even within educational type? The meritocratic argument that justifies differences of opportunity on the basis of ability, and by implication merit, has been shown not just to be hollow, but egregious for its alignment of success primarily with the attribution of ability. But is the goal of equality served best by restricting both the excellence of great institutions and the fortunes of students whose success is always predicated on an uncertain blend of luck and talent? Is the motto that Berkeley lives by – excellence and access – fatally belied by the fact that there are always limits on how accessible an institution of that quality might be to a broader public? Despite Berkeley's pervasive aversion to using the language of elitism, isn't a commitment to excellence inherently elitist, even if one might work to detach some of the effects of exclusion from the self-justificatory conceits of merit?

In the Ivy League, I had become used to the idea that the goal of diversity – diversifying both the student body and the faculty – was in effect an effort to diversify the elite. That public universities, including the flagship campuses of the most academically successful systems, would aspire to more than this somewhat limited goal was fundamental to the aspirations not just of the founders of public higher education but generations of public university leaders. And yet as more and more young people went to college in the years after the Second World War, public universities developed their own hierarchies, even as they too were increasingly limited by the realities of scale. Berkeley could diversify a greater number of the new elite than the Ivy League, but it also became increasingly selective – and elite. In effect, Berkeley was a testing ground for the ideas and strategies of what was still a "meritocratic" institution, if one with broader scope and larger scale than most.

During these same years Berkeley also became increasingly expensive; even after the tuition freeze, the cost of living in the Bay Area kept rising. This meant to most Californians that it seemed both as costly, and as difficult to get into, as Harvard and Stanford, two significant reasons for the further loss of public understanding and support. Despite increasing the size of its student body at a faster pace than most elite private universities, it simply could not keep up with demand. Add to this its continuing reputation as a politicized and belligerent campus – a reputation that was burnished during the "Occupy" protests and then exacerbated because of its serious financial problems – and its stated commitment to access seemed more and more hollow to many taxpayers.

Berkeley is an iconic symbol – both of public higher education and of elite higher education – but it is hardly unique. For that reason, it has of late become again a visible representation of a much larger crisis, and not solely because the university has become more vulnerable to political attacks. Clearly, the university writ large needs to attend to legitimate concerns that it is out of touch with the current needs and issues confronting us as we move into the middle decades of the twenty-first century; it also needs to rethink how it articulates its fundamental reasons for being. It must do this in relation to a re-evaluation of the core ideas of the university – and then accordingly reimagine what the future university should be and do. But what are these core ideas?

5

Ideas of the University[*]

~

"[There is a] recurrent need to reflect on the nature of the research university, to consider its potential strengths and to acknowledge also the limitations these impose on trying to transform it into a social utopia rather than fortifying and extending its unique purposes of education, scholarly learning, and the preservation and creation of knowledge within the conditions of the greatest possible freedom. And those purposes, I think, are surely utopian enough."[1]

Hanna Holborn Gray, former President, University of Chicago

Soon after I stepped down from being chancellor, I flew to India to attend the inaugural ceremony of a new university being built in rural Andhra Pradesh in southern India. I had received an honorary degree earlier that year at an affiliated university outside Chennai, and while there the founders asked if I would help them build a new

---

[*] For the canonic treatment of the idea of the university, see John Henry Newman, *The Idea of the University* (Notre Dame University Press, 1982)

[1] Hanna Holborn Gray, *Searching for Utopia: Universities and Their Histories* (Berkeley: University of California Press, 2011). The idea of utopia runs through my book as well. It always struck me as significant that observers as different as Edward Said and Clark Kerr used the term utopia to describe the university; though I was also struck by Hanna Holborn Gray's eloquent questioning of the value of the utopian ideal. Resolute historian as she is, Gray dismisses much of the literature and discourse of crisis, finding examples across time of just about every *cri de coeur* or warning about the contemporary state of the university; she also learned from her long and successful administrative career that excessive ambition for the university never turned out well, that indeed it was better to seek only to preserve some basic core elements of university life not just to be practical, but to stay sane. I have come to appreciate her

university in Amravati, an ancient city slated to be the capital of the newly redistricted state of Andhra. They promised me that they had the highest aspirations for this new university – that they wanted to include the liberal arts as well as engineering and science – and I was impressed by the level of funding and commitment that was being set aside to build what was slated to be an ambitious new comprehensive university.

Some years before, I had signed a memorandum of understanding with another new university, this one just outside New Delhi, called Ashoka. It was already off to a great start, attracting attention, recruiting superb faculty and receiving top notch applications from prospective students, many of whom otherwise would have tried to go to college in the US or UK. An old friend, fellow historian Rudrangshu Mukherjee, was the inaugural vice chancellor, and the board was made up of a group of benefactors who had collectively contributed the base endowment to set up the university. Some of these trustees, including Pramath Sinha, had earlier established the Indian School

---

skepticism, and I have also found myself becoming ever more concerned about the viability of the utopian idea of the university to serve the purposes for which I earlier believed it should be used. Utopia no longer, if it ever did, inspires change, but serves instead both to constitute the past as full of golden ages to which we think we should return, and to retard the imagination when it comes to changing – if only in the end to protect – the elements of the university we both hold to be so important. I might only add here that the idea of utopia tends to be used by professors, whether they go on to administrative roles or not, who have tenure at one of the most highly ranked universities. Ideas of utopia don't fit well with the working conditions of most faculty, especially non-tenured and contingent or adjunct faculty, leave alone the lived experience of most students and staff. For more on Hanna Gray, see her memoir, *An Academic Life: A Memoir* (Princeton University Press, 2018).

of Business in Hyderabad, in twenty short years already one of the leading schools of its type in Asia.

It was good to be back in India. The drive to the new campus from the nearest airport in Vijayawada was long and bumpy – we could see bulldozers laying out the foundations for what were to be new national highways that were still far from ready – as we traveled through villages that took me back to my days of fieldwork in the neighboring state of Tamil Nadu. There in the heart of rural India, I was struck by the entrepreneurial energy being invested in education. On a long flat plain not far from what was to be the main highway, I saw the outline of a building made of glass and steel surrounded by construction cranes and piles of dirt. When we first visited the site, the night before the opening event, a large crew was readying the building for the inauguration ceremony, but it was clear that the building was far from ready to house a university, even in a fledgling state. Students were already milling around, and the roadway to the campus was flanked by large posters welcoming the Chief Minister and visiting dignitaries, announcing the opening of the university with great fanfare.

The model for these and other similar ventures came from the United States. One of the prime funders and movers behind Ashoka, Ashish Dhawan, had been an undergraduate at Yale and wanted to create a college experience in India that would be comparable to what he had in New Haven. Decades before, when my father had been invited from Yale to advise Madras Christian College in its efforts to decolonize and secularize its curriculum, there were institutions that provided excellent educations – including Elphinstone College in Bombay, St. Stephens in Delhi, and Presidency College in Calcutta – but they all needed to change to adapt to the needs of a new nation. Some did so better than others.

By now, however, most of the older colleges and universities in India had fallen on hard times, without the funding they needed to compete in an increasingly global academic marketplace. The Indian Institutes of Technology that had been founded for independent India were still incredibly competitive, but they had too often become feeder schools for American graduate programs, where IIT graduates regularly went for advanced study, often on their way to help power the developing tech industry in the US. The older colleges that had been established on the British model had maintained an elite reputation but had begun a downward slide under political as well as financial pressures. Students from India were traveling abroad in ever increasing numbers not just for graduate training but for college, and now it was heartening to see a concerted effort to build top colleges and universities in India as well, often with a desire to include the liberal arts in some form or another.

I was also invited back to China to advise Tsinghua University – where I had established a joint research institute with Berkeley in Shenzhen when I was chancellor – about how to build robust liberal arts programs there. NYU and Duke had set up Chinese campuses, and now even China's best engineering and science university was working to become a fully comprehensive institution of higher education. I was even offered a chaired professorship to move to Tsinghua full time as well to help them build the humanities and social sciences. I spent time in Singapore that next year as well, where I learned more about the vibrant higher educational ecosystem being developed there. More recently, the National University of Singapore had engaged in a joint venture with Yale to create a liberal arts campus with a core curriculum developed specifically to place Asian civilizational studies at the center of undergraduate teaching, while using methods and strategies that were key to Yale's success as well. The Nanyang Technological University had expanded a new division of humanities and social science, and then developed a cutting-edge initiative around the humanities and artificial intelligence. MIT had worked with the Ministry of Education to help create the new Singapore University of Technology and Design. Even if the American university was under attack at home, whether through the defunding of public universities by states or through outright attacks from the political right, it was good to be reminded that in other parts of the world these universities still set the gold standard.

The Amaravati experiment did not go quite as planned. The Andhra Chief Minister, Chandra Babu Naidu, who had committed to the project of building the new capital city and had helped recruit the university there, was defeated in state-wide elections. This meant that the new university was stranded in a rural area that would continue to be hard to reach from neighboring cities; it initially had difficulty recruiting and retaining top faculty, especially in liberal arts fields, as its student body came predominantly from rural Andhra, where there was still only a limited understanding of what it might mean to take courses – even just distribution or foundation classes – in the humanities.

When working with universities in Asia, it was clear that America was the gold standard both because of the scale and uniform quality of its research operations and because of the increasing attractiveness of the US for international students. It was also clear that many of these universities were genuinely interested in seeking to capture at least some of what was implied by the tradition of the liberal arts in the US, although the reasoning behind that was often that they were seen as somehow associated with notions of entrepreneurial creativity and innovation. Over the past twenty years, however, as I struggled to secure adequate support not just for maintaining but continuing to build American universities, I felt a growing disconnect. What had happened in the United States to the imagination and expansiveness that characterized higher education since its heyday, beginning in the early nineteenth century and continuing until the late twentieth century? Were we really taking for granted one of our most significant achievements, and that too at a time when Clark Kerr's predictions about the "knowledge economy" had become even more salient? And why was the liberal arts writ large, and the humanities more specifically, so often on the chopping block in the US, steadily abandoned by students, administrators, and the public alike?

Instead, many of the people who might have followed in the footsteps of Hopkins, Rockefeller, and Stanford – certainly in terms of wealth and philanthropic profile – were talking about disruption instead, doing little to provide the basis for a genuinely alternative model of higher education. Few commentators, apart from humanities professors disenchanted with the turns towards cultural and ethnic studies and the occasional former college or university president, were writing about the need to reinvent the liberal arts in new institutional settings. A compelling argument for the importance of the university has been made by a sitting president, Ronald Daniels, of Johns

Hopkins, who highlights its critical role in promoting and sustaining democratic forms of social and political organization through its fundamental educational mission – all the more important at a time that democracy is under growing threat.[2] Most other recent writings about the university fall into the polarized fault lines of critique by denouncing either the leftist takeover of the college campus or the corporatist failings of the neoliberal university.

Meanwhile, the great experiment of a liberal arts college on the Yale model was disbanded by the National University of Singapore, frustrated by the tensions between the messy exercise of academic freedom and student activism and the limited tolerance of the Singapore regime for political dissent. The growing focus on conveying the moral precepts associated with the "Chinese characteristics" that undergirded many humanities programs in top Chinese universities only hastened a retreat from the further development of a robust liberal arts curriculum. And many of the new experiments in private education in India have foundered in the face of an overweening interest in narrow career preparation in fields such as business administration, computer studies, and engineering, as well as the too frequent efforts by single founders to control university management.

Even as a commitment both to teaching and research was fundamental to the development of research universities in Germany as in the United States, the model of American

---

[2] Ronald J. Daniels, with Grant Shreve and Phillip Spector, *What Universities Owe Democracy* (Baltimore, MD: Johns Hopkins University Press, 2021). For an important earlier argument about the relationship specifically between the humanities and democracy, see Martha Nussbaum, *Not for Profit: Why Democracy Needs the Humanities* (Princeton University Press, 2010).

higher education had been predicated at least in part on the assumption that some version of the liberal arts for "general" education was as critical as the development of programs to teach knowledge and skills for actual careers. Now, in the third decade of the twenty-first century, as both the humanities, and the liberal arts more broadly, seem to founder against changing social, economic, and cultural trajectories, both in the US and abroad, we need again to ask: what is the future of the liberal arts? Do they need reinvention? Are they still fundamental to the university? If, as I argue here, they are critical to the idea of the university, then we might well ask again: what would, or should, the liberal arts really look like in the twenty-first century? Can they still provide a moral function without trafficking in the religious roots of the university's emergence in the US; and can they be genuinely adapted to different global conditions in ways that might exceed their association with mere prestige on the one side or faux ideas of innovation on the other?

The liberal arts have changed significantly over time, but they have for the most part always embodied forms of knowledge that go beyond single fields or areas, and are decidedly not about teaching disciplinary knowledge per se.[3] They are often designed to expose students to histories of and debates over the forms of governance we rely on and the kind of society we inhabit; necessitate encounters with meaning, aesthetics, values, and ethics; include areas of thought and experience that raise questions of cultural difference, human universals, social justice, and the contingency of historical outcomes; and curate explorations of

---

[3] For a deeply intelligent set of reflections on the history of liberal learning in America, see Michael S. Roth, *Beyond the University: Why Liberal Education Matters* (New Haven, CT: Yale University Press, 2014).

what it means to be human, to find meaning in life both for oneself and in relation to the larger world. This implies an ethical stance, but it need not be about inculcating what ethical stance students should take. As I've made clear in this book, I have experienced the liberal arts in different forms: initially, as an undergraduate taking courses taught by professors from different disciplines who exemplified a spirit of engagement and debate, then as a set of distribution courses for students in science and engineering at Caltech. Later on, at Columbia, I saw the value of core classes taught by miscellaneous faculty with the goal of creating cultural literacy through a commonly taught set of texts and ideas. I don't think that one is inherently better than the other, but I do think that a common element to each is when faculty try to teach with intellectual rigor and a critical sensibility about large and vexing issues that extend beyond their main area of research specialization, and when students grapple with big questions that have more to do with the good life than their specific major or their aspirations to acquire skills for the right career.

Viewed this way, the liberal arts are more important than ever. They are, to be sure, the survival in some respects of older and often deeply problematic conventions of educational practice – the historical residue of the moral education used to cultivate and elevate the clergy and the elite, in what was once a combination of early modern Christian theology and classical ideals. Indeed, some of what I wrote just now has echoes of the famous 1828 Yale report,[4] which – recommending as it did the

4 Committee of the Corporation and the Academical Faculty, *Reports on the Course of Instruction in Yale College* (New Haven, CT: Printed by Hezekiah Howe, 1828).

continuation of earlier curricular standards rather than initiating (very slightly) broader programs and new elective courses – held that only a classical education would form proper character, the primary aim of education. That canonic report explicitly argued that the discipline of studying the classics through Greek and Latin would make men into gentlemen, while providing "the necessary disciplines and furniture of the mind." The Yale report held that if Greek or Latin were ever given a secondary place in the curriculum, Yale would "sink into a mere academy" and its degrees be made "valueless." It made no accommodation for the argument that education should also prepare young men (and they were all men) for any particular profession or career.

As influential as that report was, it was only one of many similar interventions in an ongoing and vigorous debate over the past two centuries about what university education should be. For those who think that the culture wars are a recent phenomenon, the historian Lawrence Levine wrote a book called *The Opening of the American Mind*[5] – specifically targeting Allan Bloom's *The Closing of the American Mind*[6] – in which he detailed some of these early wars from the early nineteenth century, showing for example that fields such as science, and even modern history, were derided as of little importance in many American colleges for years. James McCosh, President of Princeton, opined that one historian on the faculty was more than enough, as the history of one epoch after the next did not demand

[5] Lawrence Levine, *The Opening of the American Mind: Canons, Culture, and History* (Boston, MA: Beacon Press, 1996).
[6] For a detailed critique of Bloom's work, see my *Autobiography of an Archive*, pp. 321–37.

"thought"; instead, as he declared in his inaugural speech of 1868, undergraduate education should instill a "classical taste ... fostered by living and breathing in the atmosphere of ancient Greece and Rome."[7]

Harvard's Charles Eliot, who introduced the "elective" system in the late nineteenth century, argued against McCosh and others, asserting that universities "must try to teach any subject for which there is any demand."[8] For many years he was the outlier in the elite private colleges on the east coast. Instead, it was the public universities in states such as Michigan, Wisconsin, Illinois, and California and the German-inspired research universities such as Hopkins, Harvard, Chicago, and Columbia that diversified curricula (mostly at the graduate level first) and introduced serious programs in the social sciences, as well as the sciences, medicine, and engineering, and in some cases business. In the mid twentieth century, when Robert Maynard Hutchins introduced the "great books" to Chicago, his views were strongly contested by many of Chicago's faculty, despite the reputation for support of these programs it later acquired because of Allan Bloom's conspicuous role there. And at Columbia, as I suggested earlier, the core that developed in the years after World War I was subsequently maintained as much by alumni as by a minority of the faculty after any residual college-wide curricular consensus dissolved into predominantly departmental preoccupations during the 1950s.

The interwar years had witnessed not just the development in many US universities of "core" curricula that

---

[7] Quoted in Levine, *Opening of the American Mind*, p. 42.
[8] Quoted ibid., p. 43.

combined some version of "great books" with a mission of providing a moral if secular educational base for undergraduate teaching, but also the rise of the idea of the humanities as a related cluster of disciplines that supported the moral aspirations of an increasingly secular educational landscape. Building on the classical conventions of nineteenth-century moral education, as well as on the subsequent developments of what more broadly became denominated as "philology,"[9] the humanities worked to secure for themselves a solid place in a curriculum that was beginning to branch much more aggressively into the social, natural, and physical sciences. Chad Wellmon and Paul Reitter have recently demonstrated that the rise of the modern humanities took place in the context of two related developments, the first the demise of core Christian (Protestant) values as the base for moral education, and the second a concern about the rise of the research university itself.[10] They reference the significance of the concerns raised by Harvard professor Irving Babbitt, whose book, *Literature and the American College*, published in 1908, argued against Charles Eliot, and for that matter the idea of the research university then being imported from Germany, by noting that "the humanist is concerned with the perfection of the individual," rather than the "elevation of mankind as a whole."[11] In their important book, Wellmon and Reitter demonstrate that between 1930 and 1950, as a set of disciplines were

---

[9] See James Turner, *Philology: The Forgotten Origins of the Modern Humanities* (Princeton University Press, 2014).
[10] Paul Reitter and Chad Wellmon, *Permanent Crisis: The Humanities in a Disenchanted Age* (University of Chicago Press, 2021).
[11] Quoted ibid., p. 226.

grouped under the mantle of the humanities in American universities, Babbitt's insistence on maintaining an individualistic – and elitist – moral mission for collegiate education was inscribed in the justifications of the humanities and the role they played in university curricula. The humanities were fashioned as a secular substitute for Protestant values, a continuation of McCosh's elevation of classics as the basis for the cultivation of moral values.

If the humanities were indeed largely established by the mid twentieth century as the new foundation for a collegiate education, however, they mapped onto a predominantly Eurocentric view of values, with disciplines such as (western) classics and moral philosophy at the core, arrayed alongside (and taught through) a collection of departments of European languages and their literatures and histories. While the Second World War had introduced the importance of understanding the world at large to the mandarins of university life, the idea of western civilization's preeminence was undiminished by the catastrophic events of Europe's dark century, not to mention the first significant tremors of decolonization. The departments that made up the bulk of humanistic disciplines were those that divided the teaching of language and literature by national borders, with separate departments for French, German, and Spanish, with occasional forays to the north around Scandinavian languages, and to Italy in the south, all iconic bastions of European nationalism at the heart of the western humanities. When Asian subjects were brought into the mix, they were consigned to peripheral status, with vast swaths of culture and language grouped together in single programs or departments. Even today, any parallel effort to consolidate

national European languages in a single department leads
to an uproar from faculty in the affected departments who
would decry the end of the humanities as a whole.

The humanities were often defended most vociferously
by those who were concerned not just about secularization, the need to preserve western civilization, and to
control the effects of the research university – but also
by those who shared the pervasive sense that the new
focus on science and technology ignored the importance
of humanist values. For many of the old guard in the
first decades of the twentieth century, science had come
to be seen as authorizing "a misguided, dangerous view
of humanity. It delivers material progress but also sows
moral degradation."[12] As Daniel J. Kevles has shown, a
distinguished group of professors, writers, and poets, who
called themselves "humanists," charged, "frequently with
passion and eloquence, that the dominance of science and
the machine was throwing civilization into a dangerous
imbalance."[13] One such humanist was none other than
Robert Maynard Hutchins, the young and outspoken
President of the University of Chicago, who brought to
Chicago an emphasis on "great books" and "general" education. As he told a university convocation in 1933, "the
keys which were to open the gates of heaven have let us
into a larger but more oppressive prison house. We think
those keys were science and the intelligence of man. They
have failed us."[14] There were of course genuine reasons

[12] Andrew Jewett, *Science Under Fire: Challenges to Scientific Authority in
Modern America* (Cambridge, MA: Harvard University Press, 2020), p. 4.
[13] Daniel J. Kevles, *The Physicists: The History of a Scientific Community in
Modern America* (New York: Knopf, 1971), p. 181.
[14] Ibid., p. 239.

to be concerned about some of the uses of science; it had prospered in large part because of its utility during the First World War, though the development of the atomic bomb was still a decade away. And yet the rejection of the importance of scientific discoveries in fields such as physics during the great era of Einstein's insights into relativity and the subsequent development of quantum mechanics hardly cleared the way for the humanities to achieve great success in a secular and scientific age. While the disciplines of the humanities had suffered from the steady secularization of intellectual life generally and university commitments to shifting and often contradictory moral concerns more specifically, the denunciation of science left little space for those defending the value (and values) of humanistic education outside of the hoary language of civilizational collapse itself.[15]

The critique of science and technology did not abate with the Second World War. As Andrew Jewett writes, "In the 1950s and early 1960s, a remarkably broad array of mainline Protestants, humanities scholars, conservative political commentators, and even establishment liberals joined theological conservatives in arguing that science represented a moral, and even existential, threat to civilization."[16] Increasingly, the term used to attack science was "scientism," which implied a scientific world view rather than, for example, the use of newly discovered

---

[15] As Latour has written, "Is it so surprising, after all, that with such positions ... the humanities have lost the heart of their fellow citizens, that they had to retreat year after year, entrenching themselves always further in the narrow barracks left to them by more and more stingy deans?" ("Why Has Critique Run Out of Steam?" p. 239).

[16] Jewett, *Science Under Fire*, p. 4.

penicillin and other antibiotics to fight infectious disease during the same years. Jewett goes on:

The postwar period, which we now remember as the "golden age" of American science, brought a society-wide reckoning with the place of science in modern culture. Critics of varied political and religious persuasions argued that even the horrors of atomic warfare paled in comparison to science's capacity to unravel the social fabric itself. Science, they contended, replaced the familiar view of human beings as moral actors with a new conception that ignored their capacity for moral choice and reduced them to the status of animals or machines.[17]

These concerns paved the way for, and were then massively exacerbated by, the political explosions of the late 1960s and 1970s, when the military-industrial complex – and in particular its expressions around the Vietnam war – was linked by many student activists and faculty critics to big science, the malign influence of science and engineering in university life, and the extent to which faith in science had led social scientists to embrace ideas of objectivity and neutrality instead of examining their own deep implication in the cold war consensus around American exceptionalism. Many of the contemporary jeremiads about the degradations caused by research universities, e.g., Bloom,[18] Kronman,[19] Lewis,[20] and Deresiewicz,[21] echo these earlier

---

[17] Ibid.   [18] Bloom, *Closing of the American Mind*.
[19] Anthony Kronman, *Education's End: Why Our Colleges and Universities Have Given Up on the Meaning of Life* (New Haven, CT: Yale University Press, 2007).
[20] Harry R. Lewis, *Excellence Without a Soul: How a Great University Forgot Education* (New York: Public Affairs, 2006).
[21] William Deresiewicz, *Excellent Sheep: The Miseducation of the American Elite and the Way to a Meaningful Life* (New York: Free Press, 2014).

objections and concerns, though now from political perspectives far removed either from the years of the depression or the campus wars of the 1960s. They still decry the authority that had been conceded not only to the research enterprise of the university but specifically to science and technology. Kronman – a former Dean of the Yale Law School – characteristically writes, in his *Education's End* (2007), that "the preeminent authority of science is the central fact of our age and the collapse of the authority of the humanities within our colleges and universities is in part a consequence of the authority that science possesses outside them."[22] When he laments that "the modern sciences of nature surpass all other modes of human knowledge,"[23] he counters by asserting that "we need the humanities to meet the deepest spiritual longing of our age."[24] He concludes his book by stating that our colleges and universities must "be the spiritual leaders they once were and that all of us, teachers, students, parents, citizens of the republic, need for them to be again."[25]

Kronman's new faith is in the kind of "secular humanism" that he believes is taught through great books programs, whether in Yale's Directed Studies program, Columbia's and Chicago's core curriculum, or similar curricular requirements at colleges such as Reed, St. Olaf, or St. Johns. Although he seeks to restore what he sees as the rightful place of the humanities, he is deeply critical of what he sees as the recent turn to "political correctness" in humanistic disciplines, a cancer from within rather than an infection from the world of science and

---

[22] Kronman, *Education's End*, p. 208.   [23] Ibid., p. 218.
[24] Ibid., p. 229.   [25] Ibid., p. 259.

technology. But he avers that even this turn took place, and then took hold, in part because of the insidious effects of the research ideal. As he notes, "By accepting the imperatives of the research ideal and arranging their work to meet its demands, humanities teachers have therefore traded a valuable and distinctive authority for one based upon values they can never to hope to realize to anything like the degree their colleagues in the natural and social sciences can." Ideas of diversity and multiculturalism crept into the vacuum created by this crisis of confidence, "because they seemed to offer an antidote to the emptiness produced by the humanities' own endorsement of the research ideal."[26]

And yet it was precisely the continued evolution and vitality of the humanities that led many colleges and universities – in the continuation of a long process that Lawrence Levine has documented – not just to overlap increasingly with the social sciences, but to teach new kinds of liberal arts courses, including in their purview the study of slavery, exploitation, empire, and inequality, as well as considerations around the exclusions based on gender, sexuality, race, ethnicity, culture, and other insurgent identities. As the culture wars heated up in the 1970s and 1980s, when the struggles over civil rights for African Americans and equal rights for women began to be incorporated into college and university curricula in systematic ways, the backlash to these movements used many of the same arguments that had been invoked by the authors of the Yale report 150 years before. Allan Bloom's *Closing of the American Mind* became a *New York Times* bestseller in the late 1980s less

---

[26] Ibid., p. 135.

because of his arguments that classical philosophy was the only worthy discipline for undergraduate education than because of a widespread ideological reaction to the notion that young people's minds were being poisoned by "tenured radicals" teaching them revolution, disruption, and perversity.[27] Rather than the inevitable result of the yawning moral vacuum created by new social movements, however, the culture wars were animated by the recognition that education still has a moral function, which is why it has been a contested terrain since its inception.

The secularization of humanistic thought, an intellectual history that was first driven by the loss of political power and authority of the dominant Protestant elite, and then propelled by the social movements that dominated American cultural and political life in the decades during the second half of the twentieth century, did in fact create a conundrum at the heart of the debate over the place of culture in higher education.[28] In turn, humanistic disciplines were often captured either by narrow topical or methodological concerns, building on the philological turn of the nineteenth century, or by a growing consensus that critique (in the sense of emphasizing the negative and the nefarious – through the systematic unmasking of aesthetic forms and old orthodoxies – rather than the multiple levels on and through which cultural objects command attention) was the only ethical alternative.[29]

---

[27] See Roger Kimball, *Tenured Radicals: How Politics Has Corrupted Our Higher Education* (Chicago: Ivan Dee, 1990).

[28] For an important statement of values that underscores the role of reason, see John Sexton, *Standing for Reason: The University in a Dogmatic Age* (New Haven, CT: Yale University Press, 2019).

[29] Again, see Felski, *Limits of Critique*.

Inevitably, when poststructuralism became associated with these traditions of critique (and often forms of Nietzschean nihilism as well) in the 1970s and 1980s, what at the time were the most theoretically exciting tendencies in the humanities were ill equipped to take center stage in broader curricular debates, either for those who harbored left political views or for those who continued to hold onto the desire to translate religious conviction into a secular idiom.[30] On the one side, there was a growing reaction to the disabling politics of deconstruction; on the other, many believed that the apotheosis of philology into endless word play exposed the moral limits of critical theory. And yet by this time it was far too late to return to the moral certainties of earlier eras, whether the worship of great ideas as only vaguely disguised theological musings on the part of Allan Bloom or Harold Bloom, or for that matter anyone else defending the exclusive pedagogical utility of canonic "great books."

When I first went to Columbia in 1997, as I've written earlier, I was myself extremely critical of the overweening role of "Western" philosophy, literature, history, art, and music in its core curriculum. The effort I had made to provincialize

---

[30] For cogent reviews of the state of literary studies in late twentieth- and early twenty-first-century US academia, see Gregory Jones-Katz, *Deconstruction: An American Institution* (University of Chicago Press, 2021); and John Guillory, *Professing Criticism: Essays on the Organization of Literary Study* (University of Chicago Press, 2022). Jones-Katz documents the robust career of deconstruction in the American university, revealing its intellectual and political allure as well as the inevitable trajectory of its demise; Guillory intimates that the current impasse of literary studies is inseparable from its professional formations (or, inversely as he jokes, its *déformation professionnelle*), an abrupt reminder of the possible roles of the critic outside the formal channels of university life.

Kant's so-called cosmopolitan idea of "universal history" when I incorporated postcolonial and non-western perspectives into my teaching of "Contemporary Civilization" was hardly generalized across other "sections" of the core. Teaching in the core did, however, give me a sense of how to connect my own concerns about Eurocentrism with a more traditionally conceived curriculum in what I came to think were productive exercises. I became persuaded that a core curriculum, whatever its flaws, has the advantage of directing the moral debates over education to a shared curriculum in which faculty across many different disciplines have a common stake. With or without a core curriculum, there should be mechanisms that not only permit but enjoin faculty to debate the goals of "general" as well as "specialized" educational matters. For me, the critical feature here is debate, both within and about the educational process itself.

The debates continue and keep changing our sense of the terrain. During the last decade, in fact, debates over the curriculum have begun to take on a new and even more destabilizing form, extending concerns about representation and inclusion in the curriculum to the escalating effort to demand new kinds of insulated spaces for marginalized groups both in courses and on campuses more generally. Students have begun to complain about texts in courses that trigger "trauma" around sexual violence and identity, slavery and racism, among other atrocities that require some measures of protection – either "framing" troubling texts at a minimum, or "excluding" them altogether. As campuses have wrestled with issues of sexual assault and racial prejudice, new curricular controversies erupted. At Columbia, a group of students in 2015 complained about the inclusion of Ovid's *Metamorphoses* in the first-year core course called "Literature Humanities," by noting that it, "like so many texts in the Western canon, ... contains triggering and offensive material that marginalizes student identities in the classroom." For some student members of the college's "Multicultural Affairs Advisory Board," "these texts, wrought with histories and narratives of exclusion and oppression, can be difficult to read and discuss as a survivor, a person of color, or a student from a low-income background."[31] Increasingly, the language of trauma has begun to inflect the rhetoric of representation.[32] Unfortunately, some of these assertions work to dampen and even suppress debate, even as the widely circulating and sensationalist critiques of "wokeness" work in the same way to stifle disagreement and discursive engagement.[33]

As important as the development of new levels of sensitivity to the power of speech has been – along with the

[31] Kai Johnson, "Our Identities Matter in Core Classrooms," *Columbia Spectator*, April 30, 2015.

[32] For a nuanced discussion of the trajectories as well as limits of identity claims for issues of representation and expression in the art world, see Maggie Nelson, *On Freedom: Four Songs of Care and Constraint* (Minneapolis, MN: Graywolf Press, 2021).

[33] Unfortunately, even mild critiques of "wokeness" often fail to recognize the important historical and cultural reasons why representation – and forms of speech – are real and potent issues, even as some of the examples of the policing of speech can provide ready fodder for polemic, outrage, not to mention chronic alarm. As in every other political movement, however, excess comes with the territory, and it is as important to understand the reasons for concerns about speech as it is to push back against efforts to silence expression, especially when it is accompanied by respect and – of greatest importance for universities – scholarly interest in exploring difficult and even dangerous topics and ideas.

accompanying shift in thinking about the place of power in the discursive ecosystem of the university – the accompanying challenge to the fundamental commitment of the university both to free speech and to academic freedom is unresolved to say the least. Faculty and students both have begun to retreat from discussing matters that are linked to a loosely defined array of potentially traumatic subjects, for fear both of giving offense and, to be sure, getting into trouble. I understand and applaud the desire not to give gratuitous offense, but there have to be ways to study, interrogate, and understand offensive – and even potentially traumatic – ideas, and not just because the lines that demarcate offense will constantly be redrawn. The world is full of offensive things, ideas, and people, but if we avoid considering or debating them, we will give them more power. And we know that any form of censorship can empower those who wish to enforce restrictions on progressive as well as regressive views of the world; any demand for censorship will generate many more. Besides, the city of intellect does make its demands.

It is easy to forget that one hundred years ago, teaching the science of evolution was seen as offensive by many Christians, for whom any deviation from biblical authority for the story of creation was blasphemous.[34] The

---

[34] And, in fact, students continued on occasion to find a historical and "secular" account of Christianity in a classroom setting as troubling at best, and often offensive, as my colleague at the University of Michigan, Tom Tentler, routinely reminded me in the 1980s and 1990s. More recently, controversies have attended claims by some students that showing any image of the Prophet Muhammad in, say, a class on Islamic art history, is blasphemous, but contemporaneous controversies in Florida demonstrate how widespread such concerns can be, not to mention how dangerous state efforts to intervene might be.

historian Jill Lepore recently observed that the overt political effort to restrict the teaching of evolution in 1920s America has returned with a vengeance in the 2020s in the contemporary attempts to restrict the teaching of the constitutive role of race (and racism) in American history.[35] But as Hanna Holborn Gray sagely noted (though her position would seem more controversial today than when she wrote it), "education should not be intended to make people comfortable; it is meant to make them think. Universities should be expected to provide the conditions within which hard thought, and therefore strong disagreement, independent judgment, and the questioning of stubborn assumptions, can flourish in an environment of the greatest freedom." She suggested as well that "they should encourage civility," and yet she insisted that "the tendency to rule making, as in the case of speech codes designed to avoid unpleasantness and distress, elevates the model of the social community at the expense of the intellectual freedom central to a university's life."[36]

These questions migrate quickly from the classroom to the open forum of university life, and back again. As I noted earlier, they arise in especially stark ways around recent debates over controversial speakers on college campuses. When I was chancellor, I tried to call attention to the necessity of acknowledging contradictions when universities seek to uphold values of inclusion on the one side and principles of open inquiry and free speech on the other. As I wrote before the visit of Milo Yiannopoulos to Berkeley's campus:

[35] Jill Lepore, "Why the School Wars still Rage," *The New Yorker*, March 21, 2022.
[36] Gray, *Searching for Utopia*, p. 86.

The concerns around the upcoming visit of a controversial speaker to campus make it necessary for us to reaffirm our collective commitment to two fundamental principles for our campus. The first of these principles is the right to free expression, enshrined in the First Amendment to the U.S. Constitution and reflected in some of the most important moments of Berkeley's history. The second of these principles has to do with our values of tolerance, inclusion, and diversity – values which we believe are essential to making this university, and indeed any university, a site of open inquiry and learning. While both these principles are fundamental to who we are and what we aspire to be as a community, we must at the same time acknowledge that at times these principles can be in tension with or even in opposition to each other. This sometime tension between rights and values is at the heart of the current controversy concerning the planned visit to Berkeley of Milo Yiannopoulos.

Many critics thought I was hypocritical in my pronouncements about power dynamics on campus because I did not heed all of their requests (or demands), while many from the right assumed that I had cancelled Milo, and later Coulter, and that in doing so I was suppressing free speech. What I argued could be negotiated on campus as a productive tension was seen by others as an unbridgeable contradiction. It was, however, not just a sign of the times, but the prelude for my prediction that any call for censorship on the part of the left would only license the right to do far worse.

At Berkeley I neither cancelled these troubling events nor did I suppress free speech, though I tried to call persistent attention to the essential tensions between free speech and prevalent campus values. I also struggled to make clear how important it was to acknowledge that free speech did not exist independently of the relationships of power, status, and different forms of privilege. Indeed, I argued that contradictions were not just inevitable but instructive; in this sense I took a slightly different line than the one in the University of Chicago's Kalven Report from 1967, stipulating that universities should not take political positions in order to maintain academic freedom for its many constituents; I believed this report was both too simple and too constraining.[37] Universities can – indeed they always do – take moral positions. These positions are inevitably political, but they can also encourage an open atmosphere that allows fundamental debate.[38] Regrettably, conservative critics of the university, who had bemoaned for years the putative takeover of academic values and principles by the left, have relentlessly used these free speech controversies on campuses to assert that colleges and universities are propaganda machines and no longer fit to be trusted with the young people of the US. In the case of Berkeley, however, the fact that the antifa – with approval from many students and some faculty – shut the Yiannopoulos event down through their attack on the student center only provided greater ballast for the conservative attack.

[37] Kalven Committee, *Report on the University's Role in Social and Political Action* (University of Chicago Provost's Office, November 1967).

[38] The Kalven Report, which was written in 1967 by a University of Chicago faculty committee, declared that the university should almost always remain neutral on political and social issues "not from a lack of courage nor out of indifference and insensitivity ... [but] out of respect for free inquiry and the obligation to cherish a diversity of viewpoints." Nevertheless, universities are always making statements about values, even when they also wish to respect free inquiry and a diversity of thought. Neutrality is not always an option; accepting contradiction and inconsistency may be the best we can do.

If Berkeley seemed to be in the public crosshairs when I was at the helm there, it was a predicament that quickly spread. Other colleges and universities alike have since witnessed a growing litany of crises around free speech, controversial speakers, demands for safe spaces, and university-wide commitments not just to support under-represented communities but to protect them from verbal harassment and further collective trauma. Reports of these cases spread on social media and cable TV, often losing their local context and nuance, revealing the depth of the tension between traditional ideas about open inquiry and newer concerns about equity and inclusion.

Importantly, however, the blistering attacks on the university – from many political perspectives – have only gained credibility because of a growing disillusion with some of the core features of the university world, not least its commitments to forms of the liberal arts that seem to many to be luxuries at best and political theater at worst, not to mention all the internal critiques mobilized against administrators and funders. All this has fed into a growing loss of faith in the values and institutions that must provide the foundation for the real political work ahead: to make high quality education more generally available to more students, not just to make our society genuinely more inclusive, but to take on the great challenges, local and global, that confront us, which includes providing venues for deep political differences to be debated with respect and serious efforts at mutual understanding. And here the (small-L) liberal role of the university is central, as it has historically served as a model for the kind of civil society and democratic politics that includes robust intellectual exploration and argument. Unfortunately, this too includes assertions and arguments that appear (and may well be) distasteful if not offensive to many students and faculty on our campuses (not to mention others off campus). Polarization on campus as well as off has worked to displace the unique, and even foundational, place of debate and open inquiry in the liberal arts. This is a crisis both of principle and of political necessity. For the attention that is increasingly directed towards universities – especially towards public universities such as Berkeley that already grapple with precipitous declines in state funding – has contributed to a more general assault. And now the assault is about far more than political correctness, for it has turned its weapons on the whole array of commitments universities have identified with for decades: not just cultural and racial diversity, but values connected to ideas of the public good, global collaboration, genuinely critical inquiry, and – once again – science itself. Critics from the right within the university should also beware: for it is in part an attack on elitist institutions that, so goes the claim from both the right and the left, have lost touch with most of the people outside its gates.[39] Can the knowledge that is fundamental to university life be abstracted from a set of propositions about elitism that have lost favor across the political spectrum? Are the liberal arts themselves only valued when they are part of the imprimatur conferred by elite institutions, even as their elitist associations have rendered them increasingly toxic for those left out.

[39] Some politically conservative faculty may be tempted to think that new ideas like the recently announced University of Austin might offer respite from what they see as censorship, but leaving aside the fact that, so far anyway, they are recruiting a far more ideologically homogeneous group of people and supporters than any regular (in their terms "super-woke") university, they are resolutely elite in ways that will inevitably create backlash and resentment of familiar kinds as well.

It was no accident that in the same years that Milo was trolling college campuses on behalf of Breitbart News and other organizations, there was a growing move to use current controversies to regulate free speech on public campuses. In North Carolina, a bill – similar to bills that had earlier been passed in many other states, including Colorado, Tennessee, Utah, and Virginia, and that were introduced in states like Wisconsin and California – promising to ensure the free exercise of speech on public college campuses was passed in 2017 by the state legislature. When first read, this and similar bills seem reasonable, even necessary given some recent controversies. If you read carefully, however, you realize that there is another agenda altogether in some of the provisions, an agenda that has only become more explicit of late. State legislatures, in some instances, were to be given the authority to monitor free speech on campuses, demanding yearly reports, insisting on (and thus defining) administrative neutrality on all political issues, imposing new rules for student discipline (including expulsion) around any perceived disruption of free speech (again, defining what disruption might mean, as opposed to the exercise of free speech rights), and ultimately taking direct responsibility for controlling campus unrest.

The ideas in these bills drew from language developed and promulgated by the Goldwater Institute, a right-wing think tank that had been actively campaigning to introduce more conservative political views on American campuses for years. These state-level bills did much more than introduce ideas, for they were concerted efforts to take direct political control over public colleges and universities. This has only become clearer today, as in Florida for example, when these efforts turned from invoking free speech to insisting on censorship – most recently of anything that might be associated with "critical race theory," but increasingly of anything that might make some people uncomfortable. Governor Ron DeSantis of Florida has targeted everything he has grouped under the label of "wokeness" to commence his own effort to take control of the curriculum, far outdoing the left by actually using his own power to determine what words can (and cannot) be used and what ideas taught. The slide from "free speech" to "censorship" has been as steady as the move from "introducing" conservative views for the sake of "viewpoint diversity" to "suppressing" what are seen as liberal ideas because they cater too much to racial, ethnic, or sexual diversity.

Universities can hardly be sealed off from the politics of the world outside their gates, nor should they be. By the same token, universities are places where disagreements will never be resolved through resort to reason, enlightened debate, or political means alone. This is so not just because of the pervasive character of political differences – and the use of political power to enforce different views – but also for some of the same reasons that have animated the culture wars over the last two centuries. The idea of the university has been as much about holding, and defending, moral positions as it is rooted in some fundamental commitment to open inquiry. Although I disagree with Kronman about the way he frames the spiritual role of the humanities, he is right to assert that the debates that take place in universities have religious dimensions, not least because of the dogma and schisms that accompany most disagreements. This is true today, and it has roots in university life from its origins.

The transformation of the teaching college into the research university during the late nineteenth and early twentieth centuries not only changed the focus of university education but propelled the parallel shift towards a more secular outlook on the world as well. As universities shed their denominational ties, they translated their religious origins and mission into registers that invoked the broadly defined moral dimensions of the educational project. The liberal arts – and more generally the basic relationship of the humanities to the developing rationale for the liberal arts – became a new modality for teaching what once were explicitly religious values. As universities came to see their role as oriented increasingly towards specialized training and research, the place of values receded, while also raising the stakes for what would count as "general" education – the key knowledge that might be seen as necessary for all students. It was this simultaneous pressure that animated a great deal of the intensifying debate over "core curricula" and "foundational" courses. And while "great books" could no longer be justified in the old language of religion, the rhetorical force of the liberal arts resided in part in the religious genealogies of new distribution or required courses.

This transformation had personal echoes for me in the path my father had taken from the farm to the church to the university. He came to believe that he could be a better Christian – that, as he put it, Christianity itself could become more authentic – through the disciplined inquiry that was part of the process of seeking knowledge in universities. That is why he had created the journal *The Christian Scholar* in 1953. He had been influenced by Walter Moberly's important book, *The Crisis in the*

University.[40] Moberly, who had been Vice Chancellor of the University of Manchester between 1926 and 1934, and after that the Chair of the University Grants Commission in the UK, believed that universities had ceased demonstrating the moral and cultural leadership they once had, advocating that Christian academics work together to counter the disenchantment with Christianity that increasingly dominated university life – a disenchantment he felt had contributed to the moral incapacity of the university to resist Nazism in wartime Germany. By the time my father launched his journal, however, he sought instead to assert that Christian belief could be fully realized within the modern university, while also pushing the university to realize its own mission, by helping to break down barriers within the university to free and open exchange. *The Christian Scholar* argued that the academy was enhanced rather than constrained by the simultaneous commitment to ethical values and the belief that genuine knowledge functioned as an instrument of God's ultimate wisdom.

The journal captured a postwar shift in the world view of Protestant intellectuals, who were confronting not just the general process of secularization but also the changing character of the postwar university. There was a newly found sense of a vocation to be in the world, to take matters of faith to the place of teaching and learning, not just for the sake of the faithful, but also because faith – rather than existing in irreconcilable tension with knowledge – had important things to offer to the university. What this meant for my father and others of his generation was that they could leave not just their homes, but their home churches.

---

[40] Walter Moberly, *The Crisis in the University* (London: SCM Press, 1949).

They could adopt the university – and the global university community – as a new kind of mission, but one that was still continuous with the church. The journal named and then gave voice to concerns that came out of theology but were now really about the university itself: about how the mission of Christian intellectuals required that they would take the institution of the university as seriously as they took the institution of the church, how both teaching and scholarship were critical domains of religious investment in the world. My father was saying that for him the university was his new church, both his pulpit and the place for his pastoral practice. For a man who could only have left his Iowa farm to become a minister, the journal publicly affirmed his new vocation; he was fulfilling his pledge to his father after all, while also pursuing his dream of the ideal university life.

My father's generation of Protestant academics acknowledged that they had no choice but to accept the secularizing trends they encountered, though they also believed that a religious perspective would ensure that the university maintained its role as a moral force in society. In the words of historian Andrew Jewett, these "Protestants had a solid institutional core in place by the 1950s: student movements, campus ministries, and other religious organizations on campus; the Hazen Foundation, the Danforth Foundation, and the National Council on Religion in Higher Education; and the Commission on Higher Education of the National Council of Churches (whose Department of Campus Life published *The Christian Scholar*), along with the closely associated Faculty Christian Fellowship."[41] In addition to

---

[41] Jewett, *Science Under Fire*, p. 115; See also George M. Marsden, *The Soul of the American University Revisited: From Protestant to Postsecular* (New York: Oxford University Press, 1996), p. 318.

editing the journal, my father had worked for a time at the National Council of Churches, and he had long and fruitful associations with the Hazen and Danforth foundations. And it was no accident that he had studied with the three major architects of this renaissance: Union Theological Seminary's Paul Tillich and Reinhold Niebuhr, as well as Niebuhr's brother Richard, who taught at Yale.

Some of these Protestant thinkers might have agreed with Kronman about the need for humanistic disciplines to take on the mantle of spiritual leadership, but for the most part they did not wish to relinquish the role of the church to the university, nor confuse the two. Some of them believed that genuinely secular inquiry would lead them back to spiritual insight, and by implication the church. But for others, including the historian George Marsden, this process was too circuitous, fearing as Marsden did that the university had lost its "soul."[42] Although I worry about the use of this language, I understand better now how the attribution of moral qualities to the university has had important uses as new generations of humanists have sought to find an enduring place for themselves and their scholarship as antidotes to the disenchanted world.[43]

[42] See Marsden, ibid.
[43] Frank Rhodes, ever the sensible critic of university life, put his concerns about the current state of the humanities in less apocalyptic tones: "The humanities, which once inspired and anchored all the rest, are rich in learned clamor and dispute, but provide no coherent vision and address few significant questions. Yet the great themes for which they stand – the overarching issues of experience and meaning, of significance and purpose, of freedom and responsibility, of fidelity and truth – have never been more significant or more relevant." Rhodes, *The Creation of the Future: The Role of the American University* (Ithaca, NY: Cornell University Press, 2001), p. 44. Unfortunately, while he may be right in the thrust of his remarks, he also betrays his limited

I have always been clear, however, that while my academic inquiries had spiritual dimensions, neither the university at large, nor the humanities, could or should be seen as the repository of spiritual wisdom per se. Besides, I always found that disciplines in the social sciences and sciences provided just as much access to spiritual concerns as the humanities themselves. Knowledge invariably raises moral, ethical, and, yes, religious questions, whether one is studying texts from Europe or Asia, or studies of inner-city life in 1950s America, or for that matter the laws of physics or the biology of the cell. And I always believed that it was as necessary to bring the humanities into conversation with critical concerns around slavery, empire, and patriarchy as more recently we have begun to frame the human sciences in the larger context of the Anthropocene and the contemporary crises around our continued planetary existence.

While I therefore sympathize with the concerns of many critics that the mission of undergraduate teaching is often distorted by the overall preoccupations of the university and its faculty with research, both as an incentive structure and a primary preoccupation,[44] I reject the idea that the problem is with research itself. Nor is it about the growing disconnection between the humanities and western enlightenment values, or because of the larger role of science in the curriculum. Indeed, we need to continue to historicize and critique "enlightenment thought" – not

understanding – perhaps inevitable as a scientist – of the intellectual stakes of robust humanistic inquiry and debate.

[44] See for example Andrew Delbanco's eloquent, but oddly unworldly book, *College: What It Was, Is, and Should Be* (Princeton University Press, 2012).

to mention the extent to which that thought was itself linked both then and now in fundamental ways to a sense of the superiority of the west at a time of massive imperial expansion and appropriation – and we must accept that science has become fundamental to all our contemporary forms of knowledge. The problem is instead about the way in which educational thinking has become organized so thoroughly in a set of professionalized communities and protocols, disciplines in short that have segmented the university into a proliferation of discrete (and in Clark Kerr's term, "guild-like") departments, units, and schools.[45] Departmental autonomy makes it too easy to lose sight both of the larger intellectual quest that often led faculty to pursue advanced degrees in the first place and of the original meaning of the university, an institution that was meant to create a more holistic community

[45] For a good recent discussion of the professionalization of literary studies, for example, see Guillory, *Professing Criticism*. For a larger view, see Burton Bledstein, *Culture of Professionalism: The Middle Class and the Development of Higher Education in America* (New York: W.W. Norton, 1978). For an acute historical analysis of the professionalization of the social sciences, see Dorothy Ross, *The Origins of American Social Science* (Cambridge University Press, 1999). And for an intriguing assessment of the state of disciplinary life in American universities during the second half of the most recent century, see Thomas Bender, "Politics, Intellect, and the American University, 1945–1995," *Daedalus*, 126/1 (Winter 1997), 1–38. Professionalization was doubtless a critical element in the creation of the modern university, but it has had severe intellectual consequences that seem to bedevil the humanities and humanistic social sciences with special ferocity. Here I side with Guillory in thinking that the wake-up calls associated with the crisis of the university today might have at least some beneficial effects for recalibrating the ends and purposes of intellectual labor without reverting to earlier choices between a nostalgic clinging to past canons and the inevitably involutionary preoccupation with questions of method and theoretical debate.

of scholars, teachers, and students. The problem is not a loss of religious values, but of intellectual ones.[46]

Eric Hayot has recently argued that what he calls "humanist reason" needs not just to find institutional and curricular expression well outside its usual disciplinary locations, but also to pervade forms of knowledge across the university.[47] Indeed, he has challenged humanists (and university administrators) to conceive of undergraduate curricula in terms of general themes and methods – that commingle and challenge the separation of the orthogonal procedures of particularization and universalization. What he means by humanist reason maps onto a much broader sense of humanistic perspective than any single theory about either humanism or reason. He defines "humanist reason" as the study of the "lifeworlds of beings with minds" – by which he intends to capture the range of concerns across multiple disciplines that entail the building of "models of causation, of meaning, and of life, that aim to explain pasts, understand presents, and imagine futures." Hayot is not a traditionalist, as he acknowledges the lessons of recent critical theory, including those influenced by Foucault, that emphasize power over truth, and of poststructuralism, that stress interpretation over facticity. He is, however, a realist, and describes humanist practices – including the adherence of most humanists to truth claims – rather than the theoretical traffic of much recent humanistic rhetoric.

---

[46] As Nietzsche, who is invoked by Guillory in this connection, wrote in his caustic way about the scholar, "For having a specialty one pays by also being the victim of this specialty. *The Gay Science*, trans. Walter Kaufmann (New York: Vintage, 1974), p. 323.

[47] Eric Hayot, *Humanist Reason: A History. An Argument. A Plan* (New York: Columbia University Press, 2021), p. 18.

A commitment to the idea of the university as a city of intellect is not only critical for reframing the place of the disciplines, but also for confronting the contemporary crises on our college campuses around free speech and academic freedom. It is also critical for guiding how we conduct ourselves amid contradictory and troubling beliefs concerning the fundamental elements of intellectual life in the university. Hate speech – however it is defined – can cause real feelings of injury as well as offense, and minority and other groups often have neither the cultural resources and capital to thrive in the presumptively neutral cultural space of unfettered academic debate nor the structural position on campuses to feel genuinely welcomed and sustained without a great deal of supplementary support.

And yet, when Claude Steele and I were shouted down in the student-run Berkeley forum event because of the conviction on the part of many university students that it was more important to protest our speech than to hear us out and argue back, I saw this as part of a broader rejection of the idea of the university. Given the recent slide from weaponizing free speech – in the case of Milo, Richard Spencer, and others – to calls for outright censorship, it is not difficult to appreciate anew the protections that free speech affords for academic life of any kind, even if that speech might include efforts to shut down what some see as hate-filled speech. Protest is an important part of the social repertoire for free expression, but on college campuses it needs to be accompanied by the capacity to appreciate contradiction and cacophony, and most of all perhaps, impassioned – if respectful – disagreement. By the same token, efforts to discipline – or on occasion fire – faculty for expressing views that run afoul of current sensibilities risks misappropriating and ultimately compromising the necessary struggle for voice and recognition on the part of students and other constituencies, easily leading to the suppression of the core values of academic conduct, while also giving further ammunition to the right. These efforts also contradict what universities must uphold, namely their role not just as creators and guardians of knowledge, but of the process by which, as Colin Lucas has noted, "propositions are advanced, theories tested, differing interpretations contested."[48]

This is why university administrators must not abandon their primary obligation to protect academic freedom and freedom of intellectual inquiry. These principles are fundamental. There is still a great deal of disagreement about what academic freedom really means, as also about the limits (or conditions) of free speech in relation to "hate speech" and other clear markers of the university values that direct the expression and creation of a genuinely welcome space in the university for traditionally disempowered communities and voices.[49] As I struggled with these issues from the chancellor's office at Berkeley, I came to appreciate the legal rulings about "time, place, and manner" that allowed universities to control where and under what conditions protest could take place, while being clear that they were not to control what kind of protest, or speech, could be conducted in any given

[48] Colin Lucas, *What Are Universities For?* (Ranikhet, India: Permanent Black, 2017), p. 32.
[49] For a useful compendium of positions on academic freedom, see Akeel Bilgrami and Jonathan R. Cole (eds.), *Who's Afraid of Academic Freedom?* (New York: Columbia University Press, 2015).

venue. I also came to appreciate that academic freedom was designed to protect unconventional views as well as overtly – and not always civil – political speech, though in both instances with provisions about the kinds of intellectual exchanges within classroom teaching that were specifically encouraged and protected. In statements by the American Association of University Professors about classroom teaching, it was clear that professional standards were to dictate what kinds of teaching materials were discussed as well as the need to maintain to the extent possible an open and welcoming classroom environment for different kinds of views. All of these statements left large grey areas; but they also dictated that there were distinctions between and among contexts that made the contradictions and ambiguities of academic freedom and free speech more manageable as fundamental principles of university life.

All of these questions necessitate further debate and rethinking in a new era; it has been over a century since Dewey and Lovejoy commenced their effort to enshrine the ideas that need protection by these core principles. What shape will the city of intellect take in years to come? Perhaps more important than any particular outcome is the survival of a fundamental commitment to intellectual life that demands we learn how to debate and disagree, even – perhaps especially – about fundamentals. The liberal arts need to keep changing, even as they may well occupy very different institutional locations as the university becomes more a set of networks than a single, if complex, "multiversity," to use Clark Kerr's famous term. But they are a necessary proxy for the kinds of educational conversations that must take place if the city of intellect is not to disappear, only to be replaced by far more limited ambitions for what higher education is all about.

Some of the most powerful justifications for the general educational function of the university today reside in the language of civic values, a further specification of the moral purpose of education around a set of principles that are fundamentally tied to American ideas of democracy. Even though it is hardly clear that there is in fact a strong relationship between detailed knowledge of American political history and the practice of democratic values, it is tempting to believe that higher education might have some real value for teaching civic understandings, especially at a time when democracy is under such direct and dire threat. As noted earlier, Ron Daniels[50] has recently made an eloquent plea for the role of universities in teaching skills that are required for active and engaged citizenship. But he also makes the broader argument, which is demonstrably true, that universities provide a critical element for any political society, in that they are (among many other things) the most reliable arbiters of what facts mean, how knowledge is developed and evaluated, and what it means to investigate and interrogate our political institutions and protocols – and leaders. In other words, universities not only contribute to a democratic ethos, they provide an important check on the capacity of more authoritarian regimes to claim they have control over knowledge itself.

If the city of intellect shrinks to the point that it becomes the gentrified enclave of only a few elite institutions – where massive endowments will sustain them

[50] Daniels, with Shreve and Spector, *What Universities Owe Democracy*.

long beyond the possible shelf life of much of higher education, and where their prestige alone will confer significance on anything they might choose to teach – the university will lose what is even more critical: its capacity both to give lives meaning and to provide examples and educational experiences of what the rigorous and always contested pursuit of truth is all about. This is not just critical for the future of our civil society, but for a social compact in which intellectual values are considered important, both for their own sake and because critical knowledge and reflection are core elements of the human experience. Without the city of intellect, our individual lives will not just be poorer. We risk losing the capacity to imagine better ways to frame our most fundamental desires as a society with collective responsibility and moral accountability.

6

The Multiversity

~

"I ... had a vision that both placed the university at the center of
the universe and called for it, once again, to become more of a
community of people and of interacting intellectuals across fields of
knowledge ... the best of Berkeley and the best of Swarthmore ...
although this may be only unguarded utopianism."[1]

Clark Kerr

The Master Plan demonstrated Kerr's extraordinary
skill as a political actor and negotiator. It also, however,
opened him to other charges, and not that he was a utopian. In overseeing the radical expansion of the university, he was also held responsible for his role in creating
what he himself had called the industrial university, or the
"multiversity," that many student activists during his time
and critics of the neoliberal university later felt rendered
individual students mere cogs (as well as consumers) in
a corporate machine. Kerr was vocal about his views
even while he was in university administration, though
he later regretted being so outspoken before his forced
retirement. He had first aired some of his more outspoken views in his Godkin lectures, delivered at Harvard
in 1963, without anticipating that his description of the
"knowledge industry" would be used by students to brand
him as the administrator who turned the university into
a factory.

[1] Kerr, *Uses of the University*, p. 155.

Despite his great accomplishments, he spent a considerable amount of his time after stepping down defending his administrative record. Such, I fear, can be the afterlife of administrators. Kerr had coined the term "multiversity" to capture how the university had ceased being a single community, becoming instead an umbrella term for the vastly different communities of interest and practice that made up the postwar university. In part he meant a university that had a large research enterprise, the kind of university Berkeley and Stanford had become in the years after World War II when they attracted major federal funding both for individual scientists and their labs and for "big science," increasingly conducted not just in universities but in affiliated laboratories such as Lawrence Berkeley National Laboratory just up the hill from Berkeley's main campus, and SLAC, the National Accelerator Laboratory at Stanford. And in part he meant to convey the differences of scale between the Swarthmore of his undergraduate college days and the Berkeley of his days as a professor and an academic administrator. As he wrote:

The multiversity in America is perhaps best seen at work, adapting and growing, as it responded to the massive impact of federal programs beginning with World War II. A vast transformation has taken place without a revolution .... The multiversity has demonstrated how adaptive it can be to new opportunities for creativity ...; how fast it can change while pretending that nothing has happened at all; how fast it can neglect some of its ancient virtues. [2]

In invoking this idea of the multiversity, however, Kerr still meant to imply a city of intellect. The emphasis,

[2] Ibid., p. 34.

however, was now on *city* – and all the complexity and even cacophony that modern cities bring in their wake. But he was deeply worried about what this meant, especially for the undergraduate students who often seemed neglected as a result. As he wrote, "the university is so many things to so many different people that it must, of necessity, be partially at war with itself."[3] Nevertheless, he took a fundamentally optimistic view, believing that the multiversity was not just a necessity but under the right conditions could be creative, adaptive, and productive.

For Kerr, to get these conditions right required active intervention on the part of university administrators. Kerr understood that administrators typically played a largely passive role, accommodating and balancing what often were competing visions and interests. He himself did far more, doubtless a major reason he thought that administrators were more likely than faculty to move the university forward. For even as he saw the university as the successful outgrowth of a distinctive history and set of circumstances – structured to serve different and sometimes competing interests – he also recognized serious shortcomings. He was skillful in his interactions with the Regents, but he was acutely aware of the problems of public governance. He held that faculty were the heart of the university, but he was also critical when he saw many of them become members of guilds connected far more vitally to their professional cohort than the university community. Kerr eulogized the university as the "city of intellect," but he was concerned that faculty – especially at great universities like Berkeley – were

3 Ibid., p. 7.

255

not only too professionalized but also deeply resistant to change when it would be for the good of the overall institution.

Kerr wrote that in all intellectual and social revolutions, "the university, as an institution, was initially more a 'stronghold of reaction' than a revolutionary force."[4] Collectively, the faculty are rarely the agents of change, he noted, except when there are new institutes, departments, or campuses, that provide innovative spaces outside the institutional inertia of the academy. For Kerr, the imperative to change was no different than the need to stay both relevant and excellent. He believed that the challenge for university administrators was "to make the collective faculty a more vital, dynamic, progressive force as it is now only at the department level; … to make the old departments and divisions more compatible with the new divisions of knowledge; to make it possible for an institution to see itself in totality rather than just piecemeal and in the sweep of history rather than just at a moment of time."[5] But this challenge is rarely met, for reasons that have to do both with pressures on administrators and incentives for faculty. In my view this at best is an argument to encourage more faculty who might be committed to change to spend time in administrative roles, not to empower administrators with more independent authority.

Kerr was right of course to predict that the university would grow in importance as the economy itself became more and more centered around "knowledge." As he put it in 1963:

---

[4] Ibid., p. 74.   [5] Ibid., p. 90.

Knowledge has certainly never in history been so central to the conduct of an entire society. What the railroads did for the second half of the last century and the automobile for the first half of this century may be done for the second half of this century by the knowledge industry: that is, to serve as the focal point for national growth. And the university is at the center of the knowledge process.[6]

Although he worked to create a hybrid institutional form that could accommodate the liberal arts education that he had experienced as an undergraduate at Swarthmore while taking on the role of a large modern research university, he effectively predicted the role that institutions like Berkeley would play for the new economy, nowhere better exemplified than in the Bay Area itself. But in part because of his use of the language of economic needs, he was repeatedly accused of subordinating all forms of knowledge to the managerial concerns of late twentieth-century America. He was vulnerable to this critique in some ways precisely because he recognized the importance of providing access to new knowledge for as many young people in postwar America as possible, while expressing his alarm about new forms of knowledge that ended up being deeply critical of the institutions that were part of the postwar consensus.

And yet, as Kerr updated his 1963 Godkin lectures – the basis for the book he published under the name *The Uses of the University* – every decade or so up until its last edition in 2001, he did not always sound like a booster either of the university or of new economic trends. Despite his persistent optimism, he became steadily more concerned

---

[6] Ibid., p. 66.

about the future of the university given the growing disconnection of faculty from the university beyond their departments and the increased reliance on external funding, support, and outside entrepreneurial opportunities. He wrote that higher education would continue to fragment, and he noted the increased level of ethical confusion swirling around the university. Even in his darkest moments, however, Kerr did not anticipate the Berkeley I inherited ten years after his death. He would have been distraught at the steady loss of funding from the state even as the university was being put under greater and greater political supervision and control.

As Chancellor of UC Berkeley sixty years after Kerr was first in that role – confronted with a yawning budget deficit and an unyielding state government – I thought I was channeling Kerr when I suggested – given the new budgetary and political realities – a fundamental reimagining of the university. Although the times were different and I was hardly in Kerr's position either at Berkeley or at the university at large, perhaps I should minimally have learned from him to keep such thoughts to myself. For all his limitations, he was far more outspoken about his own misgivings about the university than most administrators of his time, leave alone one who made such enormous changes to the ecosystem of public higher education.

Change is more important than ever today, not just to restrain costs, and not only because of the changing nature of knowledge itself. But is change possible with current modes of university governance? Some of the problems remain the same as they were decades ago: but there are even greater reasons to be worried today about the hyper bureaucratization of university administrations, the over-professionalization of the professoriate, and the enormous chasm not just between the administration and the faculty but also between the university community and the public at large.

There is a growing library of books and articles decrying the "neoliberal" university, uniformly convinced that the privatization – or corporatization – of the university has been advanced by a new administrative class that has embraced narrow, and self-serving, instrumental ends for universities as profit centers rather than repositories of knowledge. Chad Wellmon, for example, has recently asserted that Clark Kerr's liberal belief in the power of higher education was in part responsible for the shift from state to private funding for universities. Wellmon is not wrong to see Kerr as a proponent of a general faith not just in modernity but in the economic, social, and cultural optimism of the postwar period. For all of his educational ideals, he was completely committed to ideas of American progress and exceptionalism, fully immersed in the goals of postwar global capitalism. However, Wellmon goes further, and argues that "without this faith – or, rather, credulity – the gradual shift from public to largely private financing of U.S. higher education would not have been possible. Taking higher education's liberatory promise as their premise, university leaders compared human capacities to untapped oil reserves and urged aspiring students to "invest" in themselves, to put themselves and their families up as collateral for cash to college."[7] Although Kerr, among many others, believed in the importance of

---

[7] Chad Wellmon, "The Crushing Contradictions of the American University," *Chronicle of Higher Education*, April 22, 2021.

a college education whoever paid for it, he would have much preferred for the state to continue to invest enough in the university to keep tuition nonexistent or as low as possible. Kerr was not just a victim of Reagan's political crusade against Berkeley, he became an active antagonist of the Reagan revolution that had a very different argument for wanting to defund public universities. If Kerr and his successors held fast to their convictions that college education was important for the growing economy of the US in the late twentieth century, they were hardly the intentional architects of the neoliberal university.

Critics of the neoliberal university are right, however, to castigate state governments for defunding public higher education, even if they often mistakenly assume that it would be easy for administrators to make persuasive arguments to restore that funding. They are also right when they complain that contemporary concerns with financial viability have led institutions to compromise on the core values and commitments of university education and research. And I agree with many critics who question the priorities of universities that end up, for example, producing far too many PhDs in fields where they will rarely secure decent academic positions, while balancing budgets by hiring increasing numbers of underemployed PhDs with no hope either of academic advancement or better career prospects. Meanwhile, administrators too often follow old rules that seem increasingly outworn, for example encouraging faculty to secure outside offers to get raises or promotions, rather than working with faculty leaders to reward institutional loyalty, dedicated teaching, intellectual breadth, and other values that too frequently fall through the cracks of the academic marketplace.

Too often, however, these critics only reinforce stand-ard faculty skepticism about the motives of all admin-istrators, who often move into their roles to advance shared academic goals while learning only belatedly about the impossible contradictions at the heart of what has become an extraordinarily complex institution. And their critiques rarely make positive recommendations for reform, instead recommending a return to older struc-tures (of departmental autonomy, disciplinary identity, faculty self-governance within existing academic units) as the principal keys to rescuing the university. Without a clear sense either of the reasons for the current crisis of the university, or of how the university might change to better meet contemporary challenges, these critiques ring increasingly hollow.

To be sure, administrators have become an increas-ingly timid group, in part because advocating for major change is no longer a good career move. The traditional role of university president as "public intellectual" has become much more fraught, with most significant change contested, and public statements written and vetted by public relations departments that keep a close watch on the views of multiple constituencies that are part of the university. While critics of the modern university usually insist that change should be driven by the faculty rather than the administration, the truth is that major change will only happen if both groups work together.

Lower-level administrators are hired to do a great deal of the work that used to be done by faculty (advis-ing students, for example, or handling admissions) as well as the additional burdens that steadily get mandated for universities, including many which faculty not just approve of but advocate for. These "needs" range from compliance for research to looking after the extracurricular, mental health, and the other growing needs of students – from expanding offices of Title IX, diversity, equity and inclusion, to career and personal advising, recreational sports, other student services, as well of course as the quasi-professionalized domain of college athletics. But the so-called bloat of administrative cadres is as tied to the protected role of ladder faculty and the changing mandate of universities as it is to the inexorable logic of bureaucratic expansion. Significant reductions of administrative staff would require a radical reset of the mission of the university.[8]

Senior administrators can on occasion be a progressive force for universities. They can drive new ways to enact interdisciplinarity, the use of technology, and other innovative approaches to diversify income streams to sustain faculty salaries and research. And yet when administrators champion interdisciplinarity they are seen as doing so only to cut costs, rather than encouraging change in academic and intellectual practices in positive ways. Regrettably, many faculty resist these changes at least in part because they see them as corrosive of their own identity, privilege, and security, preferring to stay firmly within disciplinary lanes. As I found out in my academic

---

[8] To be clear, I believe we need to reset the mission of the university, or at least make adjustments that would have implications for the hiring needs of administrators across the university; however, my point here is that this is easier said than done. And while faculty routinely talk about administrative bloat, they have come to rely on certain categories of administrators even as they revile them in general, accepting as they do the need for greater levels of student and faculty support than some years ago would have been considered adequate.

career, it is not easy to break disciplinary rules, whether publishing and teaching outside one's field as a member of the faculty, recruiting "outsiders" to established departments as a departmental chair, or seeking to merge distinct units together as a senior administrator.

Interdisciplinary work can be important for solely intellectual reasons, even if it can also be aligned with greater "efficiency," and therefore cost savings. And yet, financial efficiency has too often become an object of scorn by the same faculty who are most critical of university administrators. Oddly, talk of cost savings often becomes seen as a commitment to unneeded and unwelcome "austerity." This despite the low probability that either states or the federal government will dramatically increase public funding, with most indications that funding will continue to decline and pressures against charging more tuition to increase. In turn, tenured faculty too often concern themselves primarily with their own conditions of work and remuneration, as well as with parochial concerns about increasing the faculty count in their own departments, often in the fields closest to their own. They decry the language of the market unless it is used for raising their own salaries or decreasing their teaching loads when they receive offers from other universities.

This is by no means to excuse administrators or administrations from criticism, for university bureaucracies expand like all other bureaucracies, and it is all too easy for academic administrators to lose touch with the real academic mission of the university. However, many administrators protect the privileges of the tenured faculty, who themselves rarely volunteer to relinquish these privileges whether in the service of change or to equalize the burdens of teaching (and, for that matter, of administration) across all groups of university staff (including the relatively low-paid staff who have assumed most advising and student service roles, as well as the growing cadre of even more lowly paid adjunct and non-tenure track instructors). There is a glaring synergy between the goals of administrators and the career aspirations of many faculty, as both groups buy into the idea of "star faculty" and the primacy of the academic market. My priority as dean was to raise the academic reputation of different departments, which entailed buying into the reward structure of the academic marketplace and recruiting those with scholarly renown by offering generous packages and, on occasion, reduced teaching and service obligations. As old a practice as the research university (Johns Hopkins quickly established its formidable reputation by recruiting star faculty in the 1870s and 1880s), this system is deeply embedded in both administrative and faculty culture.

Administrators also, of course, cater to alumni wishes, concerns, and priorities because they depend on these alumni to support the institution financially. And if they increasingly treat students as "customers" – and please believe me I could never bring myself to use the term – they are acknowledging that at the end of the day most universities are dependent on tuition for meeting their basic revenue needs. It comes as either news or spin to many faculty that a single-digit increase in, say, their salaries, costs the university millions of dollars, or that endowments are not just pools of cash waiting to be spent on their own special projects. There seems to be a willed desire to remain ignorant or distrustful of the basic facts of university budgeting in favor of arguing that administrators are just sitting on piles of cash they reserve for their own purposes.

Even as some on the left take relentless aim at administrators,[9] the right has escalated their attacks on the left politics and political correctness of college campuses – attacks that began in earnest in the turbulent 1960s but that have been spread since then as part of right-wing culture wars, amplified by cable television and more recently by social media. The cultural swirl on college campuses has been intensified both by the larger changes in our society and economy and by the escalating crises around funding for universities. For a wide variety of reasons, the university is perhaps less understood and appreciated today than it has been at any time in our history. And while university admission is more sought after than ever, the combination of the Varsity Blues scandals on the one side and the disparagement of campus culture on the other has led to a sense of crisis both within and outside the university. Meanwhile, students have been reeling from the rising cost of college, and the recent political move for "free college" has captured wide public support for obvious reasons.

This impasse has created perverse incentives for universities, to say the least. Most top public universities make ends meet by using a standard repertoire of measures, for example recruiting ever greater numbers of students from out of state – who pay far higher levels of tuition than in-state students – subverting the original justification for having flagship public institutions

---

[9] See, as one of many examples, Francois Furstenberg, "The Era of Artificial Scarcity," *Chronicle of Higher Education*, April 8, 2021.

in each state while becoming as hard to get into as top private institutions. While many of these universities, including the University of California, do not recognize legacy status for admission decisions – not succumbing to the steady requests of alumni and donors to grant them special status – they have to do a range of other things to control costs while also protecting both the professoriate and the rankings for research excellence and productivity. Indeed, universities – public and private – hire ever more non-tenure track faculty, create new Master's programs for the primary purpose of generating tuition income, give "merit" aid rather than solely "need-based" support, and seek not just to increase their fundraising but the benefits that can come from private sponsorships and commercial opportunities – e.g., selling sweatshirts, naming departments or schools after donors, and seeking to maximize their income from intellectual property rights. You can call this corporatization, or you can call it finding ways to pay the bills, but it reflects the increasingly dismal financial environment in which universities operate. The one thing the "administration" has not traditionally done (though this could of course change) is tell faculty what to teach, what research to conduct, let alone demand that their research yield material benefits to the university. While they usually link allocations of new faculty lines on the basis in part of enrollments, using other incentives to encourage the teaching of courses that attract students, at top universities they also actively collaborate to reduce the teaching loads of faculty in some departments to stay competitive in the discipline, a function of the overweening power of the rankings for university decision-making. Either way, skirmishes over these issues work to defer serious discussion about institutional restructuring.

What is to be done? Is it the case, as was often said in administrative circles, that universities simply need to do a better job of getting their message out to the public? After all, universities change all the time, and programs ranging from affirmative action to need-based financial aid have changed the makeup of most student bodies and the nature of the experience for underrepresented students in positive ways on most college campuses. Universities do much more for students than ever before, especially important given the percentage of first-generation college students on many campuses who need far more support than other students with greater cultural experience and capital. Meanwhile, colleges and universities are often more interdisciplinary than they used to be, and there have been efforts to create new departments and programs to reflect changing times and ideas. Faculty in top research universities are more committed to teaching than in earlier years; it is increasingly rare for teaching not to be an important component of evaluation for promotion and tenure. And scholarship, research, and curricula have been transformed over and again to address current issues and public concerns. Isn't this enough to rekindle general approval?

The answer unfortunately is that all this is not nearly enough. Universities will need to change in far more fundamental ways both to recapture their original educational purpose and to secure support from the public, even if these two trajectories are not always well aligned. Instead, universities give way on the one side to student demands that they be protected from the sharp edges not just of knowledge but of life and on the other to the professional ambitions of faculty who live more in their own professional bubbles than they do in the university at large. Meanwhile, faculty too often teach undergraduates as if they are preparing them for graduate study, while using their own graduate students both to lessen their teaching load and to reproduce their own research profiles – however unlikely it is that graduate students who reproduce these models will get permanent academic positions. Universities seek to cater to the concerns of alumni and the larger public through major investments in intercollegiate athletics, an industry that has increasingly betrayed the rhetoric of "student athletes" in favor of professional entertainment, too often fundamentally at odds with the stated aims of serious education. And with all of this, the cost of higher education, even at the significantly discounted rates of public universities, has simply left the public behind, especially now that high-paying jobs and rewarding careers seem so hard to find.

What might it really mean to reimagine the university? Should we accept, for example, Kevin Carey's abrupt diagnosis (made before the pandemic) that – with some rare exceptions – we embrace the "end of college,"[10] since we now have the technological means to provide high-quality low-cost education for "all"? Is it time to accept the drumbeat of those calling for radical disruption, assuming that because of the reluctance of universities to change they will go the way of the floppy disk,

[10] Kevin Carey, *The End of College: Creating the Future of Learning and the University of Everywhere* (New York: Riverhead, 2015).

to use one of the great disruptor Clayton Christenson's favorite examples.[11]

The language of disruption is as capacious as it is ambiguous, a rhetorical pitch to herald some new idea or product more than a serious call for institutional change. And yet the disconnect between those calling for disruption – a call usually accompanied by predictions of the imminent collapse and total failure of higher education – and those content with at best minor reforms, has created a serious need for fresh thought. The growing ubiquity of rankings and league tables has helped propel a push towards uniformity in institutional form and aspiration, a process that has both retarded institutional experimentation and guided too many institutional strategic planning exercises. Too often, universities are unable to find ways to change this, given the locus of power and governance in discrete parts of the institution that are dead set against change of any kind. And there is no doubt that some of the calls for disruption around specific institutional protocols having to do with accreditation (both who is responsible for accreditation and the criteria for it), and the process more generally for conferring academic credentials, need to be taken much more seriously in the mainstream. It has seemed impossible, however, to mobilize critics from within the university to unite about such matters, given the professional and dispersed character of most university life. As Frank Rhodes, former President of Cornell, wrote more than twenty years ago: "Today's university has no acknowledged center. It is all periphery, a circle

---

[11] See Jill Lepore, "The Disruption Machine: What the Gospel of Innovation Gets Wrong," *The New Yorker*, June 23, 2014.

of disciplinary and professional strongholds, jostling for position, and surrounding a vacant center."[12] His worries seem even more palpable today, and the task of generating support for major institutional change has become even more difficult.

Over the past few years, I've taught a course on the future of higher education to recent college graduates and I've been struck by a pervasive paradox. On the one hand, most of my students have greatly valued their own educational experiences, many of them having worked with professors and mentors who lead their fields in their respective areas of research. On the other, they don't see the rationale for using university resources to support the same superb and research-intensive faculty they admired so much. They believe not just that research drives up the cost of education, but that it interferes with the commitment to teaching on the part of faculty. When I ask these students to design the higher educational institutions of the future (their capstone project for the course), they make arguments in favor of "student-centered" curricula and teaching – but seem to have little understanding of or sympathy for the perspective of faculty for whom the opportunity to continue to do research is in large part what drove them to pursue advanced degrees and enter faculty ranks in the first place. They tend to agree with the proposals of the disruptors, and increasingly see the task of the university as providing real-world skills for its students – using arguments that might be more appropriate for an enhanced form of vocational education than for the "traditional" universities they attended.

[12] Rhodes, *Creation of the Future*, p. 44.

At the same time – since these courses have recently been taught online – they are disappointed with the online delivery of education, both because it limits the character and extent of intellectual exchange and because they miss the residential component of college. But they are deeply troubled that while the cost of computers, mobile devices, and big-screen televisions is consistently going down, the cost of education only goes up at an alarming rate. Significantly, only a handful of this group of students foresee a life in academia for themselves.

Disruptors have been predicting the death of the university for some years, and in the words of Mark Twain, they have so far been premature in doing so. And yet the pandemic has exacerbated many of the issues that have been accumulating for years: who pays for higher education, how much do they pay, and do our regnant assumptions and institutions serve our present and prepare for our future. Universities with large endowments are doing fine, and will continue to have their pick of students, while offering ample financial aid, at least to undergraduates and doctoral students. These institutions provide extraordinary educational opportunities for the admitted, but in the end they accept and serve only a small fraction of our students. For many other colleges and universities, the growing pressures on finances will have severe and, in some cases, devastating effects. There is growing pressure to move to more online teaching, to use the logic of scale to produce greater revenues and reduce expenses, and to cut programs that are undergoing less and less student demand and interest.

Now that everyone in higher education has not only accepted but participated in new technologies of teaching and learning, it is much more difficult to disavow some of these possibilities of change. At the same time, we need to have more imaginative conversations about the future than simply asserting that technology is the answer. And whatever we do to change, we should ask how we might simultaneously maintain the intellectual and research function of universities while also educating many more students – from a wider range of backgrounds, with a wider range of interests, and enacting much more flexible regimes – preparing them better for the world after college without being burdened by mountains of debt.

Perhaps the time has come to consider disentangling the elements that historically, as Veysey demonstrated, became bundled together in the late nineteenth century as the sine qua non of the college experience. Might we finally try to unpack the institutional consensus that long ago congealed as the single university model, and then became the basis for the emergence of the mid-twentieth-century multiversity, an inevitable exemplification of the incoherence Veysey captured so well? The first step here might be to disaggregate the different kinds of goals we ascribe to and functions that are performed by the university. Then we could perhaps begin to design a different set of institutional options that preserve the "city of intellect" while at the same time creating more individualized – or customized – educational pathways for students across a longer swath of their lives than the customary college years?

Minimally, this would entail a proliferation of experiments in different institutional structures. With luck, we could usher in a new future of educational possibility rather than yet another moment of crisis. We might even break the stranglehold of norms and conventions – and accrediting gateways – that have been so undergirded by the power of normative rankings and rigid reputational hierarchies. All this requires an openness to change on the part of faculty and administrators, even as it may entail major shifts in the lives of students. It certainly necessitates thinking differently about the departmental organization of universities, as also the ways in which disciplines determine the value and importance of research and intellectual work more generally.

As I look back on my own educational passages, I know that I was the beneficiary of a system that worked extremely well for me. I liked to study, I thrived while doing research and writing articles as well as books, I enjoyed teaching and the opportunity to convey my love of learning to generations of students, and I found my time doing senior administrative work rewarding and fulfilling. Research work animated my teaching and was always as much a function of intellectual curiosity as of professional certification. I also had the great good fortune of studying and working in some of the top universities in the world. I've spent a not inconsiderable amount of time proselytizing for this model even when working around the globe, and it would have been easy for me to stay complacent. I worry now, however, that if even the top universities are facing the kinds of crises I outline in this book, and if those of us with academically privileged life stories like mine don't participate in reimagining the university, it will be imagined by others with different values and goals. In the worst instances, the disruption debate will be driven by those who either reject the idea of the university entirely or encourage others to do so because of narrow visions of life, knowledge, and the world. Then the city of intellect will doubtless disappear, for good.

Universities should maintain their interest in melding the pursuits of education and research. But they need to evaluate whether they are organized optimally to achieve specific institutional goals rather than the outcomes associated with high rankings by *US News and World Report*.[13] The academic department was formed primarily for graduate education, coeval with the establishment of professional organizations for the disciplines. While in early years departments were critical for developing not just graduate programs but everything from elective courses in new areas to defined "majors" in fields ranging from anthropology and psychology to the basic sciences, over time they became not just the means for the training, evaluation, recruitment, and promotion of faculty, but the basis on which the entire university was organized. The inherent tensions of the research university as it grew in the middle decades of the twentieth century were reflected in the conflict between separate graduate and undergraduate faculties at universities such as Columbia and Chicago, but have played themselves out in various guises in almost every university across the decades. And yet several notable efforts to change the status of the department, even in universities established to focus primarily on undergraduate education, have conspicuously failed.

The textbook case of this failure was Clark Kerr's experimental university in Santa Cruz. Established in 1965 by Kerr and inaugural chancellor Dean McHenry (who

---

[13] Leon Botstein, "Can We Finally Topple the Tyranny of Rankings?" *Chronicle of Higher Education*, November 28, 2022.

was Kerr's roommate as a Stanford graduate student), it was initially designed to be a predominantly undergraduate institution within the elite set of University of California campuses. Residential colleges were at the core; each one had a "provost," and all faculty had half of their appointment vested in one of the colleges, which had general themes of focus and curricular responsibility but were broadly interdisciplinary. The other half of faculty appointments was vested in what were called "boards of study," department like (but department lite) entities that played a supporting role in the hiring and evaluation of faculty and in developing curricular pathways. This bipartite structure made possible innovative and unusual courses that were taught across the curriculum, by faculty who interacted with each other as much in the residential college setting as in departments of disciplinary colleagues. The university built a few high-level graduate programs, mostly in the sciences, though also, in another grand experiment, in a program called the "history of consciousness," that spanned the humanities and social sciences. In its early years, the university attracted top faculty and students from top east coast universities. Within a decade, however, some of the faculty began to revolt against a structure that put them out of synch with other universities, even as the administration set about establishing an engineering program to take advantage of its proximity to the Silicon Valley. Soon, residential colleges lost their appointment powers (although faculty were still affiliated with colleges) and boards of study became reorganized and then relabeled as departments. Fifteen years after it was born, Santa Cruz no longer looked nearly as distinctive as when it was first established.

I followed this history especially closely because my father was a "dean" (he had the title of "vice chancellor for the humanities") at Santa Cruz during its early years. Recruited there by Chancellor McHenry in 1972, he was initially enthralled by its postdisciplinary vision for a new kind of university. But the vision quickly lost traction during the 1970s, in large part because it was difficult to maintain its unique organizational form when the rest of the university system was so uniformly normative. While other colleges and universities have succeeded in building and maintaining interdisciplinary programs and affiliations for faculty and students along with departments (including the two where I was educated, Wesleyan and Chicago), the deliberative effort to create a new kind of university in Santa Cruz – in which the new structures were at the center rather than the periphery of the institution – proved just how difficult such a venture is. In his memoir, Kerr blamed the counterculture of the late sixties and seventies for undermining his dream of "neo-classical" colleges in the redwood forest.[14] My father was clear that it was not about the counterculture; instead, he was aware that the junior faculty – and most of the faculty he recruited were at the level of assistant professors – wanted Santa Cruz to be more like Berkeley, with top-rated departments and prestige associated with disciplinary research. I think my father was right.

Fifty years later it may be that the times are more propitious, especially as all but the most highly ranked and best resourced universities face recurrent budgetary crises,

[14] Clark Kerr, *The Gold and the Blue: A Personal Memoir of the University of California, 1949–1967*, vol. 1 (Berkeley: University of California Press, 2001), pp. 235–301.

while all universities confront a more skeptical public. At long last, it may be possible for universities to offer different kinds of pathways for students – and for faculty – to accommodate the changed conditions, and needs, of our current moment. Perhaps out of crisis can come some real alternatives and advances. In the final chapter, I turn to some proposals for how we might construct a more open future for the university.

7

Reimagining the University

~

"There are two great cliches about the university .... The external
view is that the university is radical; the internal reality is that it is
conservative. The internal illusion is that it is a law unto itself; the
external reality is that it is governed by history."[1]

Clark Kerr

The Arts and Sciences are connected by being in the same
administrative unit in universities, but often this feels like
the trace result of a long-outworn history. They are seen
as representing two parallel universes, or as two cultures
in C.P. Snow's canonic formulation. When Snow delivered the Rede lectures in England in 1959,[2] he gave voice
to what by then was a common assumption of university
life, that the humanities and the sciences occupy not just
different parts of the quads, but two distinct cultures of
inquiry and understanding. He advocated for changing
the educational system accordingly. As he put it, "Closing
the gap between our cultures is a necessity in the most
abstract intellectual sense, as well as in the most practical. When these two senses have grown apart, then no
society is going to be able to think with wisdom. For the
sake of the intellectual life, for the sake of this country's
special danger, for the sake of the western society living
precariously rich among the poor, for the sake of the poor
who needn't be poor if there is intelligence in the world,

---

[1] Kerr, *Uses of the University*, p. 71.
[2] C.P. Snow, *The Two Cultures* (Cambridge University Press, 1998).

it is obligatory for us and the Americans and the whole West to look at our education with fresh eyes."[3] Snow's lecture was short on details and intentionally polemical, but he did suggest, as literary scholar Stefan Collini wrote in a later introduction to the lectures, that "we need to encourage the growth of the intellectual equivalent of bilingualism, a capacity not only to exercise the language of our respective specialisms, but also to attend to, learn from, and eventually contribute to, wider cultural conversations."[4]

The arts and sciences had been part of a single intellectual culture until the early twentieth century. Without in any way reverting to outworn epistemologies of the nineteenth century, it seems necessary – at a time of global warming, technological apotheosis, democratic crises, the decline of the humanities, and a biomedical revolution – to consider bringing the "arts" and "sciences," writ large, much closer together once again. This is important for disciplines across the entirety of the arts and the sciences, specialized areas of inquiry that had been part of a more capacious intellectual culture until the professionalizing of the disciplines. The pursuits that could be called scientific ranged across a multitude of fields and involved a wide array of questions and methods. When Alexander von Humboldt wrote his multivolume natural history entitled *Cosmos* during the middle years of the nineteenth century, he incorporated as much art as he did science, exemplifying a unity of natural and human history that has been belatedly recognized as fundamental to understanding the intertwined histories of the Anthropocene,

---

[3] Ibid., p. 50.   [4] Ibid., p. lvii.

our present age when man and the planet have become part of a single ecology.

It was only when John Dewey tried in the early twentieth century to specify a distinctly scientific method that science seemed fully constituted as a separate pursuit.[5] Thomas Kuhn, who had been trained as a physicist but was recruited by James Conant, President of Harvard, to teach a core course on the history of science to acquaint Harvard undergraduates with a broader appreciation of the importance of science during the early years of the cold war, soon began to recognize the significance of the intellectual frameworks governing scientific practice that he later called "paradigms." Kuhn's monumental 1962 book, *The Structure of Scientific Revolutions*,[6] heralded not only a new understanding of the social history of science but also a far broader appreciation for the integral unity of the arts and sciences. The historian of science Henry Cowles writes that "science has not always been 'a method only,' nor is method necessarily as flat as it seems. It is possible, as it was in the age of methods, to think of science as the flawed, fallible activity of some imperfect, evolving creatures *and* as a worthy, even noble pursuit."[7] While many scientists have tried to exempt their disciplines from the uncertainties and limitations of other forms of human knowledge precisely to elevate the epistemological foundations of science, historians such

---

[5] See Henry M. Cowles, *The Scientific Method: An Evolution of Thinking from Darwin to Dewey* (Cambridge, MA: Harvard University Press, 2020).

[6] Thomas Kuhn, *The Structure of Scientific Revolutions* (University of Chicago Press, 1962).

[7] Cowles, *Scientific Method*, p. 279.

as Andrew Jewett observe that science skepticism of the
kind that circulated across the US from the 1920s on was
not "wrong in every detail." As he writes, "science is a
messy, thoroughly human enterprise that does not, and
cannot, address many of the issues we face. Indeed, most
scientists share that assessment themselves."[8] He goes
on to argue that, "Over time, in fact, a more charitable
and nuanced assessment of science might help us liberate
researchers from the extravagant assertions of disinter-
estedness that envelop their work. It is not their claims
alone, but also the arguments and actions of many other
groups, that have trapped scientists in the cage of absolute value-neutrality."

The extraordinary advances in science during the twentieth century, perhaps most conspicuously in physics
and then in biology and information science – ultimately
spanning every possible field of scientific endeavor – soon
ameliorated Snow's major concerns, namely that science
did not have sufficient prestige in British and American
universities. Snow had worried in his day that humanists
snubbed science, and scientists, at their own peril. Things
have changed in the decades since. Now, humanists resent
the prominence of science and the research apparatus
associated with it, especially given unequal levels of university support, not to mention teaching loads and other
perquisites of university life. At this moment of science's
ascendence, even Snow would have conceded that science
needs to acknowledge the critical importance of the arts
and humanities. Meanwhile, the two cultures have become
in some ways even more incomprehensible to each other,

[8] Jewett, *Science Under Fire*, p. 260.

while the humanities have understandably become more defensive about their place in the university – especially given the constant threat of downsizing due to steadily lower enrollments and numbers of majors – resisting the sense that they are now largely irrelevant except for a basic set of courses in "general" education. In hunkering down with an eye to weathering the storm, disciplines in the humanities and humanistic social sciences have too often retreated inside their disciplinary shells, writing within and disparaging efforts to communicate to wider publics, even across the university quad.

On the other side of the quad, as the sciences have become more specialized, they have created more barriers for exchange, not least because of the sheer technical knowledge required to participate. However, there is a new openness to interdisciplinary collaboration within the sciences that is related both to the explosive growth and ubiquitous role of technology as well as the enormous power of recent advances in the biological sciences. Some scientists in cutting-edge fields, gene editing for example, have begun to advocate for greater attention to ethics and the social consequences of science,[9] while computer scientists have become increasingly concerned about questions of privacy, security, and the malicious shaping of human opinions and consciousness by ever more sophisticated self-optimizing algorithms.[10] During

---

[9] Walter Isaacson, *The Code Breaker: Jennifer Doudna, Gene Editing, and the Future of the Human Race* (New York: Simon & Schuster, 2021), pp. 333–70.

[10] See, for example, Stuart Russell, *Human Compatible: Artificial Intelligence and the Problem of Control* (New York: Penguin, 2019); and Brian Christian, *The Alignment Problem: Machine Learning and Human Values* (New York: W.W. Norton, 2020).

the pandemic, medical researchers realized the importance of cultural, behavioral, and even political factors
in public health. And yet this recognition has translated
only rarely into the structural reorganization of programs
and departments, which continue to reflect the categories
and protocols of knowledge at the turn of the last century
more than they do the forms of knowledge appropriate
for the twenty-first.

If we accept the extent to which the arts and sciences
are linked, it becomes easier to argue that different disciplines within the humanities and social sciences should
interact far more than they currently do. Departments
may need to continue to exist for graduate training, but
they should no longer organize all of college or university life, and faculty might be appointed in more than one
academic unit whenever possible. This has the potential
not just to integrate colleges and universities better into
the prevailing needs of our day, it might also free the disciplines – including the humanities – from the historical
conditions of their professional origins. As I have suggested in earlier chapters, the humanities have not only
been much too focused on the legacy of outworn ideas
about western civilization, they have also been much too
separated from the worlds of social science, science, and
engineering where they are needed (and which they need)
now more than ever. Not only does this have deleterious effects on the conduct of these other disciplines, it
cripples the humanities with the disabling belief that they
exist either as a set of disciplines in decline or, ironically,
a "service industry" for the rest of the university.

These are not merely "academic" questions.
Technological discoveries are decidedly outpacing our

advances in evaluating the social, economic, and ethical implications of these new capabilities. Now that advanced forms of natural language processing programs, such as Chat GPT, are being released – and updated at an astonishing rate – questions around not just ethics but also the social, cultural, economic, and political impact of new technologies have become ever more urgent.[11] These questions circulate not only around the rise of machine learning and artificial intelligence but also around the development of new medical techniques and procedures. This is not to argue that forms of knowledge in the humanities and the sciences are the same; it is, however, to suggest that the need to reimagine the university's organization of knowledge is of growing importance given the kinds of issues we are confronting, whether to do with pandemics, technological modes of surveillance and intelligence, the role of technology in the collapse of democracy, climate change, the implications of new discoveries in the biomedical sciences, or any number of other impending crises.

To meet these goals, however, we must do more than merely rework the departmental organization of the university. We need to provide greater flexibility in every dimension. The idea that all students should go straight from "high school" to "college," for example, needs to be rethought. For the early years, whenever students might enter college, we should continue to design courses that provide a genuine liberal arts education, through courses that can be taught by faculty from different (and

[11] See for example Ezra Klein, "This Changes Everything," *New York Times*, March 12, 2023.

disparate) fields and departments (and colleges). For later years, we need to continue to devise new kinds of degrees and certificates for areas of learning that keep changing. In all cases, we have to accept that undergraduates should not be trained as if they are going to go on for PhDs, with majors that look like miniature versions of advanced disciplinary degrees. As we mix and match course requirements and curricula, the structure of both majors and electives could still reflect common but customizable educational goals that can be mounted efficiently as well as effectively.

Many of the challenges colleges and universities confront have to do with the nature of educational training students receive in schools from kindergarten to the twelfth grade. This in turn has to do with issues that range from vastly different funding for schools in different locales to vastly different levels of social capital – outcomes too of unequal access to resources and wealth. For some students, both those from low-achieving and those from high-achieving schools, college could start earlier. There have been extremely successful efforts to establish "early college" models that take students out of schools where they are not well served (for various reasons) to begin a college experience (see Bard's "Micro Colleges"). The early college idea has the added advantage of short circuiting one of the biggest impediments to genuine educational attainment in high school – the relentless and relentlessly uniform pressures to prepare to get into college.

If college can begin early, at least for some students, it can also begin later for others. It could proceed in more discrete steps, allowing students to take time off on a more routine basis: to take gap years, to study abroad or in other institutions, engage in internships or "deep dives," in activities that will both inform their education and enliven their sense of purpose and direction before they start or as they progress. They could travel, try out jobs in areas ranging from sports to the arts, or participate in start-ups or do volunteer work in community organizations or projects. Most important, they could then re-enter the university, newly motivated, more experienced, and with a necessary kind of focus. As we devise new forms of micro-certification and "badges" across a range of subjects, institutions, and programs, student mobility and flexibility can be increased even as institutions diversify the students they admit and teach. As they do so, the debate between those who insist on maintaining the current model of higher education and those who believe we should expand vocational educational opportunities might be resolved in ways that would allow students to enter not just professional but also vocational training programs after two years of a more general – "liberal" – education.

As the boundaries of college open both at the initial point of entry and for the purposes of easy exit and re-entry, the rhetorical gestures made by so many about the importance of lifelong learning need to be built into the fundamental structures of the university, genuinely ensuring ease of access for both advanced training and general education throughout full lifetimes. Lifelong learning should entail that "students" get the mentoring and networking support they might need to shift careers as well as pursue changing interests. And we need to be more creative about finding ways to pay for higher education, through state funding, as well as through employer educational mandates and subsidies, along with subscription and sponsorship models that provide sufficient remuneration for professors and universities to build these obligations into their teaching schedules and responsibilities.

The nature of PhD training also can change. Too many of us who teach in doctoral programs think of the PhD primarily as a means to reproduce ourselves, training students to become clones of what we imagine ourselves to be. We take too long to confer degrees, and while the idea that we need to impart and then certify specialized expertise is still valid, the notion that graduate students should have to spend seven to nine years gaining that expertise, given that only one or two of them in ten will get academic jobs, is no longer viable.[12] The PhD can be both significantly compressed and transformed to train students for a variety of career goals. On the one hand, when the PhD years are extended, the temptation is strong to use the training function of graduate student teaching as a major crutch for undergraduate teaching, subverting the administrative argument that graduate students are apprentice teachers. On the other hand, the skills of specialized knowledge, original research, and critical reading, writing, and speaking are,

---

[12] As I have been completing this book, new statistics about job prospects for historians seeking tenure track jobs have suggested an even more alarming future, one in which, as Daniel Bessner recently put it, the "end of history" is all too literal. History departments are shrinking with special rapidity, while students majoring in history and related fields have dropped by one third since 2012. Bessner characteristically blames the growth of administrators for much of the loss in tenure track jobs. See Bessner, "The Dangerous Decline of the Historical Profession," *New York Times*, January 14, 2023.

it turns out, helpful for any number of pursuits,[13] but only if the training period is within reasonable limits. Besides, those of us who have PhDs should remember that much of what we studied in our own doctoral programs – whether for our "comprehensive" examinations or in course work we had to take – was hardly necessary for our research, even as much of what we learned about our professions came in lessons we received well after formal training. In any case, most PhDs spend at least a year, often many more, in postdoctoral fellowships before attaining the few academic positions out there still. If some of these postdocs included teaching, while also paying a living wage, they could also contribute to teaching needs in universities without linking those needs inexorably to graduate training, a source of growing tension in graduate programs.

To reduce costs as well as to begin to create a newly flexible architecture for university learning, we might ask whether we spend too many resources on student services – from food, lodging, athletics, cultural support, social life: if these expenditures and investments have compromised a central focus on intellectual and scientific pursuits? Some of these "other" resources can be provided outside of universities, even as communities within universities can be forged in more direct relationship to academic interests and activities. This would allow students to come and go not just to class but to college with greater flexibility: starting college earlier when appropriate, transferring in and out from other

[13] See Leonard Cassuto and Robert Weisbuch, *The New PhD: How to Build a Better Graduate Education* (Baltimore, MD: Johns Hopkins University Press, 2021).

institutions, taking advantage of study away opportunities, accepting credits for valid online course experiences, taking time off for internships and projects that don't fit within the precise structures of departmental majors, living with other students in settings that, at least for part of the time, are either off campus or on other campuses or even in remote locations disconnected from any one educational institution. Technology can help us detach the residential and community experiences of college from the academic pursuit itself. As we come to terms with the extent to which the networked university must train students for entirely different kinds of careers, we might also accept that an increasing number of students are "non-traditional" (older students who have had to take breaks in their education). Indeed, we need non-traditional pathways for all students, adjusting our calendars and requirements to allow students to take advantage of experiences outside the university along with other online resources for credit.

Technology will necessarily be an important part of the future. The experience of the pandemic has made this clear. Lectures are already regularly recorded, providing greater reach for professors, flexibility for students, and offerings for institutions. Classrooms are minimally being "flipped," with the idea that the more intensive or interactive teaching takes place in smaller in-person (or at least synchronous) discussion groups after the lecture. But much more can be done with technological innovation as well. Faculty can teach across multiple institutions, with joint appointments not just between departments but between colleges, with the added benefit of making many smaller colleges much more viable as nodes in larger educational networks. Courses can be designed in more modular ways to facilitate mobility, and they can be "stacked" in ways that permit specialization and choice to go together even in smaller institutions. If technology can be introduced to serve broader educational interests, it can help reduce costs without eviscerating the role of faculty and the significance of faculty research and intellectual life. Faculty can be encouraged to reconnect not just to their institutions beyond their singular departments but also to a wider set of institutions and publics, providing them with more rather than less demand from students for their courses.

If we can be open to new ideas about how faculty are hired, curricula are mounted, programs and departments are organized, and degrees are given, we might also think differently about institutions. We know that some colleges as well as universities will have trouble surviving in the future. In order to sustain them, we need to be open to new kinds of affiliations and mergers. Struggling campuses could be repurposed as part of larger universities for the sake of managing enrollment, housing discrete groups of students, conferring specific forms of certification, offering specialized courses and research opportunities. It could be routine to merge smaller units to create more workable structures both within and between institutions. All this should not be seen as a way to curtail faculty prerogatives, especially in fields like the humanities that have routinely been targeted by administrative restructuring efforts. However, as new institutional configurations emerge, faculty may have to give up some of their autonomy with respect to departmental or even college life, even as they gain more control over teaching and mentoring as well as over their research life.

Eliminating, streamlining, or merging academic departments, programs, units, leave alone discrete institutions, while also suggesting that curricular and teaching obligations and ownership be changed, invariably raise howls of protest from faculty and students alike. And yet, curricula and departments in most universities have remained roughly the same for the last hundred years – as have both the internal quarrels within departments and the rivalries between institutions. Building a new and more flexible academic architecture would enable better support for a proliferation of sites and venues, while acknowledging the need to find new ways to credential students as they engage in more variable forms of learning across their lifetimes. A new architecture along these lines would tap into the dynamism and innovation that take place on the edge of the traditional structures of the university, edges that are now particularly well suited for the twenty-first century. As we create more extensive networks, while also enabling more flexibility for students and professors, we could reclaim the vitality of the university's intellectual and scientific mission. This is critical if indeed the university continues to be the major curator as well as producer of knowledge, even if it will never again be the sole provider.

A new Master Plan (for California or anywhere else) would therefore need to be more flexible, less top-down – a network rather than a closed system – merging and connecting educational resources for common goals, preserving what is best about the university while jettisoning those elements that do not serve one or more of its core missions.[14] Such a plan might also allow us to rescue not just some of the colleges and universities that are facing perilous futures – unable to enroll enough students to pay tuition to fund a full slate of faculty and the full suite of student services. And if we can do that, we could perhaps use discrete campuses to create the kinds of residential communities students need, while also offering them the wider range of educational and research opportunities a much larger university provides. This will doubtless exacerbate some of the tendencies Kerr identified, creating more contradictions and tensions. But if the multiversity has become a dizzying assemblage of structures, it can no longer pretend to control all that it contains. As the institution becomes both more decentralized and more networked, it can open itself up to new opportunities, position itself more critically in the ecosystem of knowledge, and make a more compelling case for public relevance. It could also reduce expenses, which in turn would reduce the cost of university education.

Some of these changes might even allow a much bolder conversation about the way we organize single universities and fashion altogether different incentives both for administrators and for faculty. New institutions as well as new institutional arrangements might enable alternative models for academic excellence, transforming disciplinary and departmental ideas about who should be hired, how we reward academic work, and how one fashions a university community that might be joined by a common

---

[14] For an earlier set of proposals for structural transformation of higher education, see Mark C. Taylor, *Crisis on Campus: A Bold Plan for Reforming our Colleges and Universities* (New York: Alfred Knopf, 2010).

intellectual purpose while no longer participating in the older forms of the academic marketplace. In my view, this is what critics of the neoliberal university should begin to think about, even if many of these new experiments have the uncertain (and almost always temporary) fate of other utopian ventures. An example of such an experimental university can be found in Quest University Canada, which provides an original model of faculty and curricular organization while focusing on providing an engaged educational environment for students.[15] Quest has had more than its share of challenges, both because of funding difficulties and more recently because of the pandemic, but it is a concrete example of a fundamentally different way of organizing teaching, learning, and faculty life.

I am not proposing a single blueprint here; indeed, my whole point is that universities need to open themselves up to multiple options and experiments. And there are successful models now, from John Sexton's work at NYU to create a networked global university with campuses in places as far flung as Abu Dhabi and Shanghai to Leon Botstein's collection of schools, micro colleges, and campuses that are part of Bard College in places that range from the Hudson Valley to Berlin and the West Bank. Michael Crow has worked to create innovative new organizational structures for research work and large-scale education at Arizona State University, building inventive interdisciplinary programs including a College of Global Futures. The Design School at Stanford has laid out a new

---

[15] I thank my Columbia colleague, the astronomer David Helfand who served as interim President of Quest for a number of years, for giving me a stirring introduction to this exciting educational experiment.

set of principles for enhancing student engagement with the worlds inside and outside the campus. Northeastern University, a former commuter school in Boston that is now a thriving enterprise acquiring failing campuses such as Mills College in California, has regularized student internships (or "co-ops"), that involve connecting course work to short-term employment opportunities.

These examples of entrepreneurial vitality make clear that it is possible for universities to change, though these are often the exceptions that prove the rule – involving (once) lower-tier universities and bold leaders. One would hope, however, that these cases of institutional change and innovation might inspire the new generation of phi-lanthropists, foundations, or corporations who might even now start investing the wealth of this gilded moment of late capitalism into institutions that, however different they would be from the universities established in similar ways during the late nineteenth century, could once again help chart the future of higher education while also pre-serving the best of the past. If, however, potential funders start with the premise that the university can no longer adapt, or worse, should no longer be the starting point for the ideas that animate our programs of education, explo-ration, enquiry, and engagement, then we stand to lose much of the value not just of our university system, but of what undergirds our civil society as well as our moral and intellectual imagination.

The problems our universities face cannot alone be solved either by new cost-cutting measures or by mere structural reorganization. It is imperative to make the case for significantly more funding from states for public institutions, even as the time is right to revisit the role of federal support for public higher education beyond high-level research.[16] But – as I found out the hard way – to make that case effectively will require looking for new ways to control expenses, and not just from the traditional tool kit of adding out-of-state students (simply for higher tuition, that is), hiring more badly paid adjuncts, increasing faculty teaching loads, cutting or even eliminating fields that have lost majors, or commercializing every blade of grass on the campus. The cost issue is not merely about funding, or the changing career patterns or technological options (and imperatives) of the twenty-first century, or for that matter the need for serious structural reform of university governance. It is also about reasserting the fundamental purposes of education, and in the process rethinking them at a time of massive social, political, economic, cultural, and technological change. Such a rethinking can be deeply threatening to entrenched positions across the university.

Ultimately, however, it is our educational and intellectual ambitions that have become obscured in so many recent debates, controversies, and struggles. Even as we might shed some of the administrative functions universities have taken on, we need fresh thought about our intellectual mission as well. It is not sufficient, for

---

[16] For a powerful recommendation to involve the federal government again in the restoration of US public universities, as it was in the case of the Morrill Act of 1862, see Robert Birgeneau and Mary-Sue Coleman, *Public Research Universities: Recommitting to Lincoln's Vision – An Educational Compact for the 21st Century*, Report from the American Academy of Arts and Sciences, April 2016. (This report was shepherded by the two co-chairs of the project, Robert Birgeneau, former Chancellor of the University of California, Berkeley, and Mary-Sue Coleman, former President of the University of Michigan).

example, to lament the decline in humanities enrollments without being open to rethinking how humanistic
forms of knowledge and learning are critically required
to support the intellectual, cultural, economic, scientific,
technological, and political challenges we face, now and
in the future. Universities are already well positioned to
preserve knowledge of the past, through their libraries,
archives, and historical commitments. But even historical
scholarship is at its best when it is alive to the questions of
the present and the future, whether in relation to understanding contemporary questions around democracy,
race, sovereignty, empire, class, or the social life of those
who have been left obscure in the historical record. The
work of historical imagination is as relevant for our future
as for our past, as we work to create a better world in
part through the recognition of how contingent the present really is. To invoke Eric Hayot's phrase, "humanist
reason" can be of critical importance in every domain of
human knowledge, including basic and applied science.

Hayot asserts two clear, simple, and intertwined proposals: first, that "the undergraduate curriculum in the
humanities should not be organized around the institu-
tionalized disciplines," and second, that "humanist reason
should be found everywhere in the university."[17] Having
made these bold statements – supporting in theoretical
terms what I've been arguing for here – he disappoint-
ingly confesses that he thinks they are entirely impractical.
His greatest concern is that institutional reform is impossible without a major crisis – budgetary or political – and
that even then the persistent worry would be that such

---

[17] Hayot, *Humanist Reason*, p. 167.

reforms (which he acknowledges need to be driven by administrators) would lead to further erosion of faculty governance and an increase in the casualization of academic labor. Having said that, he reiterates that without major institutional change, the humanities will remain endangered. I understand the reasons for Hayot's hesitations, but I am troubled by them. The stakes for arguments of this kind are too high to allow them to languish in faculty anxiety about nefarious administrative intentions.[18]

When the Berkeley faculty responded to a major budgetary crisis by declaring their opposition to having the administration drive any academic restructuring, it would have been helpful to have faculty like Hayot step up to advance the intellectual rationale for institutional redesign. Indeed, the restructuring of the biological sciences at Berkeley in the 1980s was only successful because it was largely driven by an influential member

[18] Hayot writes, "The changes I propose in this chapter are almost certainly impossible. This is not only because they would involve a great deal of institutional work, the disruption of so many existing structures and administrative units, that the mere fact of their taking place would require years, but also, and mainly, because such changes almost always turn into reasons to reduce the power of faculty governance and to increase the university's reliance on adjunct, precarious teaching labor. We have no model in the modern university, especially in the humanities, for radical institutional revision that is not the product of a financial crisis or part of an attempt to force the work of teaching and learning into a more capitalized model (which means precarious employment for faculty and increased debt for students). So it is difficult to imagine how any change of the type I propose here could take place" (ibid.). Although I applaud Hayot for making his proposals, surely this statement reflects both a sterling example, and the fundamental limits, of our institutional imagination, in the end a retreat from any real commitment to significant change.

of the faculty, Dan Koshland.[19] Without reasoned (and public) support from faculty, we simply rehearse a polarized debate between administration and faculty. If these debates take place exclusively in the shadow of distrust around the administration, the university will continue its slow but inevitable free fall through one crisis after the next. Most faculty who wished to speak in favor of institutional change have learned that speaking out does not earn popularity, and frequently decide to avoid faculty meetings outside their departments. Many faculty came up to me during the time of greatest turmoil on campus to tell me they agreed with what I was doing, but simply didn't have the patience or interest or time to come to faculty meetings to speak their minds. Despite our understandable fatigue stemming from these crises, there is either a lack of interest in directing intellectual debates towards fundamental institutional questions or a lack of willingness to risk the kind of change that might endanger the privileges that accompany the status quo (at least for tenured faculty). Tenure should be a protection for academic freedom, to be sure, but it should also come with an obligation to take on shared responsibility for the university's future. Only then we will be able to begin to bridge the paralyzing gap between faculty and administration, or for that matter between the university and the world outside. We need humanist reason for the sake of the survival of the university itself.

Recent campus controversies have led to even more incoherence in university life, to revert to the language

---

[19] Daniel E. Koshland, Jr., Roderic B. Park, and Louise Taylor, *The Reorganization of Biology at the University of California, Berkeley* (Regional Oral History Office, The Bancroft Library, 2003).

that Laurence Veysey used to characterize the twentieth-century American university. Veysey was concerned with the incoherence produced by the distinct spheres of education, research, and student life. And yet controversies around academic freedom create even more dissonance not just around education but also the nature of research itself. How open is inquiry – and by that I don't just refer to recent controversies over speakers from outside or speech inside universities, but also to the intellectual exchange across disciplines that could better reconnect the arts and the sciences. Does a version of academic freedom attached to disciplinary protocols limit the kind of intellectual curiosity and adventurousness that John Dewey and Arthur Lovejoy wished to preserve and that we so desperately need today, a hundred years later? How can research be better linked to our educational mission and goals? Yes, we need to debate why and how to pay for research. Many critics have begun to suggest that research work in the humanities and social sciences, and even in the more theoretical sciences, is a luxury we can no longer afford, or at the very least should be funded completely outside of the educational system. Although university administrators repeat the catechism that active research makes teaching better, the burden is on us to show the benefits of our research not only to students but to the larger public as well.

Despite the real tensions between the educational and research missions of universities, I believe that it is imperative for them to continue to find ways to support intellectual inquiry and sustained research, both in the sciences and elsewhere. As we have seen, the model of the German research university when first followed by

Johns Hopkins, and then by other new universities such as the University of Chicago and Stanford as well as older universities, public and private alike, such as Harvard, Yale, Michigan, Cornell, and California, to take on the role of supporting research across the disciplines, was dramatic and hugely consequential for the emergence of the modern university. In just a few decades, America took the lead in university research, quickly developing a network of research universities that continues to be the envy of the world. Historians of higher education uniformly agree that research work in universities powered America's economic growth, and then set the stage for post-World War II investments in research through the creation of the National Science Foundation at the recommendation of MIT's Vannevar Bush. The support structure for research that was put in place after the Second World War – through the establishment and generous funding of the National Science Foundation, the National Institutes of Health, and the Department of Energy funded national laboratories – has been spectacularly successful. This structure only worked because of the growth of major research universities in the United States, and again, these universities have been successful in training and then supporting generations of scientists who have immeasurably advanced our understanding of fields across the basic and applied sciences. The Bay Area became a hub for innovation and technology because of Berkeley and Stanford; Cambridge attained the status it has in biotechnology because of Harvard and MIT; and universities such as Duke and the University of North Carolina have made incomparable contributions to the economic and social vitality of the Research Triangle, as have so many other clusters of universities across the nation. At the same time, support for research has immeasurably enlivened our intellectual worlds and discourses, across all disciplines and fields.

This does not mean, however, that our funding system for work even in the sciences and engineering is either sufficient or perfect in its functioning. There are critics who suggest that federal funding tends to privilege established researchers, who are funded to continue work they have already been successful in doing rather than branching out into new fields. These critics sometimes assert that the pace of innovation in science is actually slowing down rather than rising, even as they propose new ways to sponsor research that is "out of the box," bold in setting goals and mobilizing teams that have not been tried and tested, and oriented more towards long-term (and not easily measurable) outcomes than short-term advances. The push to diversify funding sources, procedures, and metrics is based on compelling insights and concerns, but I think it makes sense to consider these changes as supplemental and complementary rather than possible substitutes for established protocols and systems.[20]

Historically, the shift to focus more on research took place in tension with the original purpose of universities to educate (and socialize) the young. As states have retrenched from commitments to fund public universities at levels that kept tuition fees low at the same time as private universities have ratcheted tuition up to current

[20] See, e.g., Michael Nielsen and Kanjun Qiu, "A Vision of Metascience: An Engine of Improvement for the Social Processes of Science," *The Science++ Project*, October 18, 2022, https://scienceplusplus.org/metascience/index.html.

levels, the fundamental commitment to research has also, inevitably, grown increasingly contested. Our great universities, however, would lose their capacity to be real "cities of intellect" without the strong commitment to research, across all fields. In his important book on the American research university, Jonathan Cole made an inventory of the products and discoveries that were developed in university laboratories and libraries, a list of things most of us now feel we can't live without (and, in areas of biomedical research, often literally things some of us need to stay alive, or healthy).[21] As I just noted, federal support for "principal investigator" driven research on university campuses has also directed extraordinary intellectual energy to the larger world of the university. This energy and creativity will only be enhanced if we break down barriers between the "arts" and the "sciences," even as we need to press for more support for research work not just in applied science and engineering but in all fields on campus. Research, whether in the study of early Chinese literature or cosmology and astrophysics, contributes to our intellectual life at large and the campus work of teaching and learning. It especially does this when it engages, and in turn is evaluated in relationship to, a broader intellectual palette than those defined by narrow subfields and insular disciplinary enclaves.

Not all institutions of higher education, however, need to be equipped either with full-scale research facilities in every field, or with graduate training programs, at least not within their own institutional walls. The spirit of the

[21] Jonathan Cole, *The Great American University: Its Rise to Preeminence, Its Indispensable National Role, Why It Must Be Protected* (New York: Public Affairs, 2009).

Master Plan needs to be revisited more broadly, since there has been far too much uniformity in the ambitions of colleges and universities to follow a single research model to achieve higher placement in one ranking scheme or another. Even as the small college model that stresses teaching over research has been a critical part of the higher educational landscape, there should be room for much larger universities to focus primarily on teaching and learning as well. And it is important to accept that small colleges and universities that may lack resources to support research across every field are also critical drivers of intellectual activity and creativity. At the same time, there are too many clones of top research programs, and far too few opportunities within mainstream not-for-profit college and university programs for students to take a combination of high-quality liberal arts courses alongside courses that impart skills – whether in technology and data analytics, healthcare, public policy, finance, etc. – that are intellectually rigorous and yet more vocationally directed than many of the traditional "majors" have been in our leading colleges and universities.

As the American university became increasingly global it has also fallen into the fault lines of our contemporary political debate over globalization, for the important efforts to establish branch campuses and global footprints – international strategies that were inevitably as linked to the goal of attracting an ever-larger market share of international students as they were to the more noble idea of cross-cultural exchange and understanding – have been slowed by the widespread retreat across the political spectrum from the perceived cultural, economic, and political dangers (and real downsides) of the global. I experienced this in the reaction to the Berkeley Global Campus idea, but the problem has now become pervasive, even though many educators would agree that the ambassadorial role of US universities has been far more effective than any other form of world diplomacy. Meanwhile, universities in parts of the world well outside Europe and North America have become more and more competitive (especially in the sciences and engineering) with the top-ranked universities of the world, rising in the rankings and beginning to dominate in research areas such as artificial intelligence and robotics. If US universities are to remain competitive with them, they need both to continue to engage internationally, and to do so with an explicit commitment not just to global collaboration but to exchange around ideas as well as scientific discoveries. This too has been a signature part of our past and must continue to be an important part of our future. Our advantages inhere both in the openness of our universities to scientific cooperation and in our abiding commitment to academic freedom and the role of the liberal arts. No university will prosper if it restricts its academic agendas – not to mention its intake of students and faculty – to national borders.

Clark Kerr and the Master Plan were criticized because of their manifest elitism – the idea that some version of meritocratic social organization would determine who might benefit from and participate in the education offered by top research universities. And yet the idea that all students should be offered the same kind of education once they go to university has led to other forms of social sorting that end up diminishing both the quality of research in some institutions and the quality of education in others. The Master Plan may have instituted too rigid a structure, but it encoded the right set of assumptions about how not all institutions need PhD programs, large expensive laboratories or scientific equipment, etc. Research activity benefits teaching, but teaching and research also can exist in conflict with each other, either because of the time research work takes, or because research excellence does not imply or always produce great teaching. The important thing here is to ensure that as many faculty as possible are given time and resources to work on projects that enliven both their teaching and their sense of engagement with intellectual, scholarly, and research endeavors. It is often this that can pervade and improve enthusiasm about and commitment to teaching, whatever the research itself. Teaching at this level is about a calling to encounter intellectual and scientific issues in multiple ways, as teacher, mentor, scholar, researcher, and public intellectual.

And while we are at it, not all faculty need to follow the same path to secure teaching positions, apprenticing themselves through graduate training and the standard protocols of professional advancement to the academic norms of the disciplines. I found that hiring talented writers and intellectuals – without PhDs and formal academic credentials – could be enriching not just for students but for fellow faculty, even as intellectuals who write for multiple audiences (across disciplines) can, and do, work in multiple venues, from government to the non-profit world, from corporate to entrepreneurial domains. And, indeed, there are formally trained academics who have taken up employment in sectors outside the university who could become valued teachers and colleagues on a part-time basis – not adjuncts in the sense (and at the price point) of gig economy workers as much as flexible intellectuals who make their homes both outside as well as within universities. While business schools have led the way in this domain, there is no reason why other fields across the social sciences and humanities, as well as the sciences and engineering, could not employ a more flexible faculty as well to support intellectuals who could be part- as well as full-time academics, with compensation levels significantly above what is provided for adjuncts (levels that themselves need to be raised considerably).

As I write about how we might reimagine the university, I remember back to when I was chancellor, and how little time I had to think about these big questions. I was gratified by the chance to oversee a major initiative in data science that allowed faculty to create a new set of courses – now a new "division" of the university – that connected techniques and methods of data analysis with data from fields that not only bridged the arts and sciences but also traversed the full extent of the university, with lots of "humanist reason" thrown into the mix. I used seed funding to support initiatives in fields ranging from neuroscience and genomics to interdisciplinary social science and international studies, all vital intellectual projects. But most of my time was spent thinking about, say, athletics, both its enormous costs and the problems that came from the over-professionalization of intercollegiate sports – specifically problematic admissions procedures for and then the low graduation rates of the football and basketball teams. I was preoccupied with issues around finding sufficient support and new procedures for dealing with crises around sexual assault and mental health, needs around disability and diversity, and the shortage and high cost of housing. I spent a large amount of my time on fundraising and donor relations, not to mention trying to keep the schools and deans aligned with each other and with the central administration about how to approach every aspect of raising the money we needed from private sources. I expected much of this, and I don't mean to complain. What I didn't expect was how much time I had to spend dealing with these issues over and again at the level of the university system – and as a result in the full glare of political interference – which worked to regulate and control much of what we did in each one of these domains. In the midst of all of these issues, questions related to the university as a "city of intellect" were too often relegated to the bottom of the list.

The pressing issues all yielded to the constant challenges around how best to present the work of the university to our various constituents – within and outside the university. We sometimes felt as if we were held hostage by a few especially hostile reporters working for local newspapers, at the same time we were being treated as a kind of political football by the political forces of California, not least the major political players determining our lives. The biggest concern on the part of many of my staff was to keep ahead of anything that might be seen or disseminated as bad news, while working to be seen as acting on behalf of the entire university, not as a self-justifying bureaucratic elite that worked only to expand our ranks and wallets, as much press and public opinion seemed to believe and kept trying to find stories to demonstrate. Then there were the constant crises around legal issues, a sign of the role that litigation now plays in virtually every aspect of university life. There were issues too around "shared" governance. Working with the faculty senate was critical (and for the most part senate leaders worked closely and productively with us). But I felt that I had far less control over decision-making with respect to the office of the president, the Regents of the university, and the powers that sat in the state assembly, senate, and governor's office. In the midst of all of this, I tried to be as "present" on campus as possible, both at events that celebrated important people and programs in the university, and in informal gatherings of students, faculty, alumni, and others. Even as I'm sure I was less imaginative than I should have been about how to build consensus across multiple constituencies as it was facing such enormous budget problems, there was far too little time to focus on what I would argue are the genuinely central purposes of education. In retrospect, I was doubtless far too impatient to ask hard questions about intellectual priorities instead of accepting that my principal role was simply to manage as calmly as possible the regular external crises of university life.

It is difficult to reimagine the university under these circumstances, and when I invited the university community to join me in that process, that was clearly far too disruptive. Meanwhile, however, even if we remain inert, the university continues to change. While private and public interests seem to war against each other in the face of the massively rising costs and the uncertain benefits of higher education, new movements to contest the old protocols and certainties of university life have coalesced around a more general dissatisfaction with the sins of late capitalism and the cult of private accumulation. Unfortunately, our ideas of the public good differ enormously, a symptom of the increasing polarization of political thought that has invaded every part of our public sphere, necessarily and centrally involving the university. It is therefore hardly surprising that the campus culture wars resemble the religious wars and disputations of past eras, for the stakes take on moral dimensions even when (perhaps especially when) narrow self-interest is at work. And yet, no new creed has emerged that might blend the verities of earlier days with the urgent needs of the present; we feel adrift as we seek to find both a mission and a plan forward that doesn't seem to be deeply compromised by past failures and the pitfalls of our current predicament. While some of us wonder if the university will survive, others argue about whether it should.

I trust it is clear from this book that I am deeply committed not just to the survival of the university but to an even more central role for it in what will undoubtedly continue to be turbulent years ahead. The university is the vital repository of stubborn commitments to the importance of knowledge, and in its generationally transmitted protocols of inquiry, exploration, and debate it holds a critical function for any society, but especially one in which questions of truth, value, and epistemic autonomy are as fundamental as they are today. And yet it seems necessary to acknowledge fully the threats, the critiques, and the discontents that have led so many to lose faith, trust, and confidence in the world of higher education. As we will see in the conclusion, there are many sensible voices arguing against complacency, insisting that we take seriously the need for change, even if their recommendations for what needs to change might differ dramatically.

Afterword

~

"The monastic and cathedral masters of novices evolved into the
university professors of the later Middle Ages. The private- and
public-school masters of the Italian Renaissance were joined by
humanist essayists, orators, and tutors of princes .... Only in the past
century has higher education been concentrated into a strict and
exclusive system of degree-granting universities and colleges with
the goal of certifying professional status across a broad spectrum of
socially useful and creative fields of endeavor. There is no guarantee
that this short-lived, highly concentrated, complex, and expensive
system of education will or should remain unchanged."[1]

Ronald Musto

What could go wrong? Ronald Musto, in his recent book
titled *The Attack on Higher Education: The Dissolution of
the American University*, suggests in polemical but real-
istic terms that universities might disappear in the next
decades, much as the medieval monasteries of England
did when Henry VIII dissolved them in the 1530s.
Despite the immediate concerns that led to Henry's
turn away from Catholicism, he was only able to carry
off his draconian project, using Thomas Cromwell
as his muse and executioner, because of a long-term
and cumulative crisis that made his final decree in the
end a fait accompli. As Musto writes, it succeeded not
because of

---

[1] Musto, *Attack on Higher Education*, p. 295.

the actions of a few important men but a multipolar, multi-valenced unfolding of causations and a variety of human agencies that only in retrospect can be reassembled in narrative and interpreted as a "natural" outcome of personalities, ideas and larger socio-economic and cultural forces at work. We must bear this in mind when approaching and understanding events very close to us in time and space.[2]

Musto may be exaggerating the possibility of collapse to make his point, but it is well worth taking his warning seriously.

The decline of monastic institutions led to the rise of the university in Britain, and elsewhere across Europe. But it could have been otherwise. Now that the university has been targeted by similar critiques as the monasteries in their day, it is important that we use the idea of crisis not to shut down our imagination, but to direct it to possibilities that might preserve what is best about the history of the university and design what is needed to transform it in ways that will make it more vital for the future.

William Kirby's story, in his recent book *Empires of Ideas*, is far less dire, but he still makes clear that the great American research universities are losing ground, not just to China, but to their previous stature across private and public sectors.[3] He writes that rankings, however imperfect, reveal the "shifting tectonic plates of global leadership in higher education." He notes that whereas German universities would have dominated the rankings in the nineteenth century, today, "at least according to the QS rankings, Peking University and Tsinghua University outperform *every* German university. Times change."[4]

[2] Ibid., pp. 38–39.   [3] Kirby, *Empires of Ideas*, p. 16.   [4] Ibid., p. 16.

This remark frames the story he tells of Berkeley, seeing its challenges as destructive not just for flagship public universities but for their entire ecosystem. As he puts it, "There is no greater threat to the leading position of American higher education than America's growing parsimony in the support of public higher education."[5] He sees Berkeley as the proverbial canary in the coal mine, the harbinger of the damage wrought by the steady disinvestment on the part of states in their systems of public higher education. As for the University of California – the traditional jewel in the crown of public systems – he cites statistic after statistic to demonstrate the precipitous decline in state support, as well as in the university's capacity to provide genuine access either because of growing demand on the one side or the rising cost of college on the other. But in turning his focus back to Berkeley, the flagship of the system, he concedes special challenges, and not just predicated on the dysfunction of governance and declining levels of support from outside – e.g., state government, the governor-appointed Regents, and the public at large. He also asks whether "Berkeley – home to the Free Speech Movement, long traditions of academic autonomy, and insurgent citizenship – [had] finally become both ungovernable and insolvent in the face of the multiple 'new normal' beating down on it."[6] These were certainly the questions that I carried with me from my own efforts to come to terms with the "new normal" that I perhaps made the mistake of naming as a long-term condition.

For Kirby, the problems besetting Berkeley, and for that matter public higher education across the US, will come

[5] Ibid., p. 384.   [6] Ibid., p. 200.

to haunt the world of great private research universities as well. "Make no mistake," he warns, "the slow-motion defunding of US public higher education will have consequences also for the private schools, the Stanfords and the Harvards."[7] And he reminds us that while Chinese universities face all kinds of difficulties from existing in a politically illiberal system, that had not been a disabling impediment for German universities in the Wilhelmine period, when political orthodoxy was "seldom questioned." Still, he wonders, as do I, whether the reduction of the idea of the liberal arts to concerns about innovation and entrepreneurial creativity will serve the larger purpose of building world-class universities that have "comprehensive" coverage across different fields.

Kirby's pessimistic account of the current predicament of public universities is told in even starker terms by Simon Marginson, who considers the steady decline in public funding for higher education as a symptom of the loss of faith in the idea of the public good in his ominously titled book, *The Dream is Over: The Crisis of Clark Kerr's California Idea of Higher Education*.[8] Marginson, who sees Kerr as the most important thinker – and actor – in American higher education in the second half of the twentieth century, writes that Kerr was the exemplar of the "California Idea." This was the idea that public institutions had pride of place in the pursuits of the state and the beliefs of society. Marginson is more impressed by Kerr's pragmatic use of a postwar social science framework to design the multiversity than he is by his rhetoric,

[7] Ibid., p. 384.
[8] Simon Marginson, *The Dream is Over* (Berkeley: University of California Press, 2016).

and he looks back on the moment in American history when the role of the state was generally accepted across both the growing middle class and the leaders of the public as well as the private sector with understandable nostalgia. But he recognizes that no leader of a university, in California or elsewhere, has the capacity to counteract the fundamental degradation of the public idea for the university. Marginson tells the familiar story of California's tax revolts in the 1970s and how they led inexorably to the present moment, but remains hopeful that the good people of California will at some point take stock and reclaim their own commitment to funding the idea he associates with the name of their state. But the older commitment to making public institutions as genuinely open and free to the public as they are competitive with the private will not be restored in the absence of a major political reversal.

I do not by any means intend to suggest that the only model for universities is the public one that Berkeley represents. Many private universities and colleges offer extraordinary examples of cities of intellect that fulfill many of the educational ambitions I have endorsed here. But they educate many fewer students than go to public institutions, even if one simply counts the top tier of public universities. I am fully supportive of efforts by private universities to continue their efforts to broaden access by offering robust need-based financial aid while also opening their doors to applicants from all kinds of different backgrounds and experiences. I am also, however, well aware that this will hardly provide the educational opportunities that seem so urgent for a wide enough swath of the population to make the kind of difference in lives beyond a tiny elite, however much that elite might be newly diversified and changing. What has driven my sense of possibility has been the recognition that Berkeley has provided an exemplary if not singular case of an institution that can offer both excellence and access at scale – though scale of a kind that requires a much more extensive ecosystem across different types and categories of higher educational institutions to reach the public in a meaningful way. Otherwise, the kinds of justifications for universities offered here – whether my own defense of the liberal arts or others who have asserted the importance of universities for conveying the intellectual underpinnings for participation in a democratic society, the critical value of open research in university settings, or any number of other compelling arguments about the importance of university education for private benefit as well as public good – will fall even more drastically short.

Despite Musto's warning, the university is not going to disappear any time soon. It has been outliving predictions of total disruption for quite some time. In 1997, Peter Drucker, the influential management consultant, said that, "Thirty years from now the big university campuses will be relics. Universities won't survive."[9] And earlier I noted that similar prognostications in 2011 by Clayton Christenson, that within a decade the bottom 25 percent of every college and university tier would either disappear or merge, were, shall we say, vastly exaggerated.[10] But it is indisputable that the past decade has in fact been

[9] Quoted in Rhodes, *Creation of the Future*, p. xii.
[10] Clayton Christenson, *The Innovative University: Changing the DNA of American Higher Education* (New York: John Wiley and Sons, 2011).

a time of significant change and restructuring, with clear trends emerging that threaten the stability of the world of higher education. The wolf may not have come inside the door, but the effects of growing disaffection with the university across so many sectors of our society are becoming increasingly palpable and real.

In writing this book, I have tried to resist the tendency towards nostalgia about the times when the university – private and public alike – was held in higher esteem. I advocate for change here, but I know that I may not like much of what comes to pass. Indeed, I suspect we will see the loss of a great deal of what I have valued so much about the university over the years. That fear is built into the genre of this book, for it is impossible to write a personal history without some measure of nostalgia, embellished with its inevitable fictions, its excuses, its self-justifications. Autobiographical writing is, by definition, an exercise in memory, and historians know how unreliable that can be, how self-serving authors are when writing about themselves and their own times. In these pages of reflection about the university, however, I have tried to use the past to look forward. I've used my own history and experience to form a set of thoughts and even recommendations, however inchoate, about how to position the university for the demands and needs of the future. In doing so, I am aware that I would like to ensure the survival of at least some of the histories that I found so important in my own case, even as I accept that any prophecy about the future should at best resurrect only a small portion of the past, and in largely new ways.

Most of all, I write here about the importance of the intellectual modes of engagement that the university has for me represented, even – and perhaps especially – when

I struggled against its institutional rigidities. This was so during my college days when I was concerned about its implication in the military-industrial complex, as well as more recently when I've seen first-hand the extent to which the neoliberal multiversity can abandon core intellectual values. In our efforts to defend the university against its many critics and when advocating for its greater support – whether that is asking for more public (governmental) funding or by seeking to raise money from private sources – it is far too easy to lose sight of the often vexing and always complex demands of the city of intellect.

The survival of the city of the intellect, however, is not just critical, but a paramount need for the future of our society. Clark Kerr was not wrong to predict its disappearance in the twenty-first century, the fallout of the inexorable forces leading to the erosion of some of the core features he associated with his hybrid vision of an excellent liberal arts college (like Swarthmore) suffusing the intellectual character of a flagship public research university (like Berkeley). He recognized the corrosive pressures of funding crises, the new information age, competing political demands, and the entrepreneurial incentives for institutions and individuals alike to chase other forms of support. Having lived through the early years of the turbulent sixties, he did not predict the current crises around campus politics, thinking perhaps those were safely in the past, though he was aware that issues around identity and representation would accompany an expanding and increasingly diverse student body. He always worried, however, that undergraduate education would be overshadowed by the larger forces that make up the multiversity, forces that would only become over time more and more at war with the fundamental goals of education, research, and scholarship.

In histories of higher education in the twentieth century, Kerr is usually contrasted with Chicago's Robert Maynard Hutchins, architect of its undergraduate core curriculum and passionate defender of the liberal arts. Despite Kerr's clear embrace of the multiversity and the research enterprise, his fundamental agreements with Hutchins appear more salient in retrospect than his many differences of emphasis and opinion. They both, to use Frank Rhodes' term, appear increasingly like dinosaurs, seen that is from the vantage point of this side of the extinction event that transformed them – when they didn't die out completely – into species of birds. While universities have, however fitfully, begun to be genuinely responsive to the need to become more open, inclusive, and diverse, cracking the myths of meritocracy that allowed for the continuation of modes of traditional privilege in admissions and recruitment, they have also changed in less positive ways. They have too often protected the privileges of a shrinking tenured professoriate while building an entirely different institution around them through the increasing use of adjuncts for teaching and low-level staff for much else, while devoting their limited resources to enterprises both within and outside the university that go well beyond the demands of education and advanced research. Given political and economic pressures, they have been especially aggressive in developing new financial models, pursuing different strategies of engagement with government, industry, and the entrepreneurial economy, and using the vague language of skills and career training to respond to and in some cases create new student demand.

Too often, however, they have failed to provide students with the larger educational skills and aptitudes that might equip them for the many dimensions of life after college, not to mention the intellectual benefits of a broad and rigorous liberal arts education.

As I have suggested throughout this book, universities absolutely need to change, and they need to be aggressive in responding both to recurrent crises and to new conditions. They also have an obligation to train students for real careers and to expand the remit of research activity and public engagement. But even as they have resisted structural change, they have also jettisoned some of the fundamental values that could, and should, help to guide the turbulent process of change. Chief among these are intellectual values, the recognition of what is core to the promise of higher education for traditional and non-traditional populations of college students alike. These are ecumenical ideas, tied neither to my own particular Protestant genealogy nor to any other, as new cultural claimants and an expanding pool of national and social constituencies have demonstrated the compelling lure and critical importance of advanced education for all. When intellectual values are no longer paramount, other commitments – say to the professionalized disciplinary pathways that have congealed as the default means of university organization and governance – not only fill the vacuum but seriously limit our imagination.[11] Mandarins of the present day no longer seem motivated to propose

---

[11] For a recent argument that makes an insightful analysis of Weber's "vocation lectures" to assert the centrality of intellectual values in the university, see Wendy Brown, *Nihilistic Times: Thinking with Max Weber* (Cambridge, MA: Harvard University Press, 2023).

radically different structures, processes, and institutional possibilities for the creation of new cities of intellect for the future. This is where the loss of the utopian sensibility is both most apparent and disabling.

In his periodization of the history of the university, Kerr had already begun to identify the coming of what subsequently has come to be called the fourth industrial revolution.[12] Whatever term one chooses, the introduction of digital means of production and reproduction began to have enormous effects on all knowledge "industries" in the last decade of the twentieth century, only to give way to an escalating concatenation of network effects created by the Internet, new modes of connectivity and production, 3-D printing, the explosion of artificial intelligence, massive computational power, neural networks, large language models, and now the specter of advanced quantum modes of computation. Now that we have begun to witness the nature of life in the fourth industrial revolution – the increasing possibility that machine learning, structural biology, gene editing, robotics, and quantum computation will not only surpass many forms of human capacity and intelligence but fundamentally restructure knowledge, the organization of work, the economy, social as well as personal and even sexual relations, political life, the medicalized body, and the nature of what it means to be human – we should be even more concerned about the possible demise of the city of intellect. This is not the moment to yield to the technocratic ethos that devalues the epistemological domains of historical, literary,

---

[12] Klaus Schwab, *The Fourth Industrial Revolution* (New York: Penguin, 2017).

and philosophical inquiry leave alone the classic social science questions around structure and agency, cultural difference and moral universals, the relation of the individual to society, the multiple possibilities of the political imagination, the systemic effects of historical oppression or of imperial rule, or alternative economic and financial models and modes of organization. But where else will these domains of inquiry continue to thrive if we no longer build and sustain our cities of intellect?

The genuine democratization of intellectual capital is not beyond our grasp, as some public and private universities have shown now for many decades. But that we work both to deepen this capital and expand its reach is of ever greater importance. In the first instance, this means refusing to abandon the rigorous nature of humanistic and social scientific inquiry. It also means using appropriate techniques of reading, inquiry, and analysis to confront with relentless academic seriousness the escalating crises of our contemporaneous moment, whether regarding the looming threats around climate, the already terrifying effects of technological dysfunction, the global collapse of democratic values, or the glaringly manifest and steadily increasing inequities in wealth, opportunity, and voice that have become so fundamental to our current socio-economic reality. It means connecting the arts and the sciences – basic as well as applied – in meaningful, and meaningfully extensive ways, creating real bilingualism across scientific and non-scientific fields rather than allowing them to continue to be so sequestered. The success of these reforms will be measured both by the quality of the education that results, and by the extent and scale of its reach. The intellectual disfranchisement of those for whom a meaningful college education is not just unattainable but often unthinkable has had as disastrous an effect on our present politics as it will on our collective future.

My work in history and anthropology has taught me over my academic life how contingent things are, how much difference one encounters across the vast expanses of time and place, how things not only have changed, but by implication can and will change again. At a time when many of our forecasts about the future – whether we think about the state of our society, our economy, our political covenants and institutions, or our climate and the planet – evoke mostly fear and dread, I still believe in the promise of utopia, even as I hold that such a belief is especially critical at a time of dystopia. And even as there is little doubt that the word "crisis" has been consistently overused, higher education is not only at a moment of genuine crisis, but one that is unlikely to end any time soon.

Flawed though it is, the university is an institution that is driven by a noble idea and brings enormous value for individuals and society alike. Every now and then, the university lives up to its utopian aspirations, if only for a few fleeting moments, before inevitably falling short once again. If we are not to confront a future of dissolution, collapse, and failure, it is helpful to be hailed by that idea of utopian possibility, but it is far more necessary to be fully engaged in the process of institutional change that will continue to unfold, in one direction or another, no matter what we may do to try to wish it all away. The stakes are high.

ACKNOWLEDGEMENTS

This book began, uncertainly, as a memoir. I started by writing a historical essay about my father's life, based on a short autobiographical sketch he wrote for a talk he gave in Santa Cruz a few years before he died of a heart attack in 1981. Although he had been born on a farm in central Iowa to a family of German immigrants who spoke little English and had no advanced education, he was the only one of his extended family to leave home for college. He had been born with a hole in his heart, a blue baby, or "stubble cat" (a late-born kitten that usually died) as he put it. Without the physical stamina to take over the farming chores from his father, he went off to study to become a minister, with the idea that he would soon return to the German Presbyterian church that was just a mile down a dirt road from the farm. In time, the university became his new church, and he went on to earn a PhD in philosophy and teach for much of his life at the Yale Divinity School. He also spent a great deal of time traveling around the world, especially to India, and after working for a time in an educational foundation wound up as a dean at the University of California, Santa Cruz.

As I mulled over the many parallels between my own life story and his, the Covid pandemic paralyzed the world and I suddenly found myself with unscheduled time of a kind I hadn't had in years. In between zoom meetings, I started to write about my mother, my passages to India over many years, my early religious education and subsequent loss of faith, and my life in the university. I am grateful to David Hollinger and Richard Ford for reading early chapters about my parents, and to Val Daniel, Vishakha Desai, Peter Dougherty, Nick Lemann, Sherry Ortner, Michael Roth, and Eric Schwartz for reading the entire first draft of the manuscript when I finished it during the summer of 2021. They all made helpful and encouraging comments, although Michael in particular strongly advised me to consider abandoning much of the memoir and writing about issues related to the university instead to make for a more coherent book.

I took this suggestion to heart and recast the entire manuscript around a second project that I had begun earlier, when I was still Chancellor of Berkeley, about the current predicament of higher education, what I saw at the time as a general assault on the university. I had witnessed what in retrospect were the early stages of an all-out attack from the political right on universities like Berkeley, attacks that now, just after Governor Ron DeSantis signed a new bill imposing draconian forms of censorship and control over Florida's public universities, have escalated to an unprecedented level in America. But I had also experienced the challenges universities face from within, from the multiple constituencies and "interest groups" that were brought together to make up the "incoherence" (as suggested by the historian Laurence Veysey) of Clark Kerr's canonical "multi-versity," to the new pressures from students and some faculty to suspend traditional commitments to free speech. I decided to use my own life in the university to try to tell a larger story, one that would invoke both Nietzsche and Kerr around "the uses and abuses of the university." And there were things I could write, and views I could express, more freely, now that I had left my earlier roles of dean and chancellor behind.

After another year of writing, once I had written a substantially different book, I was grateful for the cogent comments I received from Leon Botstein, Drew Faust, Andrew Kinney, John Sexton, Mark Taylor, and most recently Judy Friedlander and Tim Brennan, both of whom provided extraordinarily detailed suggestions at the last minute as I was about to hit "send" to begin the copy-editing. A shout-out to Bill Kirby for sharing with me his thoughts about Berkeley in the context of writing his own book on the history and future of universities. I am also extremely grateful to Peter Dougherty (who continues to give me excellent advice from his long years in publishing) and Nick Lemann for reading through the manuscript a second time. And Alex Wright, my indefatigable editor at Cambridge University Press, has been an avid supporter and an ideal publisher for an unusual hybrid project of this kind.

This is not the place to rehearse my many academic debts across a long career, but I would like to remark a few of the people who made the ride through senior academic roles possible, and productive. First, Lee Bollinger asked me to serve as EVP and Dean of the Arts and Sciences at Columbia, and it was a privilege to work with him for close to a decade. I am also grateful to Jean Howard, Martha Howell, Alice Kessler Harris, and Ann McDermott for support in the early days of my Columbia administrative career, and to the late Alan Brinkley for his comradeship when he was provost. I learned much from other Columbia colleagues in the administration, including Carlos Alonso, Carol Becker, Susan Feagin, Austin Quigley, and Claude Steele – as well as from David Cohen, Jonathan Cole, Ira Katznelson, and George Rupp, who were always generous with their time and thoughts even though they had stepped down from their roles by the time I started. I am grateful to Mark Yudof for recruiting me to Berkeley, although he stepped down so soon I didn't have much of a chance to work with him, and to Bill Helman, for trying valiantly to persuade me to do something else. I had a terrific administrative team at Berkeley, starting with Claude Steele whom I recruited as provost, including Paul Alivisatos, Gibor Basri, Scott Biddy, Janet Broughton, Nils Gilman, Julie Hooper, Shannon Jackson, Harry Le Grande, Na'ilah Suad Nasir, the late Chris Patti, Rosemary Rae, Larry Rinder, Andrew Szeri, Matias Tarnapolsky, and Mike Williams. Jenny Hanson started with me in the Chancellor's Office and continues to work with me. I was warmly welcomed by the community of university leaders both in the US and globally and have appreciated the support and friendship of many of them: including Gene Bloch, Leszek Borysiewicz, Dick Brodhead, Ana Mari Cauce, Michael Crow, Ron Daniels, Drew Faust, Howard Gillman, Sam Hawgood, David Leebron, Pradeep Khosla, Louise Richardson, Peter Salovey, John Sexton, Brian Schmidt, Morty Shapiro, Subra Suresh, and Chorh Chuan Tan. A special thanks to John Sexton for connecting me more recently with the New York Academy of Sciences, where he had once been chair of the board. And thanks more generally to the New York Academy of Sciences for providing a unique perch from which to work on the issues and crises in the worlds of science and society today, while continuing to write about the present and future of higher education.

My two (now grown) children, Sandhya and Ishan, helped in different ways to keep me from focusing too single-mindedly on administrative duties over the past twenty years, as more recently has Zubin, who brought us all great joy – as well as considerable worry – during the final years of completing this book. Most of all, my most important thanks go to Janaki. She not only read multiple versions of the book, she lived them as well. I would never have survived the intense and often strange stresses and pressures of my time in academic administration without her full support and partnership. Along the way, we had some great times, but I also exposed her to a succession of adversities brought on by our public life that were both unfair and deeply wounding. I can't fully know how much her own scholarship and career suffered because of some of my career choices, only that they did. But I do know her love sustained me then as it does now. I dedicate the book to her.

BIBLIOGRAPHY

Act of July 2, 1862 (Morrill Act), Public Law 37-108, which established land-grant colleges, enrolled Acts and Resolutions of Congress, 1789–1996, General Records of the United States Government, National Archives.

American Association of University Professors. "Statement of Principles on Academic Freedom and Tenure" (1940).

Appiah, K. Anthony. "Neutrality is a Fiction – But an Indispensable One." *The Atlantic*, April 20, 2023.

Asimov, Nanette. "Cal Scrambling to Cover Stadium Bill." *SFGate*, June 16, 2013.

Bachman, Rachel. "Cal Football-Stadium Gamble." *Wall Street Journal*, April 18, 2012.

Baker, Lee D. *From Savage to Negro: Anthropology and the Construction of Race 1896–1954*. Berkeley: University of California Press, 1998.

Bellow, Saul. *The Dean's December*. New York: Harper & Row, 1982.

Bender, Thomas. "Politics, Intellect, and the American University, 1945–1995." *Daedalus*, 126/1 (Winter 1997), 1–38.

Bessner, Daniel. "The Dangerous Decline of the Historical Profession." *New York Times*, January 14, 2023.

Bilgrami, Akeel, and Jonathan R. Cole (eds.). *Who's Afraid of Academic Freedom?* New York: Columbia University Press, 2015.

Birgeneau Robert, and Mary-Sue Coleman. *Public Research Universities: Recommitting to Lincoln's Vision – An Educational Compact for the 21st Century*. Report from the American Academy of Arts and Sciences, April 2016.

Bledstein, Burton. *Culture of Professionalism: The Middle Class and the Development of Higher Education in America*. New York: W.W. Norton, 1978.

Bloom, Allan. *The Closing of the American Mind: How Higher Education Has Failed Democracy and Impoverished the Souls of Today's Students*. New York: Simon & Schuster, 1987.

Botstein, Leon. "Can We Finally Topple the Tyranny of Rankings?" *Chronicle of Higher Education*, November 28, 2022.

Brown, Wendy. *Nihilistic Times: Thinking with Max Weber*. Cambridge, MA: Harvard University Press, 2023.

Bush, Vannevar. *Science, the Endless Frontier: A Report to the President*, July 1945, reprinted by the National Science Foundation, Washington, DC, 2020.

Carey, Kevin. *The End of College: Creating the Future of Learning and the University of Everywhere*. New York: Riverhead, 2015.

Cassuto, Leonard, and Robert Weisbuch. *The New PhD: How to Build a Better Graduate Education*. Baltimore, MD: Johns Hopkins University Press, 2021.

Christenson, Clayton. *The Innovative University: Changing the DNA of American Higher Education*. New York: John Wiley and Sons, 2011.

Christian, Brian. *The Alignment Problem*. New York: W.W. Norton, 2020.

Clifford, James, and George Marcus. *Writing Culture: The Poetics and Politics of Ethnography*. Berkeley: University of California Press, 1986.

Cohn, Bernard S. *An Anthropologist among the Historians and Other Essays*. Delhi: Oxford University Press, 1987.
Colonialism and Its Forms of Knowledge: The British in India. Intro. Nicholas B. Dirks. Princeton University Press, 1996.

Cole, Jonathan. *The Great American University: Its rise to Preeminence, Its Indispensable National Role, Why It Must Be Protected*. New York: Public Affairs, 2009.

Committee of the Corporation and the Academical Faculty. *Reports on the Course of Instruction in Yale College*. New Haven, CT: Printed by Hezekiah Howe, 1828.

Coronil, Fernando. *The Magical State: Nature, Money, and Modernity in Venezuela.* University of Chicago Press, 1997.

Cowles, Henry M. *The Scientific Method: An Evolution of Thinking from Darwin to Dewey.* Cambridge, MA: Harvard University Press, 2020.

Daniels, Ronald J., with Grant Shreve and Phillip Spector. *What Universities Owe Democracy.* Baltimore, MD: Johns Hopkins University Press, 2021.

Delbanco, Andrew. *College: What It Was, Is, and Should Be.* Princeton University Press, 2012.

Denby, David. *Great Books: My Adventures with Homer, Rousseau, Woolf and Other Indestructible Writers of the Western World.* New York: Simon & Schuster, 1996.

Deresiewicz, William. *Excellent Sheep: The Miseducation of the American Elite and the Way to a Meaningful Life.* New York: Free Press, 2014.

Dirks, Nicholas B. *Autobiography of an Archive: A Scholar's Passage to India.* New York: Columbia University Press, 2015.

Castes of Mind: British Colonialism and the Making of Modern India. Princeton University Press, 2001.

The Hollow Crown: Ethnohistory of an Indian Kingdom. Cambridge University Press, 1987.

The Scandal of Empire: India and the Creation of Imperial Britain. Cambridge, MA: Harvard University Press, 2006.

(ed.). *In Near Ruins: Cultural Theory at the End of the Century.* Minneapolis: University of Minnesota Press, 1998.

Doob, Gabriella. "Columbia Report Addresses Anti-Semitism Charges." *Brown Daily Herald,* April 6, 2005.

Douglass, John Aubrey. *The California Idea and American Higher Education.* Stanford University Press, 2000.

Fay, Peter W. *The Forgotten Army: India's Armed Struggle for Independence against the British in World War II.* Ann Arbor: University of Michigan Press, 1994.

The Opium War, 1840–1842. Chapel Hill: University of North Carolina Press, 1975.

Felski, Rita. *The Limits of Critique*. University of Chicago Press, 2015.

Ferguson, Niall. *Empire: How Britain Made the Modern World*. New York: Penguin, 2003.

Friedlander, Judith. *A Light in Dark Times: The New School for Social Research and Its University in Exile*. New York: Columbia University Press, 2019.

Furstenberg, Francois. "The Era of Artificial Scarcity." *Chronicle of Higher Education*, April 8, 2021.

Geertz, Clifford. *Available Light: Anthropological Reflections on Philosophical Topics*. Princeton University Press, 2012.

Works and Lives: The Anthropologist as Author. Stanford University Press, 1988.

Geiger, Roger. *A History of American Higher Education: Learning and Culture from the Founding to World War II*. Princeton University Press, 2015.

Gilman, Daniel Coit. *The Building of the University: An Inaugural Address Delivered at Oakland, November 7th, 1872*. San Francisco: John H. Carmany, 1872.

Goldin, Daniel. *The Price of Admission: How America's Ruling Class Buys Its Way into Elite Colleges – and Who Gets Left Outside the Gate*. New York: Three Rivers Press, 2006.

Gray, Hanna Holborn. *An Academic Life: A Memoir*. Princeton University Press, 2018.

Searching for Utopia: Universities and Their Histories. Berkeley: University of California Press, 2011.

Guillory, John. *Professing Criticism: Essays on the Organization of Literary Study*. University of Chicago Press, 2022.

Hall, Stuart, with Bill Schwarz. *Familiar Strange: A Life Between Two Islands*. Durham, NC: Duke University Press, 2017.

Hayot, Eric. *Humanist Reason: A History. An Argument. A Plan.* New York: Columbia University Press, 2021.

Hofstadter, Richard. *Anti-Intellectualism in American Life*. New York: Knopf, 1962.

Hofstadter Richard, and Walter Metzger. *Academic Freedom in the Age of the College*. New York: Routledge, 1996.

Honan, William H. "Bowing to Pressure, Columbia President Reinstates Dean." *New York Times*, July 4, 1997.

Hynes, James. *Publish and Perish: Three Tales of Tenure and Terror*. New York: Picador, 1997.

Isaacson, Walter. *The Code Breaker: Jennifer Doudna, Gene Editing, and the Future of the Human Race*. New York: Simon & Schuster, 2021.

Jewett, Andrew. *Science Under Fire: Challenges to Scientific Authority in Modern America*. Cambridge, MA: Harvard University Press, 2020.

Johnson, Kai. "Our Identities Matter in Core Classrooms." *Columbia Spectator*, April 30, 2015.

Jones-Katz, Gregory. *Deconstruction: An American Institution*. University of Chicago Press, 2021.

Judt, Tony. "America: My New-Found-Land." *New York Review of Books*, May 27, 2010.

Kalven Committee. *Report on the University's Role in Social and Political Action*. University of Chicago Provost's Office, November 1967.

Karabel, Jerome. *The Chosen: The Hidden History of Admission and Exclusion at Harvard, Yale, and Princeton*. New York: Houghton Mifflin, 2005.

Kerr, Clark. *The Gold and the Blue: A Personal Memoir of the University of California, 1949–1967*, vol. 1. Berkeley: University of California Press, 2001.

The Uses of the University. 5th edn. Cambridge, MA: Harvard University Press, 2001.

Kevles, Daniel J. *The Physicists: The History of a Scientific Community in Modern America*. New York: Knopf, 1971.

Kimball, Roger. *Tenured Radicals: How Politics Has Corrupted Our Higher Education*. Chicago: Ivan Dee, 1990.

King, Charles. *Gods of the Upper Air: How a Circle of Renegade Anthropologists Reinvented Race, Sex, and Gender in the Twentieth Century*. New York: Doubleday, 2019.

Kipnis, Laura. *Unwanted Advances: Sexual Paranoia Comes to Campus*. New York: Harper, 2017.

Kirby, William C. *Empires of Ideas: Creating the Modern University from Germany to America to China*. Cambridge, MA: Harvard University Press, 2022.

Klein, Ezra. "This Changes Everything." *New York Times*, March 12, 2023.

Koshland, Jr., Daniel E., Roderic B. Park, and Louise Taylor. *The Reorganization of Biology at the University of California, Berkeley*. Regional Oral History Office, The Bancroft Library, 2003.

Kronman, Anthony. *Education's End: Why Our Colleges and Universities Have Given Up on the Meaning of Life*. New Haven, CT: Yale University Press, 2007.

Kuhn, Thomas. *The Structure of Scientific Revolutions*. University of Chicago Press, 1962.

Latour, Bruno. "Why Has Critique Run Out of Steam? From Matters of Fact and Matters of Concern." *Critical Inquiry*, 30/2 (Winter 2004), 225–48.

Lee, Seung Y. "Despite Improvement in Mind, Cal Football's Graduation Rates Fell to National Lows." *Daily Californian*, October 28, 2013.

Lemann, Nicholas. *The Big Test: The Secret History of the American Meritocracy*. New York: Farrar, Straus and Giroux, 1999.

Lepore, Jill. "The Disruption Machine: What the Gospel of Innovation Gets Wrong." *The New Yorker*, June 23, 2014. "Why the School Wars still Rage." *The New Yorker*, March 21, 2022.

Levine, Emily. *Allies and Rivals: German–American Exchange and the Rise of the Modern Research University*. University of Chicago Press, 2021.

Levine, Lawrence. *The Opening of the American Mind: Canons, Culture, and History*. Boston, MA: Beacon Press, 1996.

Lewis, Harry R. *Excellence Without a Soul: How a Great University Forgot Education*. New York: Public Affairs, 2006.

Lowen, Rebecca S. *Creating the Cold War University: The Transformation of Stanford*. Berkeley: University of California Press, 1997.

Lucas, Colin. *What Are Universities For?* Ranikhet, India: Permanent Black, 2017.

Marginson, Simon. *The Dream is Over: The Crisis of Clark Kerr's California Idea of Higher Education.* Berkeley: University of California Press, 2016.

Marsden, George M. *The Soul of the American University Revisited: From Protestant to Postsecular.* New York: Oxford University Press, 1996.

Mayer, Jane. *Dark Money: The Hidden History of the Billionaires behind the Rise of the Radical Right.* New York: Doubleday, 2016.

McCaughey, Robert. *Stand, Columbia: A History of Columbia University.* New York: Columbia University Press, 2003.

Menand, Louis. *The Marketplace of Ideas: Reform and Resistance in the American University.* New York: W.W. Norton, 2010.

Moberly, Walter. *The Crisis in the University.* London: SCM Press, 1949.

Montas, Roosevelt. *Rescuing Socrates: How the Great Books Changed My Life and Why They Matter for a New Generation.* Princeton University Press, 2022.

Musto, Ronald. *The Attack on Higher Education: The Dissolution of the American University.* Cambridge University Press, 2021.

Nelson, Maggie. *On Freedom: Four Songs of Care and Constraint.* Minneapolis, MN: Graywolf Press, 2021.

Newman, John Henry. *The Idea of the University.* Notre Dame University Press, 1982.

Niebuhr, Reinhold. *The Nature and Destiny of Man,* vol. 1. New York: Charles Scribner's Sons, 1964.

Nielsen, Michael, and Kanjun Qiu. "A Vision of Metascience: An Engine of Improvement for the Social Processes of Science." *The Science++ Project,* October 18, 2022, https://scienceplusplus.org/metascience/index.html.

Nietzsche, Friedrich. *The Gay Science,* trans. Walter Kaufmann. New York: Vintage, 1974.

Nussbaum, Martha. *Not for Profit: Why Democracy Needs the Humanities.* Princeton University Press, 2010.

Obeyesekere, Gananath. *The Apotheosis of Captain Cook: European Mythmaking in the Pacific.* Princeton University Press, 1992.

Price, David. *Threatening Anthropology: McCarthyism and the FBI's Surveillance of Activist Anthropologists.* Durham, NC: Duke University Press, 2004.

Reitter, Paul, and Chad Wellmon. *Permanent Crisis: The Humanities in a Disenchanted Age.* University of Chicago Press, 2021.

Rhodes, Frank. *The Creation of the Future: The Role of the American University.* Ithaca, NY: Cornell University Press, 2001.

Rosenfeld, Seth. *Subversives: The FBI's War on Student Radicals, and Reagan's Rise to Power.* New York: Farrar, Straus and Giroux, 2012.

Rosenstone, Robert. *Romantic Revolutionary: A Biography of John Reed.* New York: Knopf, 1975.

Rosovsky, Henry. *The University: An Owner's Manual.* New York: W.W. Norton, 1990.

Ross, Dorothy. *The Origins of American Social Science.* Cambridge University Press, 1999.

Roth, Michael S. *Beyond the University: Why Liberal Education Matters.* New Haven, CT: Yale University Press, 2014.

Safe Enough Spaces: A Pragmatist's Approach to Inclusion, Free Speech, and Political Correctness on College Campuses. New Haven, CT: Yale University Press, 2019.

Russell, Stuart. *Human Compatible: Artificial Intelligence and the Problem of Control.* New York: Penguin, 2019.

Sahlins, Marshall. *How Natives Think: About Captain Cook, for Example.* University of Chicago Press, 1995.

Said, Edward. *Reflections on Exile and Other Essays.* Cambridge, MA: Harvard University Press, 2000.

Schwab, Klaus. *The Fourth Industrial Revolution.* New York: Penguin, 2017.

Selingo, Jeffrey. *Who Gets In and Why: A Year Inside College Admissions.* New York: Scribner, 2020.

Sexton, John. *Standing for Reason: The University in a Dogmatic Age*. New Haven, CT: Yale University Press, 2019.

Sherman, Scott. "The Mideast Comes to Columbia." *The Nation*, March 16, 2005.

Snow, C.P. *The Two Cultures*. Cambridge University Press, 1998.

Taussig. Michael. *The Magic of the State*. New York: Routledge, 1997.

Taylor, Mark C. *Crisis on Campus: A Bold Plan for Reforming our Colleges and Universities*. New York: Alfred Knopf, 2010.

Turner, James. *Philology: The Forgotten Origins of the Modern Humanities*. Princeton University Press, 2014.

Veysey, Laurence R. *The Emergence of the American University*. University of Chicago Press, 1965.

Wallerstein, Immanuel, *et al. Open the Social Sciences: Report of the Gulbenkian Commission on Restructuring the Social Sciences*. Stanford University Press, 1996.

Weber, Max. *Charisma and Disenchantment: The Vocation Lectures*, ed. Paul Reitter and Chad Wellmon, trans. Damion Searls. New York: Penguin Random House, 2020.

Weil, Simone. *The Need for Roots: Prelude to a Declaration of Duties towards Mankind*. New York: Putnam's, 1952.

Wellmon, Chad. "The Crushing Contradictions of the American University." *Chronicle of Higher Education*, April 22, 2021.

Wilton, John. "Time is Not on Our Side." Berkeley Administration and Finance, November 29, 2013.

Zumwalt, Rosemary Levy. *Franz Boas*, vol. I: *The Emergence of the Anthropologist* and vol. II: *Shaping Anthropology and Fostering Social Justice*. Lincoln: University of Nebraska Press, 2019–22.

INDEX

Introductory Note

References such as '178–79' indicate (not necessarily continuous) discussion of a topic across a range of pages. Wherever possible in the case of topics with many references, these have either been divided into sub-topics or only the most significant discussions of the topic are listed. Because the entire work is about 'universities', the use of this term (and certain others which occur constantly throughout the book) as an entry point has been restricted. Information will be found under the corresponding detailed topics.

administrators (cont.)
  professional, 7, 180
  senior, 67, 77, 91, 119, 136,
    165, 262–63
admissions, 10–11, 81, 90, 110,
    113, 173, 186, 187, 318
  procedures, 110, 306
advanced research, 176, 184,
    187–88, 318
advisory groups, 67, 100, 118
affiliations, 38, 41, 276, 290
affirmative action, 50, 59, 80, 267
Africa, 21, 34, 38
African Americans, 13, 83, 119,
    139, 190, 199, 203, 228
African studies, xix, 57–58
agriculture, 95, 174–76, 208
Ahmadinejad, Mahmood, 78–79
alt-right movement, 162
alumni, 71, 77, 79, 95–96,
    100, 108–9, 112, 138,
    191–92, 264
Amravati University, 212, 215
American Association of
    University Professors
    (AAUP), 53, 250
Andhra Pradesh, 211, 215
Anthropocene, 245, 279
anthropologists, 21–23, 30, 34,
    37–38, 168
anthropology, 4, 21, 29, 31–34,
    36–38, 43, 44, 48, 67,
    198, 199
  departments, 4, 21, 36–37, 44,
    49, 51, 66–68, 199
Anti-Defamation League, 79
antifa, 159–62, 236
Anti-Intellectualism in American
    Life, 85
anti-Semitism, 52, 55, 93, 122
appointments, 4, 6, 26, 40, 83,
    90, 92–93, 100, 119, 122
  cross-disciplinary, 41

joint, 31, 40, 289
  senior, 63
Area Centers, 76
area studies, 20–21, 36, 74, 77,
    199, 201
Arizona State University, 293
artificial intelligence, 115, 206,
    215, 284, 304, 320
arts, xii, 44, 47–48, 50, 279–81,
    283, 286, 299, 302, 306
  liberal, xxi, xxiii, 175–76, 212,
    214–19, 237–38, 241,
    313, 315, 318–19
Ashoka University, 212–13
Asia, xx, 20, 27, 38, 70, 77, 116,
    213, 215, 245
  South, xxi, 20, 23, 43, 57–58
  Southeast, 21, 31, 34, 194
Asian civilization, 4, 23, 215
aspirations, xxiv, 3, 209–12,
    219, 269
  utopian, 111, 322
athletics, 6, 109–10, 138, 268,
    288, 306
austerity, 7, 101, 126, 129, 263
autonomy, 66, 91, 96, 137, 182,
    290, 309
  departmental, 246, 261

badges, 286
Bakhle, Janaki, 3, 4–6, 42, 61,
    85, 106, 139, 153–54,
    161, 167
balance, 11, 51, 91, 123, 147,
    150, 163
Balfour, Lord, 57
Baltimore, 176
BAMN (By Any Means
    Necessary), 206
Bancroft Avenue, 158
Barbour, Sandy, 109
Bard College, 285, 293
basketball, 110, 138, 306

Index

Index

faculty (cont.)
  tenured, 6, 32, 38, 68, 70, 85,
    122, 147, 263, 298
  top, 134, 196, 215, 275
fairness, 10, 59, 89
faith, xiii–xv, xix–xx, xxiv, 226,
  237, 242, 259, 309
  loss of, xx, 313
  religious, xiii, xix, xxi–xxii
fathers, xiii–xv, xviii, xxi–xxiii,
  20, 45, 74, 213,
  241–44, 276
Fay, Peter, 26–27
federal funds, 100, 160, 183,
  254, 301
Feinstein, Dianne, 154
Feynman, Richard, 24
fieldwork, 23–24, 28, 30, 46, 61,
  168, 213
financial aid, 51, 81–82, 90,
  127–29, 199, 204, 267,
  271, 314
financial crises, 12, 82, 136, 145,
  166, 204–6
financial viability, 144, 260
fireside chats, 3, 123
First Amendment rights, 8,
  53–55, 61, 79, 120,
  161–62, 235
flagship universities, 178, 187,
  265, 312, 317, 321
flexibility, 284–86, 288–91
Florida, 155, 239–40
food security, 13
football, 6, 95, 108–10, 138, 141,
  164, 180, 195, 306
Ford, Richard, 64
Foucault, Michel, 26, 31, 74,
  195, 247
founders, 27, 176, 209–11, 218
fourth industrial
  revolution, 320
Fox News, 9, 43, 161

Foxman, Abraham, 79
free speech, 6–8, 98, 120–22,
  154, 157–63, 189, 192,
  204–5, 233–40, 248–50
  movement, 2, 7, 97–99,
    119–20, 157, 188, 312
  rallies, 161
freedom, xiii, 8, 80, 87, 138, 179,
  234, 249
  academic, 53–56, 58–60, 80,
    84, 86–88, 121–22, 233,
    236, 249–50, 298–99
  intellectual, 234
freshman year, xii, 193
Freud, Sigmund, 74–75
friendships, 41, 50, 94
funding, 94, 96, 102–3, 114,
  117, 135–36, 141, 204,
  263–65, 294–95
  crises, 188, 196, 317
  state, xxvii, 12, 98, 131,
    135, 143, 174, 187, 197,
    203–4
  system, 301
fundraising, 118–19, 121, 126,
  139–41, 151, 153, 180,
  196, 266, 307

Gandhi, Mahatma, xix, 24, 27, 75
Geertz, Clifford, xi
Gell-Mann, Murray, 24
gender, xxiii, 14, 33, 228
General Studies, School of,
  199–200
German universities, 174–76,
  221, 299, 311–13
Germany, 37, 217, 222
Gilman, Daniel Coit, 14, 153,
  175–78, 181–82
global campus, 115–16
global footprint, 77, 107,
  114–16, 303
Godkin lectures, 253, 257

Index

Hopkins. *See* Johns Hopkins
  University
housing, 13, 117, 134, 290, 307
Howard, Jean, 63
Howard, John Galen, 106
humanism, secular, 227
humanist reason, 247, 296,
  298, 306
humanistic disciplines, 223,
  227–29, 244
humanistic education, 225
humanists, 31, 107, 172, 177, 195,
  222–24, 244, 247, 281
humanities, 10–11, 74, 75,
  204, 215, 216, 218,
  222–28, 245, 276,
  281–84, 296, 297
  and social sciences, 20, 72, 76,
  206, 214, 275, 283, 299
hunger strike, 68, 97
Husserl, Edmund, xvii
Hutchins, Robert Maynard, 221,
  224, 318

ideals, xxv, xxvii, 75, 111, 180,
  184, 219, 259
ideas of the university, 211–52
identity, 30, 33–35, 52, 91, 108,
  112, 152, 231, 262, 317
  academic, 45, 108
  fundamental, 40, 168
  groups, 203
ideological positions, xxvi, 56,
  162, 229
Illinois, xiii, 9, 122, 177, 188,
  197, 206, 221
imagination, 202, 216, 294–96,
  311, 319–21
in-state students, 131
inauguration
  ceremony, 128, 213
  speech, 14, 111, 221
incentives, xii, 256, 266, 292

inclusion, 102, 231–32, 234–35,
  237, 262
incoherence, 272, 298–99
income, 51, 128, 266
  psychic, 101, 129
India, xiv–xv, xviii–xix, xxi, 20,
  24–28, 45–46, 75, 77,
  211–14
  history/historians, 25–27, 74
  religions, xvi, 75
  southern, 20, 28–30, 211
Indian Institutes of Technology
  (IITs), 27, 214
Indian National Army, 26–27
Indian School of Business, 212
industrial revolution, fourth, 320
inequality, 13, 61, 115, 228
initiatives, 36, 52, 62–63, 77, 85,
  113, 143, 150, 198
  data science, 164
  undergraduate, 107, 111, 149
innovation, 91, 137, 198, 216–18,
  291, 294, 300–1, 313
inquiry, 238, 278–79, 299,
  309, 321
  intellectual, 249, 299
  open, xxii, 8, 234–35, 237–
  38, 240
institutional change, 269, 294,
  298, 322
  major, 270, 297
institutional life, 88, 111
institutional work, xxvii, 14, 31,
  39, 45, 199
intellectual capital, 196, 321
intellectual commitments,
  xxvi, 39
intellectual community, 40
intellectual exchanges, 250,
  271, 299
intellectual freedom, 234
intellectual historians, xi, 85
intellectual history, 19, 229

intellectual inquiry, 249, 299
intellectual life, xxiii, xxvi, xxviii,
    11, 91, 248, 250, 278,
    290, 302
intellectual values, xxiv, 158,
    252, 317, 319
intellectuals, 64, 86–88, 200, 305
interdisciplinarity, 39, 262
interdisciplinary programs, xix,
    33, 45, 276, 293
interdisciplinary work, 36, 263
interest groups, 124, 175
"interesting times", 11, 14, 119
internal candidates, 98
international students, 215, 303
international studies, 76, 114, 306
internships, 286, 289, 294
interviewers, 92, 97, 123
interviews, 92, 95, 97, 102,
    123, 144
intimidation, 55–56
intolerance, 53
investments, 21, 32, 81, 134,
    163, 183, 190, 268, 288
Iran, 78–79
Irvine, 184
I-School, 164–65
Israel, 9, 53, 56, 92
Ivy League, 63, 133, 172,
    181–82, 196, 209

James, William, xii, 180
Japan, xiv, 25–26
Jefferson, Thomas, 173
Jewett, Andrew, 225–26, 243, 281
Jewish students, 72–73
Johns Hopkins University, 216,
    221, 264, 300
    history, 176, 181–82
joint appointments, 31, 40, 289
journalists, 52, 94
judgments, 59–60, 89, 148, 234
    academic, xxvi, 59

Judt, Tony, 171
junior faculty, 40, 43, 65, 68, 70,
    74, 124, 134, 196, 198
justice, social, xiii, 218

Kanpur, 27
Kant, Immanuel, xi, 231
Katznelson, Ira, 55
Kennedy, Robert, 158
Kent State University, 194
Kerr, Clark, 14, 94–95, 98, 120,
    183–86, 188–89, 250–60,
    274, 313, 317–20
Kevles, Daniel J., 224
King, Martin Luther, Jr., 190
King's College, 174
Kipnis, Laura, 9
Kirby, Bill, 153, 311–12
Kirk, Greyson, 44
Knight, Bob, 117
knowledge, 15, 89–91, 201,
    241–49, 251–53,
    256–59, 280–84, 291–92,
    296, 320
    academic, 46, 59
    disciplinary, xxvi, 218
    industry, 253, 257
    politics of, 59, 89, 194
    process, 257
Koch, Charles, 193
Kramer, Martin, 52
Kronman, Anthony, 226–27,
    240, 244
Kuhn, Thomas, 280

labor, 9, 95
Land Grant Act, 174
Latin, 173, 220
law, 95, 148, 172, 174, 183, 198,
    245, 278
Law School, 23, 65, 104, 146–49
Lawrence Berkeley National
    Laboratory, 114, 254

New York, 42, 44, 63–66, 73,
78, 186, 190, 192–94,
197–98, 200
New York Times, 6, 65, 132, 144
Newsom, Gavin, 154
newspapers, 2
local, 135, 151, 194, 307
Newtowne, 172
Niebuhr, Reinhold, xii–xiv, 244
Niebuhr, Richard, 244
non-Brahman movements, xix
non-tenure track faculty, 84, 266
non-western civilizations, 70
North Carolina, 239, 300
Northeastern University, 294
Northwestern University, 5, 10,
37–38
nostalgia, xxvii, 26, 314, 316
NYU (New York University),
198, 214, 293

Oakland, 142, 175, 206
Obama, Barack, 12, 99, 127
Obamacare, 12, 145
Obeyesekere, Gananath, 35
occupations, 97, 120, 191
Occupy movement, 12, 97,
104, 206
occupy protests, 84, 210
Office of Strategic Initiatives,
146, 150
Office of Strategic Services,
20, 201
Olin, John M., 193
online teaching, 271
open inquiry, xxii, 8, 234–35,
237–38, 240
open-mindedness, 59
Opening of the American
Mind, 220
openness, 77, 162, 273, 282, 304
out-of-state students, 131,
196, 295

outsiders, 30, 97–98, 146, 263
overreach, administrative,
118, 145
Ovid's Metamorphoses, 232
Oxbridge model, 173
Oxford University, 171, 176

Palestine, 57, 59, 79
Palo Alto, 177
Pamuk, Orhan, 64
pandemic. *See* Covid pandemic
panic buttons, 105–6
parents, xviii, 75, 178, 227
Paris, 77, 171
particularization, 247
Peking University, 77, 311
Pell Grants, 132, 199
People's Park, 99, 102
perimeter fence, 140
personal history, xxiv, 17–
168, 316
Petrarch, 172
PhDs/PhD programs, 40, 260,
285, 287–88, 305
phenomenology, xvii–xviii
philology, 173, 222, 230
philosophers, xi, xvi, 83, 201
philosophy, xi–xii, xiv–xvi, xx, 19,
24, 45, 71, 74, 120, 172
physics, 98, 113, 225, 245, 281
Pipes, Daniel, 52
polarization, 10, 193, 238, 309
police, 13, 99, 105–6, 130,
139–40, 159–60,
191–92, 206
investigation, 161
protection, 44, 140
university, 105–6, 128, 130, 158
political action, xix, 35, 162
political agenda, 57
political attacks, 9, 59, 210
political career, 99, 189
political controversies, 61

Index